Organic
Gardener's Companion
Growing Vegetables in the West

Jane Shellenberger

FULCRUM
GOLDEN, COLORADO

Text © 2012 by Jane Shellenberger
Photographs © 2012 by Jane Shellenberger, except the following:
Photographs © Barbara Miller: vii; © Wikimedia Commons Public Domain: 19, 20, 43, 45, 120; © Library of Congress, Prints & Photographs Division: 22 (LC-USF344-003181-ZB), 23; © Jonathan D. Eisenback, www.Mactode.com: 29, 30; © Wikimedia Commons/

Goldstein lab–tardigrades: 30; © Wikimedia Commons/ninjatacoshell: 31; © Michael McCrea: 85 (left), 163; © Robyn Wallerich: 89; © James M. Knopf: 103; © Dan Moore: 110; © Karen Beeman, Wee Bee Farms: 145 (top); © Shep Gilchrist: 169.

Insect photographs © Whitney Cranshaw, Colorado State University, bugwood.org: 93, 94 (all but bottom right and second from bottom right), 95 (middle left, bottom left, and middle right), 96 (bottom left), 97 (all but bottom right), 98 (all but bottom right), 100 (all but middle and bottom right); © Frank Peairs, Colorado State University, bugwood.org: 94 (bottom right and second from bottom right), 95 (bottom right), 98 (bottom right); © David Cappaert, Michigan State University, bugwood.org: 95 (top), 99 (top and middle right); © Joseph Berger, bugwood.org: 96 (bottom right), 97 (bottom right); © Howard Ensign Evans, Colorado State University, bugwood.org: 96 (top), 101; © Steven Katovich, USDA Forest Service, bugwood.org: 99 (middle left); © Cheryl Moorehead, bugwood.org: 99 (bottom left);

© Susan Ellis, bugwood.org: 99 (bottom right); © John A. Weidhass, Virginia Polytechnic Institute and State University, bugwood.org: 100 (middle right); © H. Gross, USDA Agricultural Research Service, bugwood.org: 100 (bottom right).

"Benefits of Aerated Compost Tea," page 32, and "Roland Evans's Favorite Container Soil Recipe," page 74, used with permission of Roland Evans.

"Mikl Brawner's Energy-Saving Greenhouse," page 87, used with permission of Mikl Brawner.

"A Test for Chemical Herbicides," page 106, used by permission.

Library of Congress Cataloging-in-Publication Data

Shellenberger, Jane.
  Organic gardener's companion : growing vegetables in the West / Jane Shellenberger.
    p. cm.
  Includes bibliographical references and index.
  ISBN 978-1-55591-725-8 (pbk.)
  1. Vegetable gardening--West (U.S.) 2. Organic gardening--West (U.S.) I. Title. II. Title: Growing vegetables in the West.
  SB324.3.S54 2012
  635.0978--dc23

                          2011031537

Printed in China
0 9 8 7 6 5 4 3 2 1
Design by Jack Lenzo
Fulcrum Publishing
4690 Table Mountain Dr., Ste. 100
Golden, CO 80403
800-992-2908 • 303-277-1623
www.fulcrumbooks.com

Contents

Acknowledgments

Many thanks to Daniel Ault, Mikl Brawner, Whitney Cranshaw, Roland Evans, Matt Kelsch, Paul Lander, Kristin Lopez, Barbara Miller (my sheet mulch mentor), Penn and Cord Parmenter, Kayann Short, and Tom Theobald for reviewing and/or contributing to parts of the manuscript; to all the bugwood .org photographers for sharing their insect photos; to all of the Boulder Culinary Gardeners for camaraderie, lively discussion, information sharing, and great potlucks, especially Niki Hayden, Frank "Father Earth" Hodge, and Sandy Swegle, from whom I have learned a great deal; to generous, ebullient plantsman Panayoti Kelaidis, a giant among horticulturists; to seed-saving pioneers Bill McDorman and Belle Starr; to those of my neighbors on North 66th Street who refrain from using chemical fertilizers, pesticides, and herbicides on their property; to helpful gardener friends Michael McCrea, Jeff Pavek and Pete, Sahand Tabatabaii; to encouraging writer friends Ted Ringer and Thea Tennenbaum; to all the fearless, environmentally aware organic gardeners, permaculture practitioners, and farmers in Colorado and the West; and to Oscar, who always keeps the home fires burning and the vitality levels up. Special thanks to Carolyn Sobczak, my skilled and patient editor at Fulcrum.

Introduction

Community gardens are a great place to learn from other gardeners and share ideas and challenges.

My first vegetable garden was in a hard-packed dirt driveway in Boulder, Colorado. I was living in a basement apartment there, having jumped at the chance to come out West with a friend in his Volkswagen Bug, fleeing college and inner-city Philadelphia. I was twenty, hungry for experience, and fully intending to be a ski bum in my new life. But it didn't turn out that way.

The garden was my boyfriend's idea. He grew up on a farm in Loveland and knew just what to do. While I was off at my minimum-wage job, Randy dug the compacted ground with a shovel and pick, added bags of manure and compost, bought seeds and a hose, and enclosed the whole thing with a gated chicken-wire fence, all in one day. Before long we had vegetables of all kinds, including beans and melon vines that clambered up and over the top of the fence. I was worried about bugs, but Randy assured me they wouldn't eat much, and they didn't.

We (well, mostly he) created a striking, lush oasis on the edge of a bare and dusty driveway that connected the alley with the street. The neighborhood kids used the alley as a shortcut on their way to school. If I was out working in the garden, they might wander over to ask a few questions, so right away I discovered the social benefits of gardening.

Since my arrival in the West four decades ago, I've lived in many different apartments and houses in various Colorado neighborhoods—urban, suburban, and rural. I planted a garden of some kind at each one and often maintained a community vegetable plot with a friend too. Gardening isn't something I went to school to learn; I just jumped in, learning from my mistakes and from other gardeners, picking up tips here and there. But I was already familiar with plants and flower gardens.

My mother nearly finished an advanced degree in botany after her father nixed her

1

preferred artistic path as "too Bohemian." While I was growing up, she spent much of her time outdoors in baggy slacks with dirty knees working in the woodland gardens she created. She taught my sisters and me the Latin names of plants and helped us with our own little gardens. And my father, always a showman with an angle (often designed to keep the IRS at bay), grew flashy orchids later in life, renting them out to galleries and offices in New York and to upper crust private homes for party or holiday decor, making the deliveries personally in an old Rolls-Royce. I sometimes wonder if his routine pesticide spraying inside a small greenhouse played a role in the onset of Parkinson's disease, to which he finally succumbed.

Most of the gardeners I know had a childhood mentor or have fond memories with a parent, grandparent, or a kindly older neighbor who gardened. But as home vegetable gardens became less necessary and food became fast, more and more people grew up without an opportunity to learn about or even see someone gardening. Though gardening classes and programs have proliferated recently, many American children and some adults still don't exactly know where food comes from or how it grows. Without any fundamental experience or context, gardening can seem much more difficult than it is, especially in the semiarid West, where locals lament the challenging growing conditions.

There is a lot of information in the pages that follow, some of it complex and detailed. You certainly don't need to know all of this to have a garden, but it may explain a few things, give some context, or spark your curiosity. I've gardened in the West without using chemicals or poisons for more than forty

Cats make great garden companions. Mine love to eat grasshoppers—and cooked mashed broccoli, carrots, and squash. Well-fed cats also kill millions of songbirds, so don't allow roaming at will, especially during nesting season from late April through mid-June.

years. It's not difficult, but it helps to have a bit of education on the topic. I became a more adventurous and thoughtful gardener after reading books by the pioneers of organic gardening, and I've also learned a lot from other gardeners in my local community.

I hope to give beginner Western gardeners the confidence to get growing, plus the tools and understanding to start raising healthy, tasty food while building better soil every year and creating better conditions for bees and other creatures in the yard. At the same time, there should be plenty of material and tips for those with more gardening experience.

Over the years my priorities have shifted. As someone who always tends to throw a lot of balls into the air and then wonder why I'm juggling so much, I aim more for simplicity these days, even if I don't always accomplish it. And while I once embraced the sweaty, physical exertion involved in wielding a pick and shovel to carve gardens out of the ground, I now use, and am always on the lookout for, less strenuous methods. They are easier on the infrastructure—both the land's and mine.

There are many paths leading to a garden and many experiences awaiting those who venture in. No matter what your motive—whether to grow healthy, delicious food; spend time outdoors feeling more alive than your desk job allows; help save the planet; find relaxation, solace, or healing; meet your neighbors; get your hands in the sweet earth; or discover for yourself just how abundant and generous nature can be—a garden rarely disappoints. It's a magnet for life in all its quirky, beautiful forms.

Your leaning may be more toward science or art, but in either case you're bound to find some magic in a garden. Once you see firsthand how one tiny seed morphs into a huge, lush plant bearing many delicious vegetables or fruits, each bursting with life force and containing the seeds for its own renewal many times over, you'll know just what I mean.

Chapter 1
Saving Life on Earth with Organic Gardening

Many better-tasting heirlooms mature and ripen late. Western growing seasons aren't always hot long enough for them to produce much before frost. Save seeds from the first tomato(es) to ripen, and grow your own adapted starts each year.

M any people today are interested in food gardening, especially. The local food and slow food movements are exploding with energy and enthusiasm. Vegetable gardens are sprouting in front- and backyards and community plots everywhere. Farmers' markets and Community Supported Agriculture farms (usually called CSAs) have never been more popular. People are interested in where food comes from and how it's grown.

When I first started gardening in the 1970s, the main motivation for using organic methods was to avoid toxic pesticides. Whatever organic produce you could occasionally find in supermarkets wasn't of the best quality; I remember the aphid-covered broccoli, especially. The message seemed to be: You want organic? Then I'm sure you won't mind some bugs with your vegetables.

Today, organics commands a much bigger share of the American food market (though still just 3.5 percent), and it increases every year. The demand is greater than the supply, which is why stores like Whole Foods also import organic food from China and other countries. Pesticides are still with us, of course, and of great concern, especially with the sad plight of our major pollinator, the honeybee. But soil health, biological diversity, nutrition, permaculture, biodynamics, and sustainability have also recently entered the gardening conversation.

SUSTAINABILITY

Ecologists define *sustainability* as "the ability of natural systems to remain diverse and productive over time." Applied to humans, it usually refers to the wise use of natural resources without depleting and polluting the Earth—which hasn't exactly been our specialty so far. Sustainable agriculture used to mean systems and growing methods that champion soil and environmental health. These include, among other things, replenishing the soil and preventing topsoil erosion by nurturing the soil food web, using mulch and/or cover crops, and sustaining the invaluable honeybee, which has served us so well by pollinating a third of all food plants and giving us honey to boot.

Because *sustainability* resonates with consumers and gardeners, and young gardeners in particular, the term has so much marketing currency these days that it is very widely interpreted. It has even been claimed by the biggest ag science and biotech corporations like Monsanto and Syngenta, who have built reputations and profits as destroyers of soil life, insects, and weeds, not as restorers and renewers of life. Welcome to reframing, twenty-first-century-style.

Maria Rodale, former editor of *Organic Gardening Magazine* and granddaughter of the founder of the Rodale Institute, a nonprofit organic pioneer since 1947, points out the importance of the US Department of Agriculture organic standards as a democratically based statute that is "our only real opportunity to control the quality and safety of our food." Rodale says that because the word *sustainability* has been co-opted, appearing in so many places where it is completely inappropriate, we can't count on it. *Organic* is the only designation with any real oversight and accountability, thanks to the efforts of many people over time.

Toby Hemenway, permaculturist and author of *Gaia's Garden*, goes even further, saying, "Sustainable agriculture is an oxymoron…Agriculture takes more than it gives." Three thousand years of agriculture wrecked the fertile crescent of Mesopotamia in modern-day Iraq. In Greece, five hundred years of agriculture reduced the land to its current degraded state. The dust bowl in North America was caused by just a few decades of farming.

LIVE AND LET LIVE: A PERMACULTURE APPROACH

Permaculture, working *with* nature and using its patterns as models to design functional ecosystems, offers a solution for turning this situation around—through the creation of home forest gardens with a combination of forage food plants (like fruit and nut trees and shrubs) and vegetable and herb plants, all while building soil. A healthy ecosystem will work constantly to balance itself and take care of population explosions of any one insect species, for example, if you give it time. As a gardener, you can gently participate in this balancing effort by creating the conditions that encourage the presence and growth of beneficial microbes, insects, plants, and animals while discouraging the destructive ones.

There is no reason at all to use toxic chemicals—not even "just a little bit"—to achieve a blemish-free home garden, especially one that you plan to eat from. Instead of looking at garden visitors as pests and acting as the grand exterminator, which inevitably leads to killing off the beneficial critters too, focus on the rich diversity of species that you attract to the garden ecosystem you have created. Just as the birders and wildflower lovers do, you might think about keeping a list of all the insects and animals that show up in and around your garden.

Barbara Miller's garden scarecrow. Note thick hay mulch that covers the ground in her entire garden area. It keeps weeds out, moisture in, and allows her to walk in the garden without compacting the soil.

An insect "problem" often indicates that soil conditions are lacking or that something is out of balance: too much or too little moisture, for example. If you attack the problem instead of the underlying causes, you will only make matters worse in the long run. There are lots of preventative things you can do to avoid outbreaks. Plant pest-resistant varieties whenever possible, plus those known to succeed for you or other gardeners in your area since they have already adapted to local conditions. Use companion planting techniques. Strong-smelling marigolds and garlic can mask the scent of other plants close by, hiding them from insects that like to eat them. Rotate crops, moving them around to different spots in the garden each year. Insects usually feed on specific plants or species; they lay their eggs where they've been feeding so their offspring will have a readily available food source when they emerge. But if you move the brassicas or beans to a different spot each year, you will confuse the bugs that feed on them. Handpicking harmful insects when they first show up can avert an infestation. And there are also easy nontoxic recipes that deter unwanted invaders if it comes to that (see chapter 9, Undesirables in the Garden).

Living in tune with nature will test you, though, because living systems are complex; the good guys aren't always clearly distinguishable from the bad guys since every species has a role in a diverse ecosystem. Most people, for example, love having birds around the garden and take steps to attract them. They're pretty, they sing, and they eat lots of insects humans don't like, including mosquitoes and grubs. But what about when they suddenly polish off all the cherries or your favorite grapes?

Many people dread wasps (and often confuse them with bees), but these comprise a big family and are some of the best pest predators around. European paper wasps first appeared in Colorado in 2003, and they have proliferated to the detriment of native species, including, sadly, most butterflies. But they do keep the cabbage worms and tomato hornworms in the garden effectively under control.

Since massive spray campaigns to eliminate unwanted or destructive insects have rarely, if ever, worked in the past over the long term, and since they usually have unintended harmful consequences, I prefer a live-and-let-live approach to Rambo-style aerosol attacks. Yellow jackets with invisible nests in the ground cause the most bites to people anyway. If really necessary, it's easy enough to knock a paper wasp nest into a bucket of water and drown the inhabitants on a cool day, at a cool time of day, or at night, when they're nonaggressive and inactive. Though I have only once been stung by any of the wasps that now inhabit my yard, I would always choose to risk an infrequent painful-but-temporary sting over the possibility of slowly poisoning myself or my pet or the bees my garden depends on. Electric bug zappers are an especially poor choice for control since they kill far more beneficial insects than mosquitoes.

Impatient and short-sighted as we gadget-prone humans have become, we often ignore or dismiss the larger cycles of nature because they take too long. Instead we feel compelled to take action that gives us results we can see right away. But look at the result—our environmental record isn't exactly stellar. Maybe it's because so many of us live in cities and our interactions with the natural world are so much less common now than our instant interactions with the images on phone and computer screens.

Diverse flora and fauna are signs of a healthy, balanced ecosystem, benefiting every gardener. Even the weeds have their roles, bringing up nutrients from deep underground, feeding beneficial insects, and stabilizing eroding soil. If you want to get your kids interested in the garden, just give them a magnifying glass so they can get a

SMALL-SCALE FOOD GARDENING WILL SAVE THE PLANET, NOT AGRICULTURE

Unlike farming, horticulture (or smaller-scale gardening) has become a crucial, decentralized, environmentally sound way to produce food. It has a small footprint and supports a diversity of plants, insects, and animals. Small-scale gardening can also go beyond sustainability, becoming restorative and regenerative, especially when practiced by large numbers of individuals. We need more conscious, life-embracing, nontoxic, grassroots food gardening to save the planet,

Genetically Modified Organisms

Most processed food in the United States now contains ingredients from genetically modified organisms, or GMOs. The primary GMO food crops are soybeans, canola (much is also grown in Canada), corn, Hawaiian papaya, and some zucchini and yellow squash. Sugar beets and alfalfa are also grown as GMO crops; GMO cotton is grown extensively. Introduced commercially in 1996 and adopted widely by farmers, "notwithstanding uncertainty about consumer acceptance and economic and environmental impacts," according to the USDA Economic Research Service, GMO products do not require

special labeling in the United States. Unless a product is labeled *organic*, you cannot be certain it doesn't contain GMOs.

Many other countries have banned or restricted the import, distribution, use, and planting of GMOs, including Norway, Austria, Germany, the United Kingdom, Spain, Italy, Greece, France, Luxembourg, Portugal, Brazil, Paraguay, Peru, China, Japan, the Phillipines, Thailand, Sri Lanka, Algeria, Egypt, Saudi Arabia, Australia, New Zealand, Papua New Guinea, Fiji, Micronesia, Cook Islands, Marshall Islands, Tonga, Tuvalu, American Samoa, Nauru, and Kiribati.

close-up look at all the fascinating life-forms you're creating a matrix for out there. While you're at it, check out the Xerces Society (www.xerces.org), which has been at the forefront of invertebrate conservation for more than forty years, and the Britain-based Amateur Entomologists' Society, founded in 1935 (www.amentsoc.org). Finally, I suggest you take advantage of the hazardous household waste drop-offs that many cities now offer to purge your garage and toolshed of every toxic product you no longer have use for. That would be all of them.

and it's already beginning to happen.

The beauty of organic home gardening is that it circumvents the problems that farmers routinely face and that agriculture has historically caused. You don't need to take out a loan to purchase large machinery or equipment that depends on fossil fuels; you don't need to grow acres and acres of just one crop or uniformly shaped, thick-skinned vegetables that must hold up during machine harvesting and shipping. And despite the rows and rows of alarmingly named chemical products on display at garden centers and hardware and

In a small-scale home or community garden plot, you can easily grow plenty of vegetables for your family and have extra to give away while improving the soil every year.

home improvement stores, you don't need to buy any of these either. You also don't need to work from sunup to sundown every day.

While the big ag corporations keep telling us that the world is running out of food—promoting as the solution expensive, patented, genetically modified, Roundup-ready, monoculture cereal crops grown from systemic-pesticide-treated seeds—experienced home gardeners know better. If you simply start by building healthy, living soil, you will be rewarded with plenty of fresh produce year after year.

One of the most gratifying things about having a garden is that you will always grow enough food to give some away. Instead of worrying about times being tough and money being tight, you will have regular opportunities to experience that expansive feeling of having more than enough. If the raccoons or squirrels don't beat you to it, one plum, peach, or apple tree can supply you and several others with plenty of fruit for every conceivable use. In a small 6 x 10 foot patch, my friend Michael grew enough Spacemaster cucumber plants to produce fifty to seventy-five cukes per week during the height of the season. It isn't often that we find such an easy, tangible, satisfying way to reach out and give something of substance to a neighbor, a friend, or a complete stranger.

One final benefit: if your garden is visible from the street, you will no doubt find that your social life picks up. Gardens attract people as well as other life-forms. Passersby will say hello and stop to chat. If you prefer to keep to yourself, you had best tuck your garden into a corner of the backyard behind a fence where no one can see it.

Chapter 2

Gardening in Western Climates Is Different

Most native western soils contain very little organic matter—just 1–2 percent. This suits grasses and other western native plants, but to grow vegetables, gardeners must build healthy soil by adding materials like leaves and compost.

Growing food in the intermountain West is a whole different ball game than gardening in less-extreme environments. Vegetable gardeners need soil with lots of organic matter and good tilth, plus regular water throughout the growing season. This is the exact opposite of what occurs naturally in the semiarid western United States.

Our native steppe and alpine soils are lean, though mineral rich. We receive half the precipitation of woodland and coastal areas, and in some areas much less. Humidity is almost always low and winds are harsh and drying. Freezes often arrive late in the spring and early in the fall, so frost-free growing seasons may be shorter than plants need in order to reach maturity. During the summer, days can be very hot, while nights are often cooler than some vegetables prefer. Drought is part of the natural climate cycle, though even our typical pattern of precipitation would be considered agricultural drought in many other states.

The trick is to build soils that support soil life (see chapter 3, Soil: The Backbone of Organic Gardening) and to create protective microclimates for plants (see chapter 7, Extending the Season). But first, a basic explanation of our western climate and geography, along with some history of human settlement that transformed the region, will be helpful.

CLIMATE CLASSIFICATION

Most climate systems today are based on a classification system introduced by Russian German climatologist Wladimir Köppen beginning in 1900. According to his widely accepted model, climate determines the plant and animal life that will inhabit a given geographical area. Together, the flora, fauna, and climate comprise what are called world biomes. Within each biome there are many different ecosystems where plants and animals have adapted to specific environmental conditions.

The Great Plains of the United States are part of a large grasslands biome that extends from western Indiana to the Rocky Mountains. Moving from east to west, rainfall and humidity decreases and what remains of the native prairie changes from tall grass to short grass. Closer to the mountains the biome is characterized as steppe, with cold winters, warm to hot summers with cool nights, poor soils, intense winds, low and erratic precipitation, drought, and fires that prevented trees from growing except along rivers and streams. Grasses survive because they are deep rooted and grow from the bottom up.

Despite these harsh conditions, there is great native plant diversity (with the exception of trees) in steppe regions, though today most are overgrazed, developed by humans, and tapped for their underlying oil and gas reserves.

All steppe climates are found in the middle of continents, on the leeward or rain shadow side of high mountain ranges, adjacent to grasslands. Other steppes with cold winters are found in Eurasia, particularly in Mongolia, Siberia, Tibet, and China. All tend to have cycles of roughly ten wet years with regular precipitation followed by dry cycles and drought. In Eurasia, humans used to cope with the dry periods by moving from place to place, living as nomads, but now they dig deep wells and set up irrigation systems. In the high plains of the western United States, Montana is the one state where drought is less common.

At higher elevations, in the mountains and on the high plateaus, the climate is known as highland and the biome is alpine.

Dominated by arctic and polar air, which keeps temperatures cool to cold and subject to extremely rapid changes, mountain climates act as important water storage areas for the surrounding lower-elevation areas, releasing water slowly as snow melts in the spring.

There is an imaginary line spanning high points in North America, called the Continental Divide, that runs roughly in a north–south direction from Alaska and Canada, through the Rocky Mountain states of Montana, Wyoming, Colorado, and New Mexico, and down through Mexico. The divide marks the separation of rivers flowing west to the Pacific and east toward the Atlantic and the Gulf of Mexico into drainage basins or watersheds. Every continent has at least one continental divide. In the United States, climates to the west of the Continental Divide are usually marked by milder winters, precipitation that's more evenly distributed throughout the year, cooler summers (in general), more clouds, and lighter winds than those on the eastern side. As a rule, the western slopes of mountain ranges in the western United States receive a lot more cool-season precipitation than the eastern slopes because they face the prevailing west–east winds. As air crosses the mountains heading east, it loses most of its moisture, creating a rain shadow on the eastern slopes. In Colorado, this is why schemes to divert snowmelt water from the Western Slope to the more-populated Front Range cities are always being proposed.

HIGH SUN, LOW WATER
Our biggest western asset is sunshine, and we have plenty of it. When I first came west,

Crab apple caught in a branch-breaking snow with its leaves still on, a common occurrence in fast-changing western springs and autumns.

though our region is considered semiarid overall (having about 10 to 20 inches of annual precipitation), some growing seasons can be remarkably cool and wet, and wetter-than-average seasons come in cycles.

I live in Colorado, between Boulder at the foothills and Longmont on the plains. Though the distance between these two cities is just 14 miles, the average annual precipitation varies from 20 inches in Boulder to 12 inches in Longmont. In fact, wide variations in both precipitation and temperature within short distances aren't uncommon. The difference in annual mean temperature between Pikes Peak, in Colorado Springs, and Las Animas, 90 miles to the southeast, is 35 degrees Fahrenheit, about the same as that between southern Florida and Iceland.

During droughts and when watering restrictions are imposed, water conservation always comes front and center, but it makes much more sense to value and pay attention to water use every day. Then, when the inevitable dry cycles and restrictions come, it won't be difficult to adapt. There are gardeners in the Southwest, including the Hopi, who have been successfully growing food for a very long time with far less water than most of us can even imagine possible. (For more on water, see chapter 9).

I was overwhelmed by Colorado's sunny climate. East Coast summers were hot, muggy, buggy, and, unless you were at the beach, you glimpsed the sun through a canopy of trees if it wasn't cloudy or raining; at night it could be uncomfortably hot for sleeping.

In the West, nearly every day is sunny with wide-open cheerful blue skies. Even

WILD SWINGS AND EXTREMES

Most of the western states' population lives in a milder corridor at the edge of the plains near the foothills, where water from mountain snowmelt is tapped to quench society's thirst. Although temperatures are not as cold as the high alpine areas, winter and summer temperatures can still be extreme.

The drier, more populated cities of the Front Range depend on mountain snowmelt for water. Because they face prevailing winds, the western slopes of mountain ranges in the western United States receive much more precipitation than the eastern slopes.

The rapid temperature swings that we experience in our interior continental climate are hard on trees and other plants that haven't evolved in these conditions. Fronts blow in and out rapidly, and even more rapidly in the mountains.

In 1949 in Fort Collins, Colorado, where pie cherries were a big industry at the time, the temperature dropped 90 degrees in less than twenty-four hours, from 50 degrees Fahrenheit to −40 degrees, wiping out every cherry tree in the city. According to a Colorado Cooperative Extension Service report,

you could hear the trees cracking as they froze. The record for a twenty-four-hour chill, however, is a 100 degree drop from 44 degrees to −54 degrees, set in Browning, Montana, in January 1916.

Areas closer to the coasts and Great Lakes experience more stable temperatures because large bodies of water absorb, hold, and then release heat slowly. This moderates dramatic temperature swings as well as the hot and cold extremes at both ends.

Mountain gardeners have their own unique set of extreme conditions, which increase with the altitude. These include a shorter growing season, colder nights, almost constant wind, more-intense UV sunlight, as well as more shade from evergreen trees and canyon slopes. Wildlife is more plentiful and the animals are bigger. The threat of wildfire is constant as a natural part of the mountain ecosystem, and the fuel—trees—is bigger. Soils are leaner, rockier, and slower to warm up in the spring; however, there are also some lush valleys with rich glacial soils and pockets of sandy river bottom.

WINTER

Dry winters are the norm on the eastern steppe plains, with some below-zero cold snaps and occasional snowstorms, but we also have many warm winter days. The higher elevation and thinner atmosphere allows greater solar penetration so winters are more pleasant, even when snow is on the ground. Strong chinook winds blow down from the mountains to the eastern high plains, sometimes reaching 100 miles per hour in the foothills, where the transition is especially abrupt. These roof-ripping warm dry winds can occur in any season, but they're most common during the winter, when they quickly warm up temperatures and can make a big snow disappear in a day or two. Because chinooks don't occur on the western side of the Continental Divide, winters tend to remain cooler there.

Once in a great while, we have blizzards with big accumulations of snow that cover the ground for weeks on the plains, but usually the snow is no match for our intense sun and warm winds, so it doesn't stick around for long. High winds create fire danger both in the mountains and on the plains. While grass fires and forest fires have long been a part of the natural cycle, they are more frequent now due to human carelessness or malice, and they can be much more severe because of all the homes, propane tanks, and other combustible objects in the landscape.

In some parts of the West—Wyoming, for example—and many places in the mountains, wind is almost constant year-round. That's great for windmills but very tough on soil and vegetable plants. Dry, windy western winters desiccate and erode uncovered soil.

Added protection in the form of mulch is essential to building and maintaining a healthy environment year-round for the worms and other helpful soil creatures in a food garden. Mulch reduces evaporation and modulates the soil temperature. Whether you live in the mountains or on the plains, the simple step of covering bare garden soil with a thick layer of mulch, especially in the winter, will save you a lot of work and do more for the health of the soil life than anything else you can do. Most trees benefit from mulch too.

SPRING AND AUTUMN

Western springs and autumns don't usually unfold gradually. Instead, the temperature often seesaws back and forth between cold and warm weather, sometimes dramatically. The plains receive almost all their annual precipitation from April through September, and the Front Range usually receives more snow in early spring and late autumn than in midwinter.

Late spring freezes often nip fruit trees and unprotected warm-season crops, like tomatoes, if they are planted out before the average last frost date. Early fall freezes can put an untimely end to unprotected gardens, even though warm, frost-free weather usually continues for weeks afterward. If you can protect your garden plants during these early fall freezes, you can extend the growing season and they will keep on producing (see chapter 7, Extending the Season).

Nonnative trees are vulnerable to late-spring and early fall hard freezes and heavy, wet snows that often break limbs or damage their internal vascular systems. This is why so many western trees have odd shapes.

The timing for trees budding out in spring and losing their leaves in fall is determined both by sunlight and temperature, although the exact balance depends on the species and drought stress. Our western UV sunlight is so intense compared to low-elevation humid climates that many nonnatives are coaxed out of their winter dormancy and get caught with their blooms showing when temperatures are still too cold. I like to plant fruit trees on the north side of a building, where they remain shaded until the angle of the sun is higher later in the spring; that way they're less likely to dry out in the winter or break dormancy early and become susceptible to late freezes. Since bees usually fly only when the temperature is at least 50 degress Fahrenheit, early bloomers may also miss their pollination window if blossoms open during a cool spell. In the autumn, early freezes can cause serious damage if trees still cling to their green leaves.

Summer

Summers in the mountains are always pleasantly cool, and warm to hot during the day on the plains. Nights are usually cool,

including in the high desert. With the intensity of high-altitude western sunlight, some plants, like lettuce and basil, that do just fine in full sun in other climates will fare better here with some afternoon shade.

Hot winds and low humidity will quickly parch bare soil and stress garden plants. Drying winds can come up any time, and they are especially hard on vegetable plants with broad leaves like cucumbers, squash, lettuce and other greens, eggplant, broccoli, and sometimes tomatoes. Even well-watered plants may wilt in hot summer sun because water evaporates through their foliage more quickly than they are able to absorb it through their roots.

Due to our low humidity and rainfall, plus cold winters, there are also relatively few destructive or annoying insects in the West, though mosquito-borne West Nile Virus has taken its toll on our insect-free reputation in recent years.

Thunderstorms can materialize at any time. On summer afternoons they often

A summer afternoon thunderhead builds on the plains.

cool things off pleasantly, but sometimes they arrive with strong wind, heavy rain, and dreaded hail. The Front Range in Colorado and Wyoming has some of the most brutal hail in North America, and it's often localized to the point where it completely devastates gardens on one side of a street while leaving the other side unscathed. Hail doesn't spare the mountains either. Thunderstorms with hail are more frequent there, though they are usually less intense and the hail is smaller than on the plains.

During the growing season, it rains more frequently in the mountains, but rainfall on the plains is often more intense and confined to specific areas. Even though thunderstorms can produce heavy rain, their localized nature means they don't have much impact on the state's overall water supply.

The West Is Defined by Its Climate

In 1879, western explorer, expedition leader, and geologist John Wesley Powell sent a report to the US Geological Survey (USGS) in which he defined a line along the 100th meridian west that roughly divides the United States into east and west. The boundary marked the reach of moist air from the Gulf of Mexico and the border of semiarid land to the west, which generally receives less than 20 inches of precipitation. It also marks where the Great Plains rise above 2,000 feet in elevation in their approach to the Rocky Mountains. Today the 100th meridian west divides the Dakotas and Nebraska in half, cuts through the western third of Kansas, follows the western border of Oklahoma except for the panhandle, and divides Texas almost in half.

The landscape of the mountain West is more diverse than any other part of the United States. It includes rolling grassland plains, all of the major deserts in North America (including the largest high desert valley in the world—Colorado's San Luis Valley), the highest mountains in the country, and alpine biomes in every state. A few high-elevation places receive up to 60 inches or more of rain and snow annually.

The 100th meridian roughly divides the United States into east and west.

The semiarid portion of the western United States extends west to the Cascade and Sierra Nevada mountain ranges (which block moisture from the Pacific), north through Montana, and as far south as the northern third of Arizona and New Mexico, the panhandle of Oklahoma, and the top piece of Texas that includes Amarillo. While there is climate diversity within this semiarid region, in general, conditions are similar enough to include them within the scope of this book.

Powell, who became the second director of the USGS, had the idea to create western state boundaries based on watersheds. From his firsthand experience on expeditions, he believed that only about 2 percent of the lands in the interior West—those that are

Western United States Precipitation

Average Annual Precipitation (in inches)

- 180.1–200
- 140.1–180
- 120.1–140
- 100.1–120
- 80.1–100
- 70.1–80
- 60.1–70
- 50.1–60
- 40.1–50
- 35.1–40
- 30.1–35
- 25.1–30
- 20.1–25
- 15.1–20
- 10.1–15
- 5.1–10
- 5 and less

Explorer John Wesley Powell recommended that all but 2 percent of the western territory be designated for low-density grazing and conservation, but the land-rich railroad companies lobbied successfully for farm-based development and lured settlers with advertisements depicting lush farmland.

close to water sources—could be used for agriculture. He warned that development was likely to result in ongoing squabbles and litigation over water rights, and he recommended that most of the territory be designated for conservation and low-density grazing since there wasn't enough water to support farming. Had Powell's recommendation been followed and western state boundaries been drawn to reflect existing watersheds, today's map with blocks of rectangular states would look completely different. And had those states been instructed to limit growth to what their specific watersheds could

Horace Greeley's Reforms

The agricultural town of Greeley, Colorado, as well as towns and counties in several other states bear Horace Greeley's name. Residents today might be surprised to learn that Greeley, who lost the 1872 presidential election to Ulysses S. Grant, promoted socialist agrarian reforms such as giving free land to the poor. For several years he employed Karl Marx and Fredrich Engles as European correspondents for his paper, the *New-York Tribune*. He also practiced and promoted vegetarianism for its health benefits.

support, the current fighting over western water might have been prevented.

But the railroad companies had been granted huge tracts of western land in return for building the lines, and they pressed eagerly for growth. Lobbying successfully for development, they persuaded Congress to pass laws that encouraged settlement based on farming. Newspaper editor and politician Horace Greeley, a booster of agriculture who was also sympathetic to the desperate plight of the unemployed poor in his home city of New York, gave the famous call: "Go west, young man, go forth into the country."

A HOPEFUL FOLLY: "RAIN FOLLOWS THE PLOW"

A once popular but now discredited theory of climatology known as "Rain follows the plow" was embraced during the late nineteenth century. The theory held that turning over the prairie sod and deep tilling of the ground by "an army of frontier farmers from Manitoba to Texas" would create a new green surface of crops to replace sparse buffalo grass and that this would bring rain. Cyrus Thomas and Charles Dana Wilber were two early proponents of this theory who believed that

> No one can question or doubt the inevitable effect of this cooling condensing surface upon the moisture in the atmosphere…By this wonderful provision, which is only man's mastery over nature, the clouds are dispensing copious rains…[the plow] is the instrument which separates civilization from savagery; and converts a desert into a farm or garden. The chief agency in this transformation is agriculture. To be more concise. Rain follows the plow.

Embellishing the premise, railroad company advertisements depicted the semiarid western terrain for sale as lush farmland.

Belief in the vision grew, bolstered by what we now know was a period of unusually heavy rainfall in the 1870s and early 1880s. Some say the theory was used to justify the expansion of agriculture and settlement in the West.

Mining and homesteading had lured many people to seek their fortunes and a better life; by 1877, white settlers already outnumbered American Indians in the West by forty to one. But during the following ten years, 4.5 million more people headed west, and many of them farmed in places that were previously considered too harsh for human settlement.

The new settlers tilled the lean western prairie soils and planted crops. No one understood that deep-rooted prairie grasses and plants had been holding the soil in place for thousands of years, or that repeated deep tilling dries out soil and destroys the fabric of soil life—the bacteria, fungi, and microscopic and larger creatures that make plant life possible. Whenever the cycle of wet years came to an end, life became much more difficult on the high plains.

SOIL TURNED TO DUST

In the early twentieth century, wetter weather returned again and there were further waves of new immigrants. Automated farming techniques dramatically increased the amount of acreage under cultivation and more cattle were grazing the land too. But a severe drought hit the western plains beginning in 1930. Decades of deep plowing without any accompanying strategies to conserve or regenerate soil, or to prevent its erosion, resulted in the Dust Bowl, a period of gigantic dust storms or "black blizzards" affecting 100 million acres in the southern high plains,

Dust storm headlines from the 1930s and '40s. These "black blizzards" affected 100 million acres that farmers had deep tilled for decades. No one understood that native deep-rooted plains grasses held the soil in place for thousands of years.

especially the panhandle area of Oklahoma. Land from which the fertility had essentially been mined for agricultural production for decades without replenishment simply dried up and blew away. Huge roiling clouds of dust covered the sun and fell as black or red snow in areas thousands of miles away. Hundreds of thousands of people abandoned their homes and land and moved to other states, especially California.

As soon as he took office in 1933, President Franklin D. Roosevelt set up and implemented government agencies and programs in an intensive effort to conserve soil and encourage improved farming techniques. Five years later, the dust storms had been significantly reduced, and the following year regular precipitation finally returned to the high plains after nine years of full-blown drought. One long-term effect of the Dust Bowl was that farms in the region became bigger as those who stayed behind acquired the poor-quality land of those who had abandoned their homesteads.

Many dams and irrigation projects were constructed throughout the West during the first half of the twentieth century, providing the irrigation water that stimulated rapid agricultural growth in several western states. Population growth soon followed. After World War II, there was another boom in urban areas in Arizona, New Mexico, Utah, Colorado, and Nevada. As water and resources became strained, water was diverted from agriculture to quench the thirst of major cities and population centers, and this practice continues today, along with the pumping of groundwater from aquifers.

EFFECTS OF GLOBAL CLIMATE CHANGE

Water shortage in the West is an issue under any climate scenario. A growing population with domestic, recreational, and agricultural demands is already putting great stress on western water supplies. Even if the climate remains stable and we receive typical amounts of precipitation, future water shortages seem likely. The problem is intensified with the potential for hotter summers and reduced snowpack.

Western states depend on the runoff from melting mountain snowpack for water. Of the water we use outdoors and in our homes, 40 percent comes from snowmelt that ends up in reservoirs. But if temperatures continue to get warmer due to global climate change, more precipitation will fall as rain, and the snow that falls could melt earlier in the spring. A cover of snow on the ground keeps soil cool and reflects sunlight back into space. But early melt-outs result in warmer soils that absorb more moisture, plus greater evaporation rates. This means that less precipitation may actually reach storage reservoirs and be available during the growing season.

One of the most succinct observations about the food security implications of global climate change was made by environmental journalist Meredith Niles, citing

Dust storms like this one caused high drifts of dirt and forced many farmers to abandon their land.

research published in *Science*: "Whether you believe global warming is part of a 'natural cycle' or a man-made phenomenon is irrelevant. The bottom line is that our earth is rapidly warming, and this is going to drastically affect our food supply."

We may or may not be able to reach consensus on effective strategies for combating global climate change or implement them in time to avert a food supply crisis, but there are many things we can do to improve conditions for growing our own food in gardens. The most important place to start is in the soil.

Chapter 3
Soil: The Backbone of Organic Gardening

Soil is a complex web of minerals, organisms and microorganisms, decaying plants and animals, water, air, and the relationships and interactions between them. Lean native western soils support native plants, but food plants require more organic matter, nutrients, and water.

The most important thing to know about soil is that it is bustling with life, movement, energy, even electricity when it's healthy. Often described as a living, breathing organism, soil is in a constant state of transformation as the dead is continually reprocessed for the benefit of the living. Soil structure has been created slowly, over geologic time, through weathering and decay by microbes that have been around for thousands of years. Much more than an anchor for plants, soil is a complex web of minerals, organisms and microorganisms, organic matter from decaying plants and animals, water, air, and the relationships and interactions between them.

Western soils are typically lean, with very little organic material compared to more-humid woodland climates where lots of native deciduous trees and shrubs grow. But there are also alluvial plains and valleys with old river-bottom sandy loam. Western soils are just right for the many native plants that have evolved here and for others from similar climates that adapt easily to our conditions. In fact, if you give these plants richer soil and lots of water, they will probably die.

To grow food plants, however, our soils need added organic matter like compost. This provides the crumbly texture that allows crop roots to get a good foothold and grow, the right porosity so that the soil drains but also holds some moisture, plus the air spaces that roots need and the nutrients that support growth and fruit and vegetable formation. (Technically speaking, the tomatoes, cucumbers, squash, and so forth are the fruits of the plants.)

Our most important job as vegetable gardeners is to feed and sustain soil life, often called the soil food web, beginning with the microbes. If we do this, our plants will thrive, we'll grow nutritious, healthy

The lack of organic matter and soil critters is immediately noticeable in conventional farm soils that are dependent on synthetic fertilizers and pesticides. It's much easier to continually build healthy soil in small-scale gardens, and this is a responsibility of organic gardeners.

food, and our soil conditions will get better each year. This is what is meant by the adage "Feed the soil, not the plants." On the relatively small scale of home gardens, this is very easy to accomplish using completely organic and inexpensive materials.

Some home vegetable gardeners start out with conditions that are even more daunting than lean native soils. Housing developments are sometimes built on land that has been depleted by years of chemical-intensive

farming. When contractors dig foundations and build houses, topsoil often becomes a casualty. The hard-packed subsoil (often referred to as builders' clay), which has little if any organic material, then ends up on the surface after topsoil has been stripped away. Sod is sometimes laid down right on top of this hard subsoil.

It's not uncommon for construction debris to be buried too. When I first dug a garden at my townhouse in Boulder, I was expecting the hard builder's clay, but the jarring clang of the shovel hitting what turned out to be huge chunks of concrete was an unpleasant surprise. I was able to remove them with patience, perseverance, and a crowbar. Today I'd probably find someone else to do it. Occasionally I've unearthed old glass bottles or other "treasures," but more often curiosities, including one old shoe full of poker chips.

TOPSOIL

Topsoil supports all of our food plants. It has the highest concentration of life, both microscopic and larger, and organic material like plant debris and humus than soils lower down. But even in healthy, amended garden soil the percentage of organic matter, which is what holds water, is usually only about 5 or 6 percent. In the majority of native western soils, the percentage is 1 or 2 percent. In soils that have been worn out by years of chemical fertilizer applications, pesticides, and regular deep tilling, the percentage of organic material is even smaller, which makes them more likely to dry out and blow away.

Topsoil is typically 2 to 8 inches deep, and it only exists on about one $\frac{1}{32}$ of the Earth's surface. Incredibly, Iowa topsoil used to be 2 to 3 feet deep 150 years ago. (It's now roughly half that, and its structure and quality have deteriorated considerably.) Here's a commonly used analogy: Visualize an apple. Cut it in half, cut one of the halves into quarters, and then cut one of those pieces into quarters again. Take one of these slices, which is $\frac{1}{32}$ of the entire apple. The layer of skin on this one thin slice represents the total amount of topsoil on our planet. All the rest of the skin represents surfaces that are covered with

water, ice, deserts, mountains, roads in cities, and rocky, wet, hot, or infertile areas.

It takes roughly five hundred years for an inch of topsoil to be naturally deposited, but today 25 billion tons of topsoil are lost each year to erosion by wind or water, largely as a result of human activities, including poor land management and overgrazing, industrial-scale agricultural practices that deplete rather than build soil, and housing and commercial development. Cornell University ecology professor David Pimentel believes that soil erosion is "second only to population growth as the biggest environmental problem the world faces."

Had more of us understood in the last century just how alive and valuable the topsoil layer is, perhaps we would have refrained from declaring all-out war on it with pesticides, herbicides, fungicides, synthetic anhydrous ammonia-based fertilizers that harden the ground, and the deep tilling that rips up the tapestry of soil structure and soil life. Two world wars, plus the Korean and Vietnam wars, provided not only many of the chemicals adapted and marketed for postwar agricultural use, but also the mindset necessary to convince farmers and the public that we needed to do battle to overcome nature and her "pests," at every turn employing a chemical arsenal.

Today, more of us are aware of sounder ecological principles, including a more holistic view of natural systems, a recognition that all living things are connected, and an approach to growing that works *with* nature. An organic garden with living soil may be the single best place to gain this understanding and put it into practice.

Soil Structure

Soil with good structure has an equal amount of moisture and air in the spaces between the particles. Most plant roots need oxygen just as much as they need water. Organic matter from compost, dried leaves, aged manure, pine needles, and the like helps soil retain water rather than drying out right away, and it also makes soil lighter by creating air spaces between the particles, allowing water to drain. Rice and cranberries may grow in wet mud, but vegetables and other fruits will not.

Compacted, hard soils are difficult for growing vegetable plants. It's much easier for both plant roots and water to penetrate soil that has good structure. Since walking directly on garden soil squeezes the air out of it and makes it hard, this should always be avoided, unless you have a thick layer of mulch on top or a board you can walk on to prevent compaction.

Soils are either sandy with large particles that drain very quickly, clay with small fine particles that hold water, or something in between. Loam is the ideal soil for growing vegetables, with its mixture of different-sized particles. It has better drainage than clay and more nutrients and humus than sandy soil.

Clay Soil

Except for pockets of old sandy river bottom, much soil in populated areas tends to be clay, which means the soil particles are small and fine, and therefore more numerous, creating a lot of surface area. Clay soil holds nutrients in all the nooks and crannies between its particles so it's more fertile than sandy soils. In microscopic close-ups, clay particles appear stacked together in thin skewed layers, like mica. And if you've ever made pottery, you know that wet clay is sticky and holds together in clumps.

Most of our rain during the growing season comes in big soaking bursts and is retained by clay soils. I've driven on red clay dirt roads in southern Colorado that turn almost as thick and slippery as lava flows in heavy rain and then dry out leaving hard, heavily crusted ruts.

You might think it would be easier to get a shovel into wet soil, but if you have clay, it's best to let it dry out for a few days before working it. Otherwise, you will remove all the air pockets and destroy the soil structure by compacting it; the end result will be a garden bed full of big clumps of dry soil that are as hard as rocks.

Compost and fibrous amendments like green manures made from chopped up leaves, straw, grass clippings, pine needles, and decomposing plants will improve the texture of clay soils.

Sandy Soil

If your soil is sandy, it will drain and dry out quickly. The particles of medium-grade sand are 125 times larger than clay particles and will feel gritty and coarse in your fingers. Sandy soils are easier to work than clay and are well aerated since there is so much space between the particles, but they don't hold water and they are very lean, which means they don't hold on to nutrients. Though this can be exactly what you need for native and rock garden plants, to grow vegetables successfully you'll need to water more frequently and add more fibrous organic material to retain water, plus a richer mix of compost and nutrients.

Loam and Silt Soils

Loam and silt soils fall in between sand and clay. Often found in floodplains, silt is very light; it compacts and erodes easily. Its irregular particles are all about the same size, bigger than clay and smaller than sand, and not very good for growing vegetables. Loam, on the other hand, has a mixture of different-sized particles as well as the best permeability and water retention of any soil for growing vegetables. Gardeners in our climate who have loamy soil are extremely fortunate. The rest of us need to build it.

Humus

While clay soils hold the nutrients in our semiarid western climates, natural humus, the spongy dark layer of organic material just under surface leaf litter, is the major nutrient storehouse in more humid climates where rainfall and woodland vegetation are plentiful. But unlike clay, humus also greatly improves the physical condition of soil. Through a natural process called humification, organic material, including plant, microbe, and animal remains, breaks down, providing nutrients for plants and conditioning the soil in the process. By adding compost, moisture, and mulch we can create this active humus in our garden soils. It is also sold as a soil amendment that's rich in microbial life.

But humus can get to a point where it is chemically stable, meaning it will remain intact for eons without breaking down any further. This stable humus can be thousands of years old, and it doesn't provide any nutrients at all for microbes or plants. Mountain peat is an example of stable humus. Not only does it make a very poor soil amendment, mountain-peat mining is extremely

disruptive to fragile mountain ecosystems. It is an irreplaceable, unsustainable resource that has no place in a garden. Ask questions before buying bagged soil mixes that simply list "peat" as an ingredient.

The life cycles of thick native prairie grasses and other plants of the Great Plains accumulated organic matter as humus in the soil over a long time, creating some of the richest, most productive topsoil in the world. Just fifty years ago, the rich midwestern topsoil was still fertile and spongy, with air and water able to move easily through it. Today farmers complain about its hard, cementlike properties.

Soil Critters
Microbes (or The Microherd)

Biodynamic gardeners, always mindful of the cosmic big picture, remind us that the minerals in our soils were once stardust. And thanks to electron microscopes, we now have a close-up view of many fantastic microcreatures that populate our soil, including microarthropods like springtails and pseudoscorpions, protozoa, microscopic worms and nematodes that sometimes get cinched in fungal lassos, mites of all kinds with scary-looking

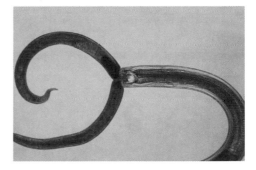

A microscopic monochoid nematode (roundworm) eats a different type of nematode. Some species are sold as beneficials for gardens.

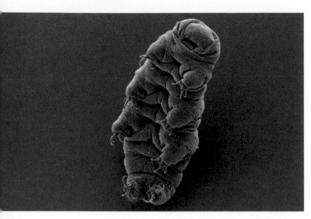

Water bears are named for their slow-gaited walk. Also known as tardigrades, these microbial extremophiles can survive a range of temperatures from near absolute zero (−459.67 degrees Fahrenheit) to 304 degrees, plus 1,000 times more radiation than other animals.

jaws and claws, and tiny puffed-up water bears that hang out in damp, mossy places like miniature versions of the giant tethered inflatable characters in parades.

In the last twenty years, microbes with exotic metabolisms have been found miles underground, living in more-extreme conditions than were ever before considered possible. The discovery of these extremophiles has changed scientists' notions about the thresholds and origins of life on our planet. Some live off hydrocarbons in oil and coal deposits, others off the organic carbon from meteors that crashed deep into the earth long ago. Remarkable "rock eaters" (lithotropes) harvest energy by snapping up electrons from the atoms of inorganic minerals in rocks or from gas atoms like hydrogen, nitrogen, and sulfur.

E. O. Wilson, the ecologist and entomologist who invented the term *biodiversity*, says that we have catalogued almost 2 million species on Earth but almost 10 million have yet to be discovered, most of them microbes.

The host of tiny microscopic beings that live in soil—invertebrates, fungi, and bacteria—are transformers and decomposers. They scavenge underground for minerals and the organic remains of plants and animals, which they consume and excrete as nutrients in a form that plants can easily absorb. Microbes are the most efficient recyclers on the planet, and there are billions of them in a handful of healthy soil.

FUNGI AND BACTERIA RULE

We have been taught to fear fungi and bacteria as nasty germs that cause disease, yet there are many more beneficial than harmful types, and they are the most numerous members of a healthy soil food web. In fact, some researchers suggest that living too clean deprives our immune systems of the training that comes with routine exposure to harmless microorganisms like the ones that live in soil. Playing in dirt, something most kids used to do, may be the best training there is. Without it, our immune systems apparently don't learn to tell the difference between the good guys and the bad guys and instead react defensively to benign substances, like pollen and pet dandruff, to which we "become allergic."

Recent studies show that one species of soil bacteria, *Mycobacterium vaccae*, works a lot like antidepressants to stimulate serotonin activity in the brain. It's easy to ingest the bacteria in a number of ways, by breathing it in, drinking water that contains it, or simply by eating plants picked from your garden. This means there is a measurable physiological effect—happiness—that comes from direct, hands-on contact with soil, as long as there's life in it. If you kill the microbes with chemicals, you're out of luck.

Soil fungi and bacteria help soil particles clump together and decay the bodies of dead plants and animals. Sometimes, in the process, they tie up or immobilize nutrients like nitrogen and phosphorus in their bodies, robbing plants of nutrients temporarily, but keeping the nutrients in the soil, accessible to plants in a slow-release form over time. This is also the reason why carbon-rich mulches like fresh sawdust and wood chips are discouraged in the vegetable garden. They stimulate the microbes to tie up nitrogen while decomposition takes place, making the nitrogen less available to growing

plants. But if there's plenty of time for the material to decompose in an inactive part of the garden, about six months to a year or more—depending on the amount, the size of the chips, and how much moisture they receive—the nutrients will again become available for plants and the soil tilth will be much improved.

Plants secrete carbohydrates and proteins called exudates through their roots to attract beneficial fungi and bacteria, which in turn nourish the plants and protect their roots. Mycorrhizal fungi cover and extend many plants' roots, especially those of trees and shrubs, with a network of fine, lacy filaments, building connecting bridges between soil and the host plants' roots. This significantly

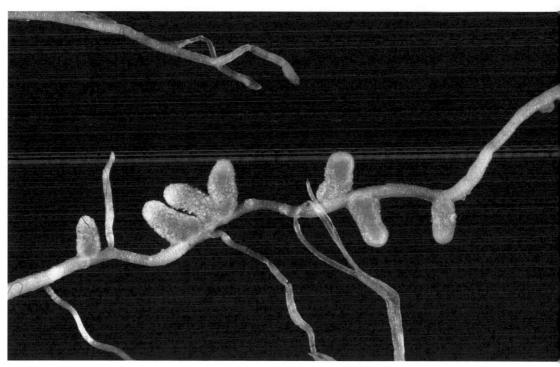

Nitrogen-fixing nodules on the roots of a legume. Once the plant dies and decomposes, the accumulated nitrogen becomes available to other plants.

Soil: The Backbone of Organic Gardening 31

Benefits of Aerated Compost Tea

By Roland Evans

Using aerated compost tea is a simple and effective way to bring your soil to life. High-quality compost tea teems with trillions of beneficial soil microorganisms. Once in the soil, these microbes work hard to increase fertility and transform nutrients into natural forms that are easiest for plants to use.

Aerated compost tea is brewed by bubbling water through a container of water into which a microbial starter and special nutrients have been added. Because beneficial microbes are aerobic (oxygen loving), it is essential to aerate the water for the whole brew time of about twenty-four hours using an aquarium air pump. This will provide the microbes with a perfect environment so they can reproduce at the highest rate.

The quality of compost tea depends primarily on the diversity and concentration of beneficial microbes in the starter. This can be well-finished compost, worm castings (vermicompost), or a proprietary starter such as Alaska Humisoil. Use the highest quality available.

In addition to oxygen, microbes need food—sugars and proteins for bacteria, fibrous materials for fungi. You can create your own nutrients from ingredients such as molasses, fish powder, bran, and kelp, or you can purchase ready-made products. The Internet provides useful information, but again, use the best-quality products obtainable; don't scrimp on quality.

Once brewing is completed, spray the diluted compost tea all over your soil and plants. Foliar spraying creates a biofilm of living organisms on the leaves that protects the plant from attack. Research has shown that aerated compost tea has many benefits:

- Faster-growing, healthier plants
- High-quality nutritious vegetables and fruits
- Increased resistance to pests and disease
- Reduced watering and fertilization needs
- Enhanced sustainable soil ecology

Using aerated compost tea will transform your soil ecology and may possibly change the way you think about gardening.

increases the roots' surface area and enables them to spread farther in search of water and nutrients. One of the most dramatic effects of mycorrhizal fungi colonization is the increase in phosphorus uptake for the host plant in soils that are low in this nutrient.

Bacteria are the oldest form of life on Earth with the biggest populations in soil. These single-celled organisms are the major food energy source for larger soil microbes, making them an essential building block of the soil food web.

Some bacteria create nodules that fix (i.e., hold and accumulate) nitrogen on the roots of legumes like peas, beans, clovers, and alfalfa. When the spent legume plants are turned in or left to decompose in the soil, the accumulated nitrogen becomes available to other plants. Instead of pulling up pea and bean plants when they stop producing in the garden, cut them off at soil level and leave the roots to enrich the soil with their nitrogen nodules.

Larger but still microbial nematodes and protozoa eat soil bacteria and fungi and then are eaten by larger microbes and arthropods as the soil food chain progresses. There is a lot of action in the plant root zone (rhizosphere) as all the complex members of the microherd both help and compete with each other to cycle nutrients.

Soil fertility problems are frequently the result of an imbalance of soil life, and this occurs with repeated use of chemical fertilizer salts that deplete soil microbe populations and dry out soil. Fungi and bacteria break down organic matter and hold on to nutrients in the soil, but they must then be eaten by larger microbes before the nutrients are released and become available to plants. Adding compost or compost tea to soil is the best way to introduce the microbes necessary to regain a healthy balance. Mulching helps keep them there. Compost maintains soil porous enough for some of the larger predatory microbes to flourish, and these will keep plant parasites in check too. If you create the conditions for a healthy, diverse population of critters to thrive both in your soil and around your garden, very few problems will develop, and if they do, they will usually be resolved without intervention.

Soil from an organically rich, heavily mulched garden is loaded with worms. Their presence also indicates a healthy population of microscopic soil critters.

EARTHWORMS

The underground soil residents most familiar and visible to gardeners are earthworms. They play several crucial roles in soil health, first recognized by Charles Darwin, who spent much of his life studying them. In a long-term experiment, he spread a layer of chalk over a grassy field and then, over a period of twenty-nine years, measured how deeply it was buried and how much humus (he called it "vegetable mould") was brought up to the surface. Astounded by the results, he concluded that "all the vegetable mould over the whole country has passed many times through, and will again pass many times through, the intestinal canals of worms."

Earthworms drag food (plant debris) down from the ground's surface into the soil and deposit castings (worm poop) that are loaded with nutrients that are especially beneficial for plants. Tireless tillers,

earthworms continually aerate and mix the soil while creating channels for plant roots as they tunnel deeply and extensively underground. They move forward by secreting a nitrogen-rich slime, which stays in the soil for plants and helps soil particles cluster together. They eat protozoa, fungi, and other microorganisms, often helping transport them by dispersing them alive in their castings. A healthy earthworm population greatly decreases soil-borne diseases and indicates that a healthy herd of microbes also inhabits the soil.

According to studies from one of the world's oldest agricultural research stations in England, the number of earthworms beneath rich fertile farmland is estimated at up to 1.75 million per acre and could weigh more than the farmer's livestock on top of it.

Most animals have lungs of some kind on the inside of their bodies. For earthworms, the entire body surface is its respiratory organ, and it must stay constantly moist at all times to do its job. Secretions accomplish this for the most part, but since earthworms need surrounding moisture to thrive and can quickly perish in dry conditions, they burrow deeper into soil whenever the top layers dry out. They can plug their burrows as protection against incoming water, but when it rains hard (or if we water too fast and heavily) and that soil becomes saturated, especially clay soil, which has few air pockets, earthworms come up to the surface to find oxygen. Then, as temperatures warm up and the soil dries out, they can dry up and quickly die, especially if they get stranded on a hard surface like a sidewalk.

Earthworms are very sensitive to temperature, pH, salts, soil texture, chemical fertilizers, and pesticides, so if they don't appear and stick around, you'll know that something isn't quite right in your garden. What's good for the earthworms is also good for the microbes and the plants you're growing. An organic garden enriched with compost and covered with mulch to keep the surface from drying out creates ideal conditions, allowing worms to continue improving the soil for you.

Darwin discovered lots of fascinating things about earthworms. They are blind, but they can sense light, becoming more active in its absence. They are deaf, but they retreat from even the tiniest vibration. They are hermaphrodites, but most species mate with a partner and each worm gets to experience sex as both a male and a female simultaneously, in languid sessions lasting about an hour. They can double their population every two to three months (no wonder!) and live for fifteen years or more.

My garden helper, Florentino Martinez,

told me his wife fried up and ate earthworms when she didn't have enough breast milk for their child. He says it's a common practice in Mexico and it works. In other parts of the world, earthworms are considered a protein-rich delicacy, and lots of animals from bears and foxes to birds, frogs, turtles, and snakes also depend on them.

Some worm species, like red wrigglers and others sold specifically for worm- or vermicomposting, won't survive in soil. These must be kept and fed in boxes or bins; only their castings go in the garden. Likewise, terrestrial earthworm species live in the ground and won't survive confined in bins.

SINGING THE SOIL ELECTRIC

Not only are there chemical relationships between plant roots and microbes, but electrical exchanges are also continually occurring underground. In soil science this is referred to as cation exchange, and it's all about moving electrons around. Tiny particles called ions are groups of atoms (compounds) with a positive or negative electrical charge. Cations are the positive ions (easy to remember if you like cats), and anions are negative.

As with magnetic forces, opposites attract and attach to each other. Tiny humus and clay particles both carry a strong enough negative charge to attract and efficiently absorb positively charged plant nutrient ions as they travel through soil dissolved in water. But some nutrients like nitrate, sulfate, and phosphate carry a negative charge, so they are repelled by soil particles. With nothing to hold on to, they are easily washed away when it rains or when you water the garden, which is why soil sometimes lacks these particular nutrients.

Plant root hairs have a positive charge. This makes it possible for them to exchange some of their positive hydrogen cations in trade for the nutrients held by negatively charged humus and clay particles. This exchange is how plants eat. Soil with a lot of clay and/or organic particles has a high cation exchange capacity (CEC), providing more nourishment for plants. Since sand particles are too large to carry a charge, sandy soils have a low CEC, meaning low fertility and less food for plants.

Soil pH

In chemistry, pH is a measure of acidity and alkalinity on a scale of 1 to 14, with 7 considered neutral. What's really being measured is the concentration of hydrogen ions. A low pH, with relatively few hydrogen ions, is acidic. A pH of 14 has an extremely high concentration of hydrogen ions and is extremely alkaline (also called basic). The pH affects the solubility and availability of minerals and nutrients to plants. Most vegetables prefer a slightly acidic to neutral pH of 6.2 to 7, because that's the range where nutrients and minerals become most available to them.

Alkaline soils are dominated by bacteria, which vegetables like, while acidic soils, which most trees and woody plants prefer, are dominated by fungi. However, healthy soil usually contains a mixture of both.

Our drier western soils are more alkaline than the woodland soils of humid regions. The good news for vegetable gardeners is that adding organic material and good-quality compost (without salts) will almost always bring the pH just where it needs to be while also improving soil texture.

Salts

Ask a knowledgeable person about the biggest problem with western soils and the answer you'll probably get is salts. In Colorado alone, nearly a million acres of irrigated land are affected by salt buildups. You can sometimes see a white crust on top of soil, indicating a high salt content. People often think this is an alkaline crust, which is different, though salts and alkalinity often go hand in hand.

Too much salt causes chemical imbalances and prevents plants from absorbing water. Seeds don't germinate and plant growth slows significantly. The leaves on plants sprinkled with salty water often appear burned.

Salts tend to accumulate in our soils for several reasons. One is the natural weathering of minerals and fossil salt deposits from ancient seabeds. Since our climate is semi-arid, dissolved mineral salts accumulate in the soil as water evaporates because there isn't enough rainfall to leach or wash them out. Drainage problem areas, where the water table is high, for example, can also lead to salt accumulation. Another reason is that all over the West, water has been diverted from rivers and streams to basins and reservoirs for irrigation. In the process, water evaporates and salt levels become more concentrated. As irrigation water moves through canals and ditches and across dry fields and pastures, it often picks up more salts from fertilizers that have been applied.

All chemical fertilizers are salts. Their names end in *-ate* (phosphate, nitrate, and so on). Since typical plant uptake of these fertilizers is only 20–30 percent at best, even when applied at recommended rates—and many people overdo it, thinking more is better—the rest accumulates in the soil in a solid form that plants can't use, especially where rainfall is too low to wash it away. The fertilizer salt granules absorb any surrounding water, sometimes including water from the living cells of soil microorganisms, through osmosis, which kills them. Adding more chemical fertilizers makes things even worse. When chemical fertilizers are applied year after year to land where salt buildup

East near the Dead Sea that are managing to regenerate some of the saltiest, most degraded soils on the planet.)

A salinity test only costs a few dollars more with a regular soil analysis, so if you suspect a problem, it's well worth it. If salt levels are high, the test will indicate a high electrical conductivity (EC) rate. Salt-stressed plants will appear to be water stressed—because they are. The high salt level prevents them from taking up the water they need. Western well water often has a high salt content, so it should be tested before using it on gardens.

Some organic manures, composted manures, and topsoil mixes that contain these manures can be loaded with salts, especially if they're from animals confined to feedlots. It's worth asking if these sometimes expensive amendments have been tested for salts. If they haven't been tested, and especially if you plan to buy a large quantity, getting a salinity test first is a good idea. Western gardeners need to be especially careful about adding soil amendments that put any more salt into the soil.

Best Ways to Nurture the Soil Food Web

- Add organic material like compost, chopped-up leaves, grass clippings, straw, etc., to your soil and water it in.
- Use thick mulch to hold in moisture and condition soil.
- Use organic fertilizers and amendments that release nutrients slowly in a form plants can use.
- Use green manures made from plants and/or yard waste.
- Use compost tea as a drench to add lots of microbial life to soil.
- Make sure any added animal manures don't have a high salt content, even if they're composted.
- Keep poisons like pesticides and herbicides out of the garden.
- Use nontoxic solutions for pests if necessary, but be patient and learn to rely first on healthy soil and the natural balance to overcome pest problems.
- Avoid synthetic chemical fertilizers.
- Avoid compacting the soil by stepping on it.
- Don't rototill or deeply hand till after the first year the garden is established.

NUTRIENT-RICH SOIL AMENDMENTS
COMPOST
You can never have too much compost. Just about all your yard waste (fall leaves, prunings from trees, stalks from deadheading, old vegetable plants that aren't diseased) can be easily composted by putting it in a contained pile and watering it. Chop up branches and plant stalks into small pieces first so they'll decompose faster. A layer of chopped-up small branches works well at the bottom of a layered compost pile too, allowing air circulation from the bottom up. Many municipalities

in the soil is already an issue, the resulting accumulation can create a big problem that's difficult to fix. Nothing will grow in these soils. (I was pleased to watch Internet videos of permaculture projects in the Middle collect leaves and branches from residents and compost them. You can buy this yard-waste compost for a very reasonable price.

There are many books, pamphlets, videos, and classes that can show you how to compost. The basic idea is to layer the materials, alternating "green" nitrogen-rich pieces (food scraps, grass clippings, green weeds) and "brown" carbonaceous stuff (fall leaves, wood chips, twigs, branches), and keep them moist, but not soggy. The pile also needs some air, but not too much, and enough mass—roughly 3 to 4 feet around—to generate the heat needed to kill weed seeds and pathogens. Most compost contains 1–3 percent nitrogen. Don't use any materials that have been treated with chemicals since they kill off the microbes. In our climate, compost needs to be enclosed or covered so that it doesn't dry out.

Good compost can provide your soil and many plants with all or most of the nutrients they need, though heavy feeders will require some organic fertilizer.

MANURES

Manures are becoming harder to find. Both the chicken and turkey plants where I used to sometimes get manure have closed. But there are still horse barns around where you can often get manure for free, plus some dairies that have compost operations, and they usually have a loader too, so if you have access to a truck you will only have to unload at the other end. Make sure to ask if they will load your truck when you're inquiring. Sometimes you can find people who will deliver for a price too.

Llama manure is great in a garden. It has more nitrogen than other types but it's not

Manure Tea

One of the easiest and most effective ways to add nutrients in the vegetable garden for plants that are heavy feeders is to create and apply simple manure teas. Put a shovelful of aged cow or horse manure in a 5-gallon bucket and fill it with water. (Adjust proportionately for larger quantities—it isn't necessary to be exact.) Stir it well for a minute or two, and use it to water newly transplanted plants at the soil level, and again as plants flower. Some gardeners prefer to let it sit for a few days or up to two weeks before using. In this case, be sure to stir it for a few minutes every day to incorporate oxygen for the microbes.

Save manure tea for the heavy feeders: asparagus, broccoli, Brussels sprouts, cabbage, kale, cauliflower, collards, melons, squash, pumpkins, corn, eggplant, peppers, tomatoes, and celery. Light feeders like beans, peas, radishes, turnips, beets, alliums, greens (except spinach and kale), carrots, and sunflowers won't appreciate it.

To grow "killer tomatoes," Don Eversoll, author of *Secrets from My Grandma's Garden*, suggests adding two tablespoons of Epsom salts (for calcium, to avoid blossom-end rot) and several dried corncobs to the mix. After stirring and soaking, pour the tea, including some corncobs, into deep planting holes, then cover with good planting dirt and plant your tomatoes. The corncobs soak up the tea and release it slowly to plant roots. You can also use manure tea to give plants a boost a couple of times during the growing season.

"hot" like poultry manure and won't burn plants. Manure from animals that stand around in feedlots instead of wandering around pastures has a higher concentration of salts, which is not good for soil life or for your plants. The best time to apply manure that isn't already composted is in the fall so it has plenty of time to break down and mellow. Dried manure has a higher nutrient content than fresh. Hot composted manure is much

Average Nutrient Concentrations of Organic Materials and Their Relative Availability for Plants*

Material	% Nitrogen	% Potash (Potassium)	% Phosphate	Availability**	Notes***
Alfalfa hay	2–3	0.5–1	1–2	slow/moderate	
Bone meal (raw)	2–6	15–27	0	moderate	alkaline
Bone meal (steamed)	0.7–4	18–34	0		
Blood meal	2	1–2	0–1	rapid	acidic
Cottonseed meal	6	2.5–3	1–1.7	slow	acidic
Composts	1–3.5	0.5–2	1–2	moderate	alkaline
Feather meal	12	0	0	moderate	
Fish meal	6–14	3–7	0–5	rapid	acidic
Grass clippings	1–2	0–0.5	1–2	moderate	
Grain Straw	0.6	0.2	1.1	very slow	
Hoof/horn meal	12–14	1.5–2	0	moderate	alkaline
Kelp (powder)	1–1.5	0.5	4	moderate	zinc, iron
Kelp (liquid)	negligible	negligible	negligible	rapid	micronutrients, trace minerals, plant growth hormones, helps plants w/stress
Leaves	1	0–0.5	0–0.5	slow	
Legumes	2–4	0–0.5	2–3	moderate	
Manures—Undried**					
Cow	0.5	0.3	0.5	moderate	weed seed
Horse	0.5	0.3	0.6	slow	weed seed
Llama	1.6	0.6	0.6		
Pig	0.6	0.5	0.4	rapid	
Poultry	0.9	0.8	0.4	rapid	
Sheep	0.9	0.5	0.8	moderate	weed seed
Manures—Dried					
Cow	2	1.5	2.2		
Sheep	1.9	1.4	2.9		
Poultry	4.5	2.7	1.4		
Mushroom compost	0.4–0.7	5.7–6.2	0.5–1.5	slow	high salt, use from organic mushroom production systems
Pine needles	0.5	0	1	slow	acidic
Rock Powders***					
Greensand	0	0	7		trace minerals & micronutrients, but potassium already plentiful in many western soils research
Rock phosphate	0	27	0		shows rock phosphate is unavailable in alkaline soils w/pH 7 or above unless in colloidal form
Sawdust	0–4	0–2	0–4	very slow	untreated, unpainted wood
Seaweed extract	1	2	5	rapid	zinc, iron
Soybean meal	6.7	1.6	2.3	slow/moderate	
Straw/corn stalks	0–0.5	0–0.5	1	very slow	
Wood ashes	0	1–2	3–7	rapid	highly alkaline, so not recommended for alkaline western soils, wood stove ash often contaminated w/colored paper, plastics

*Remember the rule of thumb for organic gardening: It's better to fertilize more often with fewer nutrients than less often with more nutrients.

**Approximate rate of nutrient release from the material—percentages of plant nutrients are highly variable

***Special properties or characteristics of the material

****Uncomposted animal manures should be incorporated into soil a minimum of four months before harvesting vegetables. Manures vary widely depending on age, animal setting, and feed. Salt content can be high.

*****Rock powders contain minerals and micronutrients, and some gardeners swear by them. Because many alkaline western soils already have high mineral content, adding more isn't usually recommended, especially greensand and others that supply potassium. Colloidal phosphate is a slow-release natural phosphate product that may be more useful to vegetable gardeners in the semiarid western United States.

different than aged manure. It has been heated up enough to kill pathogens and weed seeds.

People who keep chickens regard them as an integral part of their garden because they are such great soil builders. Not only do they eat pest insects like grasshoppers, they continually scratch and turn the soil, incorporating leaves and other organic matter, including their own manure. Beekeepeer Tom Theobald says if he were to redesign his garden from scratch, he would put the chicken coop in the middle with garden beds radiating out from it like sun rays. That way he could turn his chickens out on one ray or section to improve the soil while others were in production or growing a cover crop like buckwheat, then rotate the chickens around to the next ray.

COVER CROPS AND GREEN MANURES

Cover crops play an important role in sustainable farming. By definition, a cover crop is any plant or group of plants that is grown to provide soil cover, whether or not it is later turned into the soil. Sometimes they are grown primarily to prevent erosion or to suppress weeds. Nitrogen-fixing legume crops add fertility to soil. Cover crops are also used as catch crops, to pick up the extra nitrogen and other nutrients that usually remain in soil after a main crop like corn is grown with synthetic fertilizers. This prevents the nutrients from leaching into and contaminating groundwater.

Some crops are incorporated into the soil while still green or shortly after they flower to improve or enrich it. Known as

Plant buckwheat as a fast-growing cover crop anytime during the warm growing season. Its white flowers are beloved by bees, it makes a great soil conditioner, and it provides supplemental phosphorus for subsequent plants when turned under.

green manures, these particular cover crops have caught the interest of home gardeners, who often consider them an easier way to amend and improve their soil. After all, not everyone has a truck or a strong enough back to move loads of compost and manure around, and some animal manures come from feedlots and contain too much salt.

I read about the benefits of cover crops and knew farmers and gardeners who always planted some. I'd seen vibrant green ryegrass coming up in early November and again in early spring, and summer-blooming buckwheat patches alive with so many pollinators they were getting in each other's way. So I bought a small bag of annual rye seed and a big bag of buckwheat. I planted them both—rye in the fall, buckwheat in summer—in an overgrazed, underwatered, compacted section of pasture adjoining the garden, where I planned to expand the garden eventually. Big mistake. What I hadn't realized is how much water these crops need, especially in that situation, or how much backbreaking work it can be to turn them under by hand (rye has an extraordinary network of roots).

I had expected, unrealistically, that they would make improving the hard-packed soil easier by doing much of the remedial work *for* me. But that didn't prove to be the case in such extreme conditions. I've planted buckwheat ever since, though, because it's an excellent forage plant for bees and a great soil conditioner when it's turned under. Now I grow it in better conditions with a different expectation—and get some help with the turning under part. I gave up on rye because thick hay mulch proved to be a much easier and less strenuous way for me to build healthy soil and prevent it from drying

out and blowing away.

If you plant green manure crops in soil that's already been worked, turning them over won't be so difficult. Use a good quality fork or sharpened shovel to make the job easier.

Most farmers who grow cover crops don't do the work by hand. They work on a much larger scale and have *equipment*. Those who don't farm organically often use herbicides to kill the vegetation once a cover crop has served its soil-holding or catch crop purpose. While cover crops do protect, rejuvenate, and nourish soil and are very important in this role, home gardeners should know that growing them is not a silver bullet that eliminates hard work, as I naively assumed.

Having said that, from my own perspective as a mature gardener who is seeking out less-arduous methods, I also know some gardeners who embrace growing all types of cover crops for their many benefits and do it well. Roland Evans, an upbeat, accomplished mountain gardener, says this about green manures:

> My longtime favorites are barley and white clover planted together very early in the spring. After I turn the crop over in late April, the soil will sparkle with new life and texture. In the hot summer months, a fast-growing crop of buckwheat is useful to supplement soil phosphorus. As fall approaches, my fallow garden beds are sown with alfalfa and rye to clothe the soil during winter. There is a cover crop for every season and use.

I can almost hear him whistling while he works—and more power to him.

But there are ways to make it easier

for those who, like myself, are no longer gung-ho wielders of the fork and shovel. Take winter or annual rye, for example. It's inexpensive, prevents erosion over the winter, and adds valuable humus to soil once it's incorporated, but its roots are extensive and deep. It needs to be turned over so it has several weeks to die and break down before you can plant. If you mow, then cover the ryegrass with an old piece of carpet or a tarp to block the light, it will die and start to break down, making it easier to turn in. You can also hire someone to do the job by hand. Or you can use a rototiller (or hire someone who has one), but if you understand the harm that regular tilling inflicts on soil life, you'll see that by doing so you may be offsetting some of the benefits you set out to gain.

All green manures add organic matter to the soil, and whenever a young, still-lush crop is turned under, there is a surge of microbial life. Cereal crops like oats, rye, and barley prevent erosion and weed growth by covering bare soil, plus they contribute humus once they are turned under, which creates better soil tilth. Buckwheat and sweet clover attract pollinators, suppress weeds through their growth, and extract phosphorus from soil, accumulating it in their tissues. When these crops are turned under, the phosphorus becomes available for other vegetable crops. Rye has allelopathic properties, meaning it releases natural toxins that inhibit the growth of other plants, so it's especially good for suppressing weeds. Legumes like clover, ground or field peas,

and vetches are important nitrogen fixers (as are garden beans and peas). But vetch can become a rampant weed and must not be allowed to go to seed. Red clover attracts a lot of pollinators but its roots grow 5 to 7 feet deep! Mustard is a specialty crop that fumigates soil and provides plenty of organic material, useful in beds where root crops, especially potatoes, will be grown.

Make sure you turn these green manure crops under before they form seeds. Some can become firmly established with extensive and/or deep roots, and others will readily self-sow if you don't. Mow them first so they'll break down more quickly when they're in the soil.

Best Green Manures for Home Gardeners
Legumes that fix nitrogen
- Field peas (plant in early spring; easy to kill and till)
- White clover (plant any time; attracts and feeds pollinators)

Cereals for organic matter
- Oats (plant in early spring or fall; easy to till)
- Barley (early spring or late summer; shallow roots; easy to till)
- Winter rye (plant in fall; deep roots)

Specialty crops
- Buckwheat (plant in late spring or summer; attracts and feeds pollinators; accumulates phosphorus)
- Mustard (plant in spring; fumigates soil; good before root crops; catch crop for other brassicas)

Chapter 4
A Brief Natural History of Nitrogen

Red tide off Scripps Pier, La Jolla, California. Synthetic urea-based fertilizers now account for half of global nitrogen fertilizers. Since the algae species that produce red tides (toxic algal blooms) favor this form of nitrogen, they are increasingly occurring worldwide.

Nitrogen is by far the most abundant element in our planet's atmosphere. Oxygen makes up 21 percent of all air molecules, but inert nitrogen gas (N_2) makes up about 78 percent. Every breath we take contains mostly nitrogen, though we can't make use of it. N_2 molecules have an extremely tight chemical bond (triple covalent) so they don't combine with other molecules to make compounds.

THE NITROGEN CYCLE

Nitrogen is continually recycled through the environment by plants and animals in a process called the nitrogen cycle. Soil bacteria and blue-green algae are the only organisms capable of fixing nitrogen, which means they can break nitrogen gas molecules apart and convert them into reactive nitrogen in the useful form of ammonia or nitrate. A small amount of useful nitrogen is also released very slowly as minerals break down in the soil.

The only other way that useful nitrogen reaches the earth is through lightning, cosmic radiation, and meteorite trails that fix nitrogen in the atmosphere, causing nitrate to fall to the earth. The amount of nitrogen that falls to earth and is added to soil from lightning is about twenty pounds per acre per year. *Rhizobia* bacteria that have a symbiotic living arrangement with legumes—plants that make seeds in pods, like peas, beans, alfalfa, and clover—fix significantly more, up to five times as much.

But the main source of nitrogen nutrients in soil is the ammonia produced by bacteria as dead plants and animals decompose,

N itrogen is a major building block for life. It is in amino acids, RNA, and DNA, in all plants and animals. Every organism needs nitrogen to grow and to reproduce. One of the three macronutrients required for plant growth (nitrogen, phosphorous, and potassium, or NPK), nitrogen fuels the green, leafy growth of plants.

43

a process called nitrification. Another type of bacteria then breaks down ammonia to form nitrite (NO_2), and a third type breaks down nitrite to form nitrate (NO_3). Nitrate is the form of nitrogen that plants are able to use for growth. Fungi and bacteria that need oxygen can get it from nitrates, breaking them down to nitrogen gas (N_2). This process, called denitrification, completes the nitrogen cycle.

Debunking Green Revolution Myths

The generally accepted textbook version of the Green Revolution is that it helped "save the world" by dramatically increasing food production in Mexico and Asia. In his new book, *The Hungry World,* University of Indiana historian Nick Cullather offers a very different picture starting at the beginning in Mexico, where oil fields once controlled by Standard Oil, a major source of funding for the Rockefeller Foundation, principal bankroller of the Green Revolution, had been confiscated.

Farmers there were already supplying adequate food for the population plus plenty for export to the United States, he says. The Mexico Agricultural Program created a model for the export to Asia of one-size-fits-all agribusiness based on petroleum inputs—and the push continues for Africa today. According to Cullather, the program was shaped at least as much by foreign policy as by idealism and had dire negative results including "narrowing of (Mexico's domestic agriculture) genetic base, supplanting indigenous, sustainable practices; displacing small and communal farming with commercial agribusiness; and pushing millions of peasants into urban slums or across the border."

SYNTHETIC NITROGEN CHANGES EVERYTHING

For most of human history, the nitrogen in animal manures and decaying plants has been used to increase soil fertility. These are still the best nitrogen sources for organic gardeners. But after two German chemists discovered a process to make synthetic nitrogen in the form of ammonia in the early twentieth century, things changed. The Haber-Bosch process was used to make explosives for two world wars, but also to produce synthetic nitrogen–based fertilizers.

Along with high-yield hybrid seeds, new irrigation infrastructure, and pesticides, the new fertilizers were used to increase food crop yields in Mexico in the 1940s and India, on the brink of famine, in the 1960s. These technological innovations marked the start of the Green Revolution (so-called because green is the color of nitrogen and having no relation to the twenty-first-century meaning of *green*) at a time when fossil fuels, on which fertilizer and pesticide production and the entire modern industrial food system depends, were cheap and plentiful.

Today, chemical nitrate fertilizers have completely taken the place of organic fertilizers in what is called conventional agriculture. Since 1985 especially, production of synthetic fertilizers has increased dramatically. And farm equipment is now bigger, designed specifically for large-scale applications.

THE COSTS OF NITROGEN POLLUTION

Over the last sixty years or so, the positive result of synthetic nitrogen–based fertilizers has been to increase crop production, creating more food for more people. However, there is now a huge surplus of nitrogen-rich nutrients in our environment, and they are wreaking havoc.

As production and use of synthetic nitrogen has skyrocketed, so has nitrogen pollution. Nitrates from animal and human waste (treating water converts ammonia to nitrate, but doesn't remove the nitrate) are another contributing factor. Almost all of this excess nitrogen escapes into the environment, eventually ending up in the atmosphere, in groundwater, lakes, rivers, and oceans. Some also winds up in our food. If nutrients are good, we now definitely have far too much of a good thing.

In the last decade there has been a major shift to synthetic urea–based fertilizers, which now make up more than half of global nitrogen fertilizer. Though urea used to be considered a minor form of the nitrogen found in coastal waters, new research shows that it exists in much higher concentrations and that algae, especially the species that cause toxic algal blooms or red tides, prefer it. As urea use increases, more toxic algal blooms are being seen throughout coastal areas around the world, especially in Southeast Asia, where fertilizer use is rapidly increasing, but also in the United States, in New England, the mid-Atlantic, Florida, and the West Coast.

There is an 8,000-square-mile dead zone in the Gulf of Mexico caused by nitrate fertilizer runoff from the Mississippi River watershed. Other oxygen-depleted dead zones are appearing in the Baltic Sea, the Adriatic Sea, the Gulf of Thailand, the Yellow Sea, and the Chesapeake Bay. The number of dead zones has been doubling every decade since the 1960s, and oceanographers

report a total of 405 today, covering about 152,236 square miles of our planet's oceans. In Norway, nitrate levels doubled in one thousand lakes in less than a decade. About half of all lakes in the United States are now eutrophic. This means they contain excessive amounts of nutrients (nitrates), are subject to algal blooms, and are deficient in oxygen. Nitrate in drinking water is linked to cancer.

Algal bloom. Synthetic nitrogen fertilizer runoff is the primary source of excessive nutrients that cause algal blooms and oxygen depletion in bodies of water. Roughly half of all lakes in the United States are now eutrophic, or oxygen depleted.

Airborne nitrogen compounds that create smog and acid rain are increasing too. Nitrous oxide (N_2O) is a greenhouse gas three hundred times more potent than carbon dioxide. Agriculture, including corn-ethanol production, is responsible for 80 percent of all human-caused N_2O. Vehicle emissions and fossil fuel combustion are another minor source. In the western United States, nonnative invasive grasses that thrive on airborne nitrogen pollution are wiping out native plants that don't adapt to nitrogen-rich soil.

From Battlefields to Fields

There is a long association between the agricultural and military use of reactive nitrogen. Both potassium nitrate and sodium nitrate are used as ingredients in fertilizers and explosives. Sodium nitrate is used to make potassium nitrate.

Significant natural deposits of potassium nitrate (known as saltpeter or niter) were found and mined in China, India, the Arabian Peninsula, Hungary, Spain, Poland, Lithuania, Russia, Chile, and Peru. Scholars credit Chinese alchemists in the ninth century with the invention of explosive black powder using niter.

Huge natural mineral deposits of sodium nitrate, often called Chile saltpeter, were found in a narrow 1,400-mile strip of Chilean desert in the early nineteenth century. One theory says they were created during a huge electrical storm, described by the Inca of Peru: "Fire came down from heaven and destroyed a great part of the people, while those who were taking to flight were turned into stones."

Mining began in 1812 in what was then Peru. In 1879, demand for this valuable South American resource and a struggle for its control caused the five-year War of the Pacific, or Saltpeter War, between Chile (backed by European capital), Peru, and Bolivia. Ultimately, Chile annexed territory from both Peru and Bolivia, gaining control of the mines.

In 1909, German chemist Fritz Haber discovered how to produce biologically available reactive nitrogen in the form of ammonia from atmospheric nitrogen. Another German chemist, Carl Bosch, ratcheted up the process for industrial-level production. Its first large-scale use was during World War I, when the Allies cut off the supply of Chilean nitrates to Germany. The ammonia produced was used to make explosives for the German war effort.

The Haber-Bosch process of making synthetic nitrogen, for which both men won the Nobel Prize, defined the Green Revolution in the mid-twentieth century because synthetic nitrogen—based fertilizers dramatically boosted food yields in many parts of the world. With the mass production of synthetic nitrogen, the nitrate industry in Chile collapsed.

Most of the big agricultural companies today were once also in the business of warfare. Many of the chemicals developed for the battlefield were later adjusted and marketed for agricultural and civilian use at home. Herbicides, for example, originally used to defoliate jungles in the Vietnam War, are now the most widely used chemicals on farms and lawns.

There has been a tenfold increase in the use of nitrogen-based chemical fertilizers since the 1960s, and while the benefits of increased food production are substantial, the long-term environmental cost has been extremely high. Scientists consider nitrogen pollution a far more serious problem than carbon dioxide.

THE NEW GREEN

Some techniques are now being implemented to reduce nitrogen use and waste in agriculture (only about 20 percent of correctly applied synthetic nitrogen is actually taken up by plants). Cover crops are making a comeback. Dairy farmers in California are figuring out how to apply their nitrogen-rich wastewater on fields without impacting water quality and, in the process, eliminate the need to buy commercial fertilizer. Some large dairy producers have installed methane digesters, and one smaller dairy in Montana is turning methane gas from manure into electricity.

Home gardens fit into this picture the same way they do in regard to pollinators. We need to step back and view urban and suburban lots and the impact of our individual practices as a larger whole. Chemical use, including chemical fertilizers, is more intensive today in many urban and suburban areas than in rural areas, and the main crop is still lawn. Yet it is much easier to grow plants and food organically on the small scale of a home garden than on farms.

The extraction of natural resources to fuel and advance industry without much regard for long-term environmental consequences characterized the twentieth century, and it still continues. In hindsight, the Green Revolution that provided so much benefit can also be seen in this light. *Green* has a new meaning in the twenty-first century. It's about living more sustainably for the long term: consuming less to conserve natural resources, using renewable nonpolluting resources, giving back at least as much or more as we take from the earth, reducing negative human impacts, and supporting diverse life forms, not just humans.

Chapter 5
The Plight of Pollinators

Nigella with California poppies. Brighten edible gardens by providing flowers for bees, butterflies, and other pollinators. All are under dire environmental stress today from habitat loss and pesticide use. Gardeners must support their survival and advance their protection.

Pollination, the transfer of pollen from the male to the female part of the plant, is how most plants reproduce. For 90 percent of all flowering plants, this is accomplished with the help of an animal, usually an insect, most often a bee. Without it, many fruit trees and food plants will not set any fruit, and others, strawberries, apples, and cucumbers, for example, need multiple bee visits to do so. Some plants that don't *require* animal pollinators, like peaches and beans, usually produce a better crop when they do visit.

Over millions of years, flowers and bees have developed together in a complex dance of interdependency. Rooted to the ground, many plants have adapted to attract the attention of bees and other pollinators with fluttering flower petals, fragrance, and color, exchanging pollen and nectar for reproductive services. Plants and insects that evolved together in the same climate and location have synchronized their life cycles for mutual benefit over hundreds or thousands of years. During the sometimes brief window when a plant is in bloom, its specific pollinators emerge and show up on time to eat and transfer pollen.

Plants, algae, and bacteria are the only organisms on the planet that are able to convert solar energy to food, which they make available to animals. In the process of photosynthesis, plants also release oxygen. So not only are they the most basic food source on Earth, they make the planet habitable for the rest of us. And insects don't just pollinate plants; they also provide the basic protein source that almost all of the animals higher up in the food chain depend on. Without plants and insects, our animal and human world would completely collapse. Yet, without much concern or awareness about the implications of our actions, we dig up, pave over, and develop most of the places where wild plants, animals, and insects live in order to build *our* houses and grow *our* food.

Remember how bugs used to splatter all over the windshields of cars in the summer? That rarely happens anymore. Now we're faced with diminishing numbers of insects in general, and pollinators of all kinds in particular. Some say we've reached a tipping point. Our once wildly abundant and biologically well-endowed continent has lost so much of its uncultivated, natural land that the insects and wild animals that we continue to displace don't have anywhere to go. Native plants have been replaced with suburban landscaping that doesn't support native insects, and this means there is a lot less food for birds and other animals.

Farms used to provide food and a living for families, along with diverse habitat for lots of pollinators and other animals. When farms were smaller and everyone had home gardens, wild honeybees and native bees were able to pollinate all of our plants, even if no one in the area had a managed hive. They had some help from other winged creatures—butterflies, flies that look like bees, some wasps and beetles, hummingbirds, a few moths, and, for night bloomers, bats and all the other moths.

As farms gave way to monocultures, the focus shifted from raising several crops and animals to higher yields and greater precision with one crop. Corn is now sold by the kernel instead of the bushel and planted in perfect patterns using tractors with sophisticated GPS systems and steering-assist features. Exact amounts of fertilizer are dispensed to each plant. Something called Smartdust, a radio frequency–powered network of tiny wireless microelectromechanical sensors that can be planted into soil to detect and monitor light, temperature, chemicals, humidity, and even vibrations,

is now in the pipeline. As you can imagine, in such precise scenarios designed for maximum production, the natural areas and hedgerows at the edges of fields where native plants (including weeds) grow and insects and birds once congregated have become minute or have disappeared completely.

HONEYBEES

The honeybee is such a special pollinator that humans have enjoyed a unique relationship with it for thousands of years. Honeybees not only pollinate most of our flowering plants, including a third of all our food plants, they also manufacture honey, one of the most amazing substances on the planet, a sweet, high-energy food that never spoils. And they make plenty to share with humans and other animals.

Honeybees were imported to the East Coast of North America from Europe beginning in the 1600s, and colonies were shipped west by railroad car in the mid-1800s. Native Americans called the honeybee "the white man's fly." Many swarmed to form wild colonies, which proliferated and thrived until recently. In the first half of the twentieth century, when sugar was scarce, you could order a beehive from a Sears Roebuck catalog. Almost everyone knew where to find a wild colony, usually in an old tree, as well as how to transfer the bees into a hive and, later, collect the honey.

But, of course, honeybees are much, much older than that. Bees first appeared on Earth about 80 million years ago. We know that ancient Egyptians, Greeks, Chinese, and Europeans all kept bees, but the invention of the Langstroth hive in 1851, with its specifically defined "bee space," revolutionized beekeeping and honey production by enabling a beekeeper to easily remove frames of comb with honey. Before that, the entire colony—bees, comb, and hive—was often demolished in the difficult process of getting at the honey.

Echinacea purpura, the native purple coneflower, is one of the great medicinal plants and a favorite of butterflies and bees. Breeders have produced many hybrid versions in different colors and forms, but the original species is usually best for pollinators.

A German botanist named Joseph Gottlieb Kölreuter discovered that bees pollinate flowers in 1750 (though it's difficult to believe no one else figured this out during the thousands of years humans have been observing and keeping bees). Several decades later, another German, naturalist Christian Konrad Sprengel, studied and researched insect pollination extensively, but since his contemporaries viewed the idea of sexual reproduction in flowers as outlandish and obscene, his work wasn't accepted or considered proper science. Darwin's book on insect pollination, *Fertilisation of Orchids,* came seventy-five years later, in 1862.

No one seems to have thought too much about the critical importance of bees in agricultural pollination until very recently, when individual crops became huge monocultures requiring outside pollinators for fertilization. In the early 1980s, beekeepers first began to notice that bees were disappearing and dying in greater numbers than usual.

VANISHING BEES, COLONY COLLAPSE DISORDER, AND THE PESTICIDE PROBLEM

In the mid-1970s, I rented a rundown old farmhouse east of Boulder, Colorado, with a friend for eighty dollars a month. Surrounded by a hundred acres of cornfields leased to a farmer, the house lacked insulation, window screens, and running water, but had a screened-in porch, an outhouse with a view, plum thickets, and lilacs. The driveway was lined with huge old cottonwoods that sometimes filled with blackbirds, thousands of them, roosting for a few hours or a day before moving on. We had raccoons in the attic and all kinds of other critters outside, including pheasants, which you very rarely see in Boulder County anymore.

I've never seen so many bees of all kinds in my garden before or since. This was in part because a beekeeper named Harlan Henderson had several hives and rented a former milk house on the property for his honey house. Harlan and I became friends despite a forty-year age difference and I "helped" him occasionally when he was extracting and bottling honey. To demonstrate that bees are gentle and won't sting if you remain calm, he once walked me into the middle of a buzzing cloud of thousands of bees and neither of us wore any protective clothing.

One warm July evening, I found Harlan outside the honey house, looking forlorn. Most of his bees were dead. The cornfields had been sprayed with Penncap-M. This scenario was not at all uncommon and it continues today. Because of its lethal toxicity to birds, mammals, and fish, the use of Penncap-M was limited to certain crops in 1999, but those crops still approved for use today include the most widely grown: corn, soy, canola, sugar beets, sunflowers, wheat, and several others. It is just one of many insecticides in use today that harms or kills bees. As insects develop resistance, new insecticides are developed. When pollen and wax from several different honeybee colony sources were analyzed at a USDA lab for a 2007 study by entomologists at Pennsylvania State University, single pollen samples were found to contain up to seventeen different pesticides.

Cereals and grasses like wheat, rice, and corn rely on the wind instead of insects for pollination. But corn produces enormous quantities of pollen, which bees love to gather. Even if a pesticide doesn't kill adult bees outright, some, including Penncap-M, are applied as microcapsules, which unsuspecting worker bees collect along with pollen grains and bring back to the hive to make bee bread for the brood. This can prove fatal for the larvae or disrupt their development into healthy adults.

THE NEW SYSTEMIC NEONICOTINOIDS

Neonicotinoids are a newer class of pesticides that work systemically, expressing themselves in all parts of the plants to which they are applied, including the nectar and pollen, even when it's just the seed that's treated. They are the most widely used pesticides today worldwide. Because at least two, imidacloprid and clothianidin, manufactured by Bayer CropScience, have been linked to honeybee colony collapse disorder, they have been banned or restricted in four European countries. And where they've been banned, bee populations have bounced back quickly. Another neonicotinoid, known as Movento, recently approved in Canada, also has beekeepers worried.

Nine years ago the Environmental Protection Agency (EPA) granted a conditional registration for clothianidin, allowing it to be used in the United States, over the objections of some EPA scientists who were concerned about massive bee deaths in France, with the condition that Bayer submit life cycle studies on the product's impact on bees. Two years later, Bayer was granted an extension, which they also failed to meet. This continued for several more years while clothianidin was applied to millions of acres worth of corn seed. Because the EPA still refused to disclose the results of the studies or confirm whether they had even been submitted, the National Resources Defense Council (NRDC) sued the EPA.

In the fall of 2010, Bayer applied for an expansion of the use of clothianidin on cotton and mustard. As part of the process, two EPA scientists reviewed the life cycle study, which Bayer had finally submitted in 2006, declaring it to be scientifically unsound, even though another EPA biologist had approved it. This information was released to Colorado beekeeper Tom Theobald, who served as the Boulder County bee inspector for decades until the position was retired and who has been in contact with the EPA for decades expressing beekeepers' concerns. Theobald passed the EPA memo on to the media, where it has generated a great deal of controversy and a thus far unheeded call to remove the registration of the pesticide.

In 2009, 99 percent of commercial corn seed grown in the United States was treated with neonicotinoids. Since it's also used extensively to treat the seed of sunflowers, soybeans, cotton, sugar beets, canola, spinach, and many other crops, it's very difficult to avoid these pesticides if you're a bee. In some cases they are also applied as a drench to soil and plant leaves, even as a preventative measure, and they are used on lawns and golf courses and by tree-care companies. According to the EPA's own documents, there is evidence that clothianidin is persistent and cumulative in soil, water soluble (it can reach groundwater), and irreversible, meaning that even small doses over time can produce a dramatic effect.

Many beekeepers now believe that pesticide-contaminated pollen collected by foraging honeybees from neonicotinoid-treated crops, especially corn, is a root cause of bee and bee brood deaths. There is also increasing concern, confirmed by recent lab research, that very-low-level and even undetectable doses of pesticides, often in combination, are impairing bees' behaviors and immune systems. The perspective that has been completely absent in the process of determining pesticide toxicity to honeybees is the consideration of the colony as a whole instead of the effects on individual adult bees.

The kinds of issues affecting bees today were inconceivable a hundred years ago:

industrialization of agriculture, which has necessitated the industrialization of beekeeping for pollination; widespread loss of habitat and destruction of plant species; and regular, heavy use of systemic poisons on plants that bees visit. As bees struggle with weakened immune systems from environmental causes, parasitic mites that have been around for two decades and bee diseases, like Nosema, have become more of a problem. Throw climate change into the mix and you can see what bees are up against. Most of the wild honeybee populations in the United States are already believed to be gone.

In the late twentieth and early twenty-first centuries, it became much more profitable to move bees around in semitrailers pollinating huge seasonal crops than it was to produce honey. Questions have been raised about the effects of this migratory, pollination-for-profit, monocultural lifestyle on bees' health, including a few beekeepers' practice of substituting corn syrup or sugar water for honey to feed bees (the ultimate in exploitation). There is such huge demand for pollination services on crops that would fail if not for migratory beekeeping, like California almonds and New England blueberries, that beekeepers find themselves in a quandary. Those who pollinate for a living are increasingly boycotting growers who use toxic pesticides. Meanwhile, to rebuild the strength of their colonies, they are taking their bees to the woods to forage on wildflowers so that the bees are completely removed from conventional chemical-intensive agriculture.

Most small-scale commercial beekeepers with one hundred or fewer hives produce artisan-quality honey, have many years of experience, and take good care of their bees, but they, too, have been losing entire colonies. Many US beekeepers don't accept that increasingly large bee losses and colony collapse disorder are primarily a bee lifestyle problem, even if some less than desirable large-scale migratory pollination practices are taking their toll. Instead, those who have been on the front lines of beekeeping for decades see pesticides at the top of the list of causes. Scientific research that substantiates this is increasing, but thus far the responsibility for proof has been on the shoulders of beekeepers, who are not well-funded.

But why are small-scale beekeepers in more-urban areas, away from commercial agriculture, also losing a lot of bees? It seems mysterious at first, until you consider the following:

- Neonicotinoid insecticides are widely available to home gardeners and added to several commercial home lawn and garden products made by Bayer.
- Tree companies routinely use imidacoprid for systemic insect control.
- Neonicotinoid concentrations allowed for home garden use are much greater than for agricultural use (about seventy-five times greater, according to Dr. Vera Krischik, professor of entomology at the University of Minnesota).
- Seeds of many common bedding plants, and even fall bulbs, are now treated with imidacloprid.

Add this to all the other factors affecting bees, including massive herbicide use that destroys the wild plants bees used to depend on and new hybrids that contain much less

pollen and nectar, and it's not difficult to understand why pollinators are vanishing.

HONEYBEES ARE WHAT THEY EAT

Honeybees are our most important pollinator today because, unlike native bees, they are active throughout the growing season and, being superorganisms (or, social insects), their numbers are huge—up to fifty thousand inhabitants per colony at their peak during the growing season. They are also generalists, visiting the flowers of many different plants, though usually on different foraging trips.

Pollen is their main protein source, which the worker bees collect from flowers, pollinating them in the process. Honeybees have an electrostatic charge that attracts and holds grains of pollen. They comb it back across tiny hairs on their body and push it into pollen baskets on their back legs. When the baskets are full they return to the hive and drop it off.

Guard bees act as bouncers, checking incoming honeybees at the hive entrance and ejecting intruders. Foragers return with yellow pollen in baskets on their back legs, or with flower nectar, which they regurgitate from special honey-storage stomachs.

Honeybees depend on a few species of common plants that are abundant at different times and offer lots of nectar and pollen. From nectar, bees make honey, an all-purpose food for adult bees. Pollen is protein-rich nourishment for the brood. Scientists have found that bees add glandular secretions and microorganisms to pollen as soon as they touch it on a plant, along with nectar to make it sticky. They also remove any undesirable microbes.

Back at the hive, most of the pollen that's dropped off is mixed with honey and packed into cells next to the developing brood, where it undergoes chemical changes to become bee bread (it tastes like bread). Like butterflies, bees undergo a complete metamorphosis from egg to larva to pupa to adult. The task-oriented caste system of the honeybee is created by a very specifically timed diet regimen, with pollen as the essential building block of bee life.

Young nurse bees eat bee bread and mix it with secretions to create royal jelly, which they feed to the brood for two days, followed by a different secretion, and after the fourth day their diet is changed to a pollen/honey mixture. Queen larvae and adult queens are fed royal jelly exclusively for the duration of their lives. In an emergency or when a new queen is needed, worker larvae can be converted into queens with fully developed ovaries by feeding them royal jelly.

Adult bees also need to eat pollen for protein (and honey for carbohydrate energy) so they can create beeswax comb. By producing one pound of wax in 35,000 hexagonal cells, bees can store twenty-two pounds of honey.

While honeybees ensure that many food plants will be pollinated and bear fruit, it's the lowly dandelion, clovers, and, in irrigated areas of the West, alfalfa that actually sustain them. Dandelions kick off the honeybee season as the earliest major foraging crop, blooming in mid- to late April on the plains and later at higher elevations. Dandelions enable a colony to make thirty to forty pounds of honey, build their population, and sustain the hive until the next major food source comes into bloom in mid- to late June. Beekeeping and honeybee survival would be impossible without this bright yellow weed that is routinely exterminated with 2,4-D, often mixed with fertilizer in benign-sounding "weed and feed" lawn treatments.

Yellow sweet clover in June and white sweet clover in August are two other primary bee food sources (and also targets for 2,4-D). Alfalfa, if it isn't cut too early, can be another, though the flower has a trip hammer that bops honeybees on the head, so it's not their favorite. Imported alfalfa leaf-cutter bees, which don't seem to mind, are increasingly being used to pollinate alfalfa. Unfortunately, these bees don't make honey.

In addition to these major food sources, a colony of honeybees will also visit hundreds of other plant species in order to get a balance of essential nutrients, vitamins, minerals, and enzymes to properly nourish all the hive members, especially the ongoing successive brood of developing bees and the queen. When they're not pollinating agricultural monocrops, bee diets are extremely diverse.

TIRELESS WORKER BEES

The vast majority of honeybees are females with undeveloped ovaries—the workers. They live for roughly three to six weeks in the summer, so new brood is always needed to replace the old. In the fall, the brood develops into bees that will live several months longer than summer bees to carry the colony through the winter.

We don't know very much about male bees or drones, but it is thought that their only job is to mate with the queen. The workers do everything else: feeding and rearing the young, taking care of the queen (who mates once and spends the rest of her two-to-four-year-life laying eggs), building honeycomb, making honey, guarding the entrance and removing intruders, protecting the living and removing the dead, heating the hive when it's cold, and cooling it when it's hot.

After two or three weeks of hive duty, the wax glands and baby-food-making glands of nurse worker bees atrophy and they are recruited for foraging outside. When older workers find a good flower food source, they return to the hive to communicate its location in a waggle dance. Experiments suggest that bees practice spatial thinking and use mental maps to communicate information. Though bee behavior is instinctive and genetically programmed, they also demonstrate a well-developed ability to learn, remember, and solve complex mathematical problems even though their brains are tiny.

Bees know to fly into the wind as they leave the hive so that on their return flight, when they are loaded down with pollen or nectar, the wind is with them. Exposed to pesticides, predators, and dangerous weather conditions while out foraging, it's in bees' best interest to make efficient use of flying time.

In order to accomplish all their tasks, the adult workers visit thousands of individual flowers to gather food every day. To make a pound of honey requires tapping 2 million flowers.

NATIVE BEES

Bumblebees are also important social insect pollinators, but a mature colony usually contains fewer than fifty bees. Some types can fly in colder weather and live at higher altitudes than honeybees, and most have longer tongues so they can reach into flowers that are difficult for honeybees. Because bumblebees have a unique ability to buzz pollinate (vibrating flowers to dislodge pollen), which especially benefits plants in the nightshade family, they are raised to pollinate greenhouse tomatoes. There are roughly two dozen species of the fuzzy natives in Colorado alone, but several are endangered.

Solitary native bees make a very significant contribution too, and some are much more efficient than honeybees. But there are fewer of them, they fly much shorter distances than honeybees, and their habitat in the United States is vanishing rapidly. The vast majority of bee species are solitary rather than social. This usually means that the female mates and creates a nest by herself, lays eggs, and then dies before the larvae emerge. "Gregarious" solitary bees nest close to others of their kind. All the solitary bees are nonaggressive since they don't have a colony to defend, and they rarely sting except as a last resort. There are more than 3,500 species in North America.

The life cycle of the natives is a few weeks, much shorter than honeybees, and is usually tied to the blooms of specific plant species. Shiny dark blue orchard mason bees emerge in early April along the Colorado

Front Range and stay around for four to five weeks while cherries, early apples, and native fruits are blooming. They nest in pre-existing holes in old wood, which gardeners can also drill for them. Increasingly raised for agricultural pollination, mason bees, and nesting boxes for them, can also be purchased for home gardens.

Gentle and extremely efficient leafcutter bees (150 of them do the same amount of work as 3,000 honeybees) cut out perfectly round and oblong holes from plant leaves and use them to line their nests. Squash bees are active at dawn, before honeybees, gathering pollen and nectar, and pollinating cucurbits until midday, when the leaves begin to close. Fuzzy sunflower bees only visit flowers in the sunflower family.

Along with growing fruit and vegetables for food, and flowers for honeybees, it's more important than ever that we also grow western native plants to sustain the bees and hover flies and butterflies that have evolved with them. Native plants are much more widely available than they used to be. Think of it as restoring some of the habitat that preceded your house on the land.

ATTRACTING POLLINATORS AND GIVING THEM WHAT THEY NEED

If you want to attract and feed honeybees, give them what they need: an abundance of flowers that provide nectar and pollen at different times and over as long a period as possible, a shallow source of water or one with floating islands or sloping sides so they can drink without falling in, and places to rest. Use perennials, trees, and shrubs, especially natives, to connect the garden areas of your landscape, providing shelter and food for

A pollinator station at Laura and Tim Spear's Forest Edge Gardens pairs favorite bee and butterfly plants (yellow parsnip and pink *Melica* grass) with a shallow water source. Bees drown in deeper saucers without reliable floating islands.

pollinators as they move through it. Also consider the bigger picture surrounding your yard, including your neighbors' property and plants. See it the way pollinators do, as a continuum.

Gardens with ten or more species of plants that bees like have been shown to consistently attract the largest number of bees, and gardens with a little mess—leaf litter, twigs, some weeds like dandelions and clover—are consistently preferred over the tidiest plots. Old wooden fence posts and patches of untilled (and unmulched) bare ground give native bees a place to nest.

Bumblebees nest in the ground and in bunch grasses. A queen starts a colony by herself, brooding her eggs the way birds do, keeping them warm on a ball of pollen with her abdomen. To maintain the heat they require, she must visit thousands of flowers for nectar without leaving the eggs for very long, so it's essential that the nest be near a source of rewarding flowers. Bumblebees will pollinate red clover, alfalfa, field beans, peas, runner beans, tomatoes, potatoes, eggplant, peppers, raspberries, apples, plums, sunflowers, strawberries, currants, and many wildflower species including lupine, aster, and willow.

Many hybridized flowers look pretty but don't support pollinators. Their nectar-producing ability may be reduced and their fancy forms—double-flowered varieties, for example—can make it so difficult for bees to find their reward that they won't bother trying. To attract and feed bees, it's best to stick with heirlooms, natives, and flowers that are close to the original species. Most herbs offer a lot of food for bees because they haven't been genetically manipulated. Those with blue flowers—mints, lavender, veronica, salvia—are especially attractive.

During the height of the growing season, your garden will be competing with all the other plant sources available to honeybees. Sometimes they're out gathering nectar for the adults, and at other times pollen for the larvae. One lavender plant won't be nearly as attractive to them as a whole border of lavender because they usually won't mix pollen or nectar types on one trip; plus, they won't have to learn how to find the pollen and nectar each time, as they would on different species.

Honeybees will be drawn to flowers in gardens at times when major food sources are scarcer, in early spring, midsummer, and fall. Relatively minor sources like home gardens can make a difference in bees' overall health and survival, especially if a major bee food source should fall short or fail. This is why a range of bloom times is important.

A border of blanketflowers (*Gaillardia*), coneflowers (*Echinacea purpura*), and red *Crocosmia* 'Lucifer' nurtures pollinators and delights onlookers. Squash feeds the gardener and provides a mating spot for squash bees in its flowers.

In the vegetable garden, warm-season crops—squash, beans, cucumbers, tomatoes, peppers, sweet corn, melons, and the like—and all fruit trees, even those listed as self-pollinating, will depend on, or at least benefit from, insect pollination. Many of the cool-weather crops like onions, carrots, beets, chard, parsley, and all the brassicas except broccoli are biennials (they take two years to flower from seed). Even though you may not see the results of pollination for these vegetables unless you grow them out and collect the seed, without bees there would be no vegetable seeds to plant. In addition to broccoli, cool-season greens like lettuce, arugula, cress, spinach, and bok choy will flower and set seed during the first season. Yellow broccoli flowers attract lots of bees in my garden, so I always leave a few for them.

Gardeners have the opportunity and, increasingly, the responsibility to reshape meticulously neat human landscapes, usually dominated by lawns and a few shrubs and trees, into diverse habitat that can feed our families while also supporting the broader community of biological life. If we step out of our isolationist, self-centered mentality and take a cue from the social honeybee, perhaps we might learn something about sharing the Earth's resources with our fellow creatures through cooperation.

Some backyard beekeepers have rediscovered the more rudimentary top-bar hive, which has been around for thousands of years and is still commonly used, especially in nonindustrialized parts of the world. They see it as a less managed, less industrial, less intrusive alternative to the traditional Langstroth hive, and one that enables a honeybee colony to live more by instinct, creating a natural comb each year as bees do in the wild. Most of these beekeepers don't believe in "inputs" like treating bees with medicines. Top-bar hives are also popular because they don't require the heavy lifting that comes with Langstroth hives.

Beekeeping sanctuaries are now cropping up too. The most noteworthy example is Gunther Hauk's organic, biodynamic Spikenard Farm in Virginia, which has much to teach new beekeepers. In the midst of steep declines and colonies collapsing, dedicated, aware, backyard hobbyist beekeepers have become extremely important in the effort to keep honeybee populations going.

GROW LOCALLY AND SUPPORT OTHER SPECIES

Everywhere you look there's another compelling reason for all of us to grow more of our own food organically on a small scale, and to do everything possible to sustain biological diversity by creating better habitat in our individual home landscapes. Over-the-counter pesticides, many of them toxic to bees and other pollinators, line the shelves of home improvement stores, and many homeowners don't hesitate to spray ornamental trees and lawns, and even bees, regularly. Some tree-care companies inject chemicals into tree trunks as a safer, more environmental approach, but if they use imidacloprid, the pollen and nectar in the tree's blossoms will be harmful to pollinators.

It may seem like a drop in the bucket, but if more and more of us can stop using pesticides altogether and look at healthy gardens and yards as part of a larger whole, we'll be creating a small but vital continuum of unsprayed habitat with food and shelter, like a series of dots for pollinators to connect. All of them, including the busy honeybees that sweeten our lives and make it possible for us to grow a variety of nourishing foods, require and deserve our protection.

Chapter 6
Creating a Vegetable Garden

An enclosed, mulched, weathered-wood bed provides a defined space for beets and green beans. Raised beds warm up faster in the spring but also dry out more quickly.

Now that you understand how alive and vital healthy soil is, and what a huge advantage it is to be growing food on a small scale as a home gardener, you can begin to create your garden. There are many ways to do this and as many opinions on which is the best method. My answer: it all depends. It depends on how much space, time, and experience you have, where you live, what you want to grow, how strong you are, and how hard you want to work, just for starters.

Right now there is a lot of emphasis on growing a big yield in a small space in enclosed raised beds, which makes sense since most of us have limited space, limited time, and a desire to keep it simple. This can be a great way to start. Raised beds warm up more quickly in the spring than an in-ground garden, but they also require more water. Every method has advantages and disadvantages. You may swear by one technique for a few years and then find another way that's even better. Or you might try out several in different beds to see which works best for you. Gardeners are always learning from each other and from their own experience since the growing season varies every year.

Ideally, you would begin building your garden in the fall, when so many leaves are available and free for the taking. If you set up your garden six or seven months ahead of the growing season, the organic materials you add will have time to break down and change into humus, helped by the freeze-thaw cycle of winter. Your soil will be more alive if you can give it plenty of organic matter, plus enough time to weather, coalesce, activate, and come into balance through the unfailing help of the microorganisms. Then, once spring arrives, your seeds and seedlings will have a nicely prepared bed all ready to call home, with a healthy population of active soil critters, including worms. Fall is also a great time to apply a soil drench of compost tea to introduce microbes that will establish themselves and spark the decomposition and transformation process.

Since our region usually has plenty of warm spells throughout the winter, you will have other opportunities to get started if you can't get to it in October; but don't procrastinate too long and do save or gather bags of leaves when they're available. Leaves are one of the best materials for humus building in the garden and provide nutrients that soil microbes and worms convert into food for plants. You can also use them as mulch throughout the growing season.

Green ash and cottonwood leaves are plentiful where I live, but because they are alkaline (as are willow and linden leaves), some people say not to use them with our already alkaline soils. I have shredded and mixed them with other types of leaves for many years without paying much attention to this, using them in compost, forked directly into the soil, and as mulch, and I've never had a problem. They all break down in the end.

Various mineral nutrients (nitrogen, phosphorus, potassium, calcium, and so forth) become available to plants within certain pH ranges, mostly close to neutral. They become available through the biological action of soil microorganisms. So if you create the best conditions for a healthy population of microorganisms, they will bring the pH into the neutral range, where it needs to be, and keep it there. They know what they're doing so just give them a hand. Get a soil test if you suspect a problem or if it makes you feel better. But otherwise, delegate! Give the microorganisms what they need and let them do the heavy lifting and soil management for you.

Collect leaves, manure, composted manure, grass clipping from untreated lawns, yard waste compost, pine needles, straw—whatever organic materials are handy or available—for your garden. You don't have to chop up leaves if you're using them as mulch or for compost, but they will decompose a lot faster if you do. Leathery cottonwood leaves, especially, can take a long time to break down and, like grass clippings, they mat and clump together when they get wet, so air can't circulate through them. The microbes that break them down need air. You can run a lawn mower over dry leaves a few times (I hear it's pretty hard on mowers, though), or just jump on the bags to crunch them up once they're dry. If you didn't rake them yourself, watch out for rocks, chunks of wood, tennis balls, and the like.

I like to use an electric leaf vac, which is one of those obnoxiously loud leaf blowers with a reverse vacuum setting. Mine cost well under a hundred dollars and lasted eleven years before it conked out. They suck up the leaves and shred them into an attached cloth bag with a zipper. I unzip and dump the shredded leaves into a plastic garbage can with wheels so they're easy to move around. It takes about four big bags of leaves to fill one garbage can. I always use earplugs, a bandanna, and wraparound sunglasses when I'm using the leaf vac. It may sound like an ordeal, but it's not a heavy or dangerous tool and it does the job pretty quickly, so it seems well worth it to me.

Shredded branches and wood chips are another readily available material for your garden, but they need much more time and moisture than leaves to break down well in our drier climate. Dug into soil fresh or even somewhat aged, wood chips will *temporarily* rob the soil of nitrogen because the microorganisms consume it while decomposing the wood. But since microorganisms hold nitrogen in their bodies, given enough time—a year or two or more, depending on the size of the chips and the pile—it is eventually released back into the soil, so wood chips can be a great soil builder. It's best to dump them in a spot where you eventually want a garden bed and spread them out so the pile isn't too deep—no more than a foot or two high. Soak the pile periodically to speed up decomposition, and cover it, especially during the heat of summer. In a year or two the volume will be greatly reduced and the soil underneath will be fantastic. If your pile is too deep (a mistake I've made), it will be harder to work with, and it will take that much longer to break down. Meanwhile, mold can build up, so wear a dust mask if you decide to move the wood chips around.

If you happen upon a tree-trimming company in action, ask if they'd be willing to dump a load of shredded branches in your yard. Needless to say, first make sure you have enough room and that they'll be able to dump it where you need it.

Converting Lawn to Garden
Sheet Mulch Composting

Most western urban and suburban yards are covered with bluegrass, so chances are that any new garden will be replacing some lawn. This means that you will need to get rid of or cover the grass.

After trying many different digging and tilling methods over the years, I have become a convert to the no-till sheet mulching (or sheet composting) approach because the results are spectacular. Though I also grow some vegetables and herbs in containers, I think sheet mulching is by far the least strenuous way to create healthy garden soil on top of grass or in raised beds. It does take time, eight months to a year or longer, for everything to break down completely and mix together, and it's not always the tidiest method, but it effectively smothers grass and weeds without any herbicides or digging, while building, conditioning, and moisturizing the soil. The one drawback I can see is that ground-nesting bumblebees and native bees won't be able to find a home if an entire yard is mulched. To create habitat for these important pollinators, leave some areas uncovered.

During one particularly warm, dry, windy winter I was able to create loamy chocolate-cake soil loaded with worms in three large dried-out and neglected raised beds simply by spreading a thick (6-inch) layer of chopped-up leaves on top, watering well, and covering with flakes of hay. All winter I dumped my kitchen scraps

A thick layer of well-watered fall leaves covers the vegetable beds. I top them off with flakes of spoiled hay.

under the hay flakes. At first I loosened some soil with a garden fork and covered the scraps, thinking that the animals out here might catch a whiff and head for the garden, but more often I just lifted a flake of hay, dumped the scraps underneath, and replaced it. It doesn't get much easier than that, and in four years no varmints have ever bothered my garden, though we have fewer raccoons here than in the city. I use an inexpensive stainless steel compost bucket with a filter in the lid, purchased through MotherEarthNews.com. It works great for the kitchen, looks good, and never smells.

Mulching the garden with thick hay was originally Ruth Stout's method, which she popularized in the 1950s in *How to Have a Green Thumb Without an Aching Back* and later in *Gardening Without Work*. Both are great reads, though pricey since they're out of print. A few years ago, Patricia Lanza, who told me she had never heard of Ruth Stout, refined the mulch layering method for urban gardeners in her book *Lasagna Gardening*.

Flakes of moldy hay cover the leaf layer. I expanded the bed beyond its enclosure without tilling by covering the ground with cardboard to stop weeds, spreading shredded leaves and manure, and adding hay mulch on top. Brussels sprouts, in back, produced into November.

There are also lots of videos you can watch on YouTube that will show you exactly how people are creating layered, no-till sheet-mulched gardens, step-by-step. Essentially, you compost right on top of your lawn and, in the process, compost your lawn. "No work" isn't completely accurate because you do need to gather and assemble the materials, but compared to the hard work of digging or even pushing a rototiller around, this really is easy.

Steve Solomon, who has written some very fine vegetable gardening books and who gardened for many years in western Oregon, where winters are wet and soils hold more moisture, disputes the benefits of thick vegetative mulch in climates where there aren't enough hard freezes to control insects. But in our region we have plenty of hard freezes, and keeping soil from drying out is more of an issue than insects. (Solomon now lives in Tasmania but is very willing to communicate about gardening, within reason, through e-mail.)

Whenever I describe the thick-mulching method to someone who's unfamiliar with it, the insect question inevitably comes up. During unusually wet springs and summers, I have sometimes seen more earwigs in my garden than usual, but so have others who don't use thick mulch. I haven't found slugs to be a problem any more than I occasionally did in a wet year before using hay mulch. Insects haven't been an issue for me or for other sheet mulchers I know in the semiarid West. But one gardener friend who directed the gutter downspout into part of her veggie garden on top of thick mulch during a particularly wet growing season noticed that something not visible during the day was eating her plants. When she investigated at

night she discovered thousands of roly-poly bugs under the mulch. Horrified, her quick-thinking solution was to plug in the vacuum cleaner outside and suck them all up, which proved effective, except her neighbor complained mightily about the noise. In a dry year, the gutter extension might have been a good idea, but that summer the soil just stayed too wet.

The other sheet mulch question I usually hear is "But isn't it too dry here for the thick-mulch method?" Answer: absolutely not. In fact, our climate makes it even more compelling and effective. And it's important to keep soil from drying out during our typically dry winters as well as during the growing season. I keep my vegetable beds thickly covered with fall leaves (shredded, when I can get around to it) and a top layer of hay over the winter every year. Don't worry about growing a new crop of hay if you mulch thickly enough. The few sprouts that pop up will be easy to pull.

Tough weeds like bindweed and thistle are ubiquitous. Dan Johnson, native plant curator at Denver Botanic Gardens, was dismayed to find them on a recent trip to Patagonia. Every year, a couple of my neighbors apply tanks of herbicides to kill these and other weeds on their five-acre properties, but they never get rid of them long term. Smothering weeds with mulch is a more effective control and much easier in a relatively small area (not to mention mulch's soil-nourishing benefits, or recent studies showing that herbicides are not as short-lived or benign as we've been told). A few strands of bindweed are inevitably going to poke through here and there; just cut them off or pull them out when you see them. I've read their roots can be as deep as 27 feet! Cutting off the top growth prevents photosynthesis and deprives the roots of energy.

NO-TILL SHEET MULCH METHOD

(This sheet mulching method can also be used on existing garden beds. Just skip steps 1 and 2.)

1) To convert your lawn or part of it into a garden without rototilling or using herbicides, mow the grass as short as possible where you want your garden beds. If you do this when it's hot and dry and you've stopped watering the lawn for a while, it will already be semidormant. If you can't mow, proceed anyway and don't worry about it.

2) Spread overlapping sheets of newspaper (at least eight sheets thick), cardboard, or burlap coffee sacks (don't cut, keep them double) to smother the grass and weeds and create your bottom layer. A lot of colored ink is now soy based and lead free so it's fine to use in the garden, but if you're not sure, call the publication first to find out. Don't use plastic or old carpet or weed barrier; you want this layer to decompose eventually. Wet it down well before adding the other materials on top.

3) Spread any of the following materials in alternating layers on top of newspaper or cardboard, wetting down each layer or every few inches of material:
   - dried leaves
   - pine needles
   - grass clippings (be certain that no herbicides have been used on them—they can harm soil microbes and growing plants)
   - shredded newspaper or junk mail

- finished green compost (made from yard waste or plant debris—again with no herbicides)
- composted or dried manure
- coffee grounds, tea bags, any nonmeat, nondairy kitchen scraps
- chopped-up yard waste, including weeds before they set seed
- straw
- hay
- dog, cat, and human hair

Keep layers of grass clippings thin enough to break down without matting. You are better off shredding any leathery cottonwood leaves in this application, or mixing them with other leaves and keeping them for the top layer, especially if you don't have hay or straw. Without worrying about it too much, try to alternate more dry brown material (straw, dried leaves, shredded newspaper) with any green material (grass clippings, green leaves, kitchen scraps) as is recommended for composting.

4) Place flakes of hay or straw, branches, and/or some plastic bags full of leaves on top to hold everything down and keep it from blowing away in strong winter winds, while also allowing water to infiltrate. Throughout the winter you can place all your vegetable kitchen scraps under the top layer. If it's very dry, water occasionally under the top layer of mulch to help the materials break down. Keep some liquid (old tea, coffee, juice, or the like) along with the scraps in your kitchen compost container so you will be adding some moisture each time too.

5) During your first growing season you will simply pull the top layer of hay or

straw mulch away in order to dig holes in which to plant vegetable starts. As all the moist leaves, grass clippings, compost, and other organic materials that you layered on top of the cardboard (and under the hay or straw mulch) break down in the process of becoming soil, their volume is greatly reduced. As you dig the holes you may have to poke through some remaining leaf fragments and scraps of moist cardboard at the bottom. Where you want to plant seeds, remove the top layer of hay or straw mulch and scatter some finished compost, scratching it in lightly with a fork to blend with the top layer of soil. This creates a better texture (if you need it) for seeds to root and sprout. Put seeds on top, cover with sifted or sprinkled compost or soil, and press down. Water well, spraying with a fine mist twice a day until seedlings appear. When they have two true leaves (these come after the initial two seed leaves) you can pull the mulch back in closer around the plants. Your garden may look like a bed of mulch with uncovered islands of planted seedlings. Leave the surrounding mulch in place.

6) During the second year and thereafter, and for existing garden beds, continue adding a thick layer of leaves every fall along with any other materials you have easy access to: grass clippings, manure, compost, and so forth. Fork these in if you want, or just leave them on top. Water well and, ideally, cover with flakes of hay or straw through the winter to keep leaves in place, hold in moisture, and prevent grass and weeds from growing. The flakes may seem light, but they won't blow away.

To cover an 8 x 20 foot bed you will need about seven bales, which should last you at least through an entire growing season. If you don't have hay or straw, use a layer of cottonwood leaves or put a couple of medium-sized branches or plastic bags of leaves on top if your neighbors won't see them and object. Dump all your nonmeat, nondairy kitchen scraps from your kitchen compost bucket onto your beds under the flakes of hay or tucked under the leaves; bury them more deeply if you're worried about animals. Each year as your soil gets darker, crumblier, and starts to teem with soil life, it will be easier to plant and sustain healthy, delicious vegetables. Anytime you want to expand your garden a little, just start again with cardboard on the bottom to smother any existing grass or weeds, and add layers of leaves and hay or straw on top.

Thick mulch lets you walk in the garden without compacting the soil. Move mulch aside to plant. Leave it on throughout the growing season and during winter to keep soil from drying out and to maintain a healthy home for soil critters.

A drawback to using thick mulch is that your covered soil will probably take a little longer to warm up in the spring, especially if the weather is cool. If you live in the mountains, this is even more of an issue. Where you want to plant crops that like warmer soil, use Wall o' Waters (water tee-pees) or pull some of the mulch back to let the sun warm up the soil during the day for a few days. A temporary cover of weed barrier or black plastic will hold in moisture as the soil warms. It's amazing how fast uncovered soil dries out in our climate, causing worms and other soil critters to vanish (they just go deeper).

Consider Your Neighbors

If you live in a city or residential neighborhood, some neighbors or neighborhood associations may get nervous about what you're doing, especially if it's in a visible front yard where neatness is an issue. You can usually head off any unpleasantness by talking to them first and explaining what you're up to. You might also want to put up a nice looking sign that says No-Till Mulch Garden in Progress. Consider the materials you plan to use, especially for the top layer. Plastic bags of leaves are not the best choice in this situation. Keep it as tidy and composed as you can to avoid any hassles, or put the sheet-mulched beds in the backyard.

A Word about Hay and Straw

Where I live in Colorado there are still a number of productive hay farms. The price for horse hay usually varies from $5 to $8 per small rectangular bale depending on the quality, weight, and time of year. (In California my sister has paid up to $14 a bale.)

Farmers prefer to sell in some quantity, but feed stores sell individual bales. Cow hay has usually been rained on and costs less, $2 to $3.75 per bale, and sometimes, if you're lucky, you can find really funky hay for even less. This is the stuff you want for a garden. I see straw selling for $5 to $8 a bale in town.

Before I understood how to use thick mulch, I used old hay for a lighter, thinner layer of mulch and always ended up growing a nice new green crop of hay in the garden. Straw is not supposed to contain seeds but it often does too. The trick with sheet mulching is to use the hay thickly enough so that any grass and weed seeds in the ground, as well as any hayseeds that may drop down onto the soil, won't be able to germinate and grow up through the mulch. My hay layers are 6 inches thick or more, which is thicker than the usual recommendations for mulch. I find that hay holds together better in flakes, whereas straw flakes are usually thinner, lighter, and they tend to fall apart and blow away more easily. But straw is better for digging directly into soil to lighten and loosen it up, especially for growing potatoes, corn, and squash.

You'll need roughly one bale of hay or straw to cover 18 to 20 square feet of garden space. Leave the flakes intact but fill in any gaps or holes with loose handfuls.

OTHER LAWN-TO-GARDEN CONVERSION OPTIONS

If you're starting in the spring or you can't wait nine to twelve months for the sheet-mulch compost process to work on top of your lawn, you'll need to try something else. Here are some other options:

Double-Digging

Dig out the grass by hand and double-dig the soil with compost as instructed below. Depending on your soil, this can be really hard work but it's effective, satisfying, and only needs to be done once. If you're strong and macho, you'll probably enjoy it. Get out your pick and shovel, take your vitamins, and have plenty of water handy. Some energetic music might help. Do it in stages and take extra calcium/magnesium afterward so you won't get sore. Smaller beds equals less work. Put the grass in your compost pile. (Don't have one yet? This is a good time to start.) As you work, pull out as many roots as you can. One gardener friend digs all his beds 3 feet deep—or I should say, hires someone else to dig them, then amends with lots of composted manure.

If you plan to move and compost your dug-up clumps of grass any distance from the bed you're digging, it saves some work to have two wheelbarrows for this job. If you can't borrow a second one, just dump the grass clumps in a pile and move them when you're finished and the wheelbarrow is empty again.

1) Mark the outline of the bed.

2) Remove a 1-foot strip of grass or sod across the width of your bed and put the clumps and roots in a wheelbarrow or a pile.

3) Dig and remove soil 1 foot deep and 1 foot wide underneath the bare strip where you removed the grass and put it in your empty wheelbarrow.

4) Using a sturdy garden fork, loosen soil another foot deep (under the soil you just removed) by inserting and rocking it back and forth.

5) Shovel a few inches of compost or a mix of compost and shredded leaves on top of the soil you just loosened.

6) Remove a second strip of grass/sod next to the one you've just dug and put it in the wheelbarrow to dump for composting (or on the pile to move later).

7) Dig out the soil a foot deep under the removed grass, shoveling the soil into the first trench, on top of the compost.

8) Use your fork to loosen the soil a foot deep under the soil you just dug out and moved into the first trench.

9) Add some compost in the second trench on top of the soil you've just loosened.

10) Remove a third strip of grass/sod next to the second one, dig out a foot of soil and move it into the second trench, on top of the compost, then loosen the soil another foot deep in the third trench.

11) Repeat this process until you reach the end of the bed and fill the last trench with the soil in the wheelbarrow dug from the first trench.

Because your new soil level will be higher than ground level, you can enclose the bed with a wood frame if you want, but this isn't necessary. Add more compost, plus shredded leaves, dried manure, or whatever organic material you have and fork it in, then water and cover with mulch.

I like to use sturdy plastic edging to line the inside perimeter of the bed and keep surrounding grass from invading. The edging is 6 to 8 inches deep (the deeper the better) and comes in rolls. Cut the length to fit, and work it in gradually as you dig and fill each strip, keeping the top slightly above ground level. If you have a 3 x 5 foot bed, cut a single 16-foot length of edging. Some gardeners use strips of old carpet or scrap plastic (potting soil bags that you overlap and cut off near ground level when you're finished). Don't use metal edging, because you (or someone) can easily get hurt stepping on it barefoot. In my experience, weed barrier cloth doesn't work nearly as well as edging because the surrounding grass eventually comes through it.

Rototilling

Rototill the bed, chopping up the grass and tilling it in with compost. To break up the grass roots, a thorough tilling is needed. Remove as many clumps of roots by hand as you can. Rototilling is harmful to the established network of soil life, especially mycorrhizal fungi and earthworms, but sometimes it's the only reasonable choice for a brand-new garden. It should only be done once to establish a new garden, and definitely not every year as is often recommended or done automatically at some community gardens. I find these machines cumbersome and difficult to use, though I'm always told how easy they are.

Sod Cutting

Cut out the grass first with a sod cutter, then rototill or hand dig the bed. If you double-dig so that the soil is loosened under the top 12 inches that you till and amend, your hard work will pay off for many years to come. A sod cutter is a machine that looks easy to use on the Internet, but I wouldn't touch one with a 10-foot pole. Get some help with this one unless you really know equipment.

Raised Beds

If it's November, December, or later and you want to plan for the up-and-coming growing season but you don't want to dig, the easiest way to make a garden is to create enclosed raised beds and fill them with good topsoil and compost. First decide how many garden beds you need. You'll want to be able to easily reach the far side of each bed, so keep the width to about 2½ to 3 feet, especially if it's against a wall or a fence. You won't want to crawl in there. If it's a freestanding bed, a width of 3 to 5 feet will allow you to reach the middle easily from either side, but keep

Raised beds are easy to fill with organic materials and create a well-defined, orderly appearance, but they require more water than inground gardens. Make them narrow enough that you can reach the middle from both sides.

the length reasonable too. Accessibility is key. Use string to outline the beds on the ground first so that you end up with a configuration that works for you.

Build one or more bottomless wooden frames at least 12 inches high. You can usually find recycled lumber, and though it's an easy do-it-yourself project, don't hesitate to get some help if you need it; just make sure your helper sticks to your carefully considered design. Don't use any treated wood in the garden. It has a green tinge and leaches arsenic into the soil. Cedar and redwood are rot resistant, but just about any wood boards except plywood will hold up well in our climate for five to ten years or more. By then you will be a well-seasoned gardener and probably itching to revamp your plots anyway.

Once your raised-bed frames are built and in place, cover the grass or ground inside the planting area with pieces of overlapping cardboard, newspaper, or burlap coffee sacks, making sure the material extends a few inches beyond the outside edges of the frame to keep the grass and weeds from moving in. Have your materials at hand and ready to lay down once the beds are built.

Cinder blocks can make good raised-bed enclosures too. One gardener I know covered two layers of cinder blocks with stucco, creating some really attractive, well insulated raised planting beds. Or you can make use of the center holes by filling them with soil and planting herbs, flowers, or more vegetables inside. Be sure to lay your bottom-layer cardboard or newspaper down first and build the beds on top of it so you won't have to move all those cinder blocks again.

Finally, fill the beds with planting mix. Buy it in bulk from someone reputable or buy topsoil and compost and customize your own mixes. After filling with good soil, water the beds thoroughly, and cover with mulch until planting time. If any weeds sprout, they will be easy to pull.

If you live in the mountains, site beds for maximum sunlight, warmth, and wind protection—against a south-facing wall, for example. Place rocks around beds to absorb and radiate heat. In spring, temporarily cover the planting area with dark plastic to help it warm up. Use floating row cover over planted beds to keep warmth in. Creating more warmth for as a long a growing season as possible will be your top priority.

Judy Seaborn, who owns Botanical Interests seed company with her husband, Curtis Jones, has dozens of raised beds in her backyard. She likes the manageability of so many different boxed beds because she can spread out her workload, just tackling two or three a week. She covers the walkways in between with lawn clippings throughout the summer, and after walking around on them all during the growing season they dry out and break down, so they're perfect for adding to the beds in the fall. She puts the

Judy Seaborn, co-owner of Botanical Interests seeds, mulches paths with grass clippings all summer, then adds them to raised beds in the fall.

Creating a Vegetable Garden 71

boxes to bed for the winter one at a time by cleaning out dead plants and layering leaves and lawn clippings, compost and organic fertilizer. In the spring, she turns the soil and covers each bed with a fresh layer of compost and/or mulch.

Gardening in Containers

Even if you don't have a yard, you can still be a gardener. You can grow food that you like to eat in containers as long as you have some sun. Some people even grow rambling vegetables like cucumbers, squash, beans, and melons in containers by thinking vertically and providing a supporting trellis or teepee-shaped poles. When it comes to gardening, it never hurts to jump in

A round onion flower nods gracefully next to well-constructed bamboo bean teepees in Lele and Thea Tennenbaum's diverse biodynamic garden.

and try something new. And contrary to what beginners may think, there's no one "right way" to grow things. If you live in the mountains where deer and elk are plentiful, growing food in containers on a deck may be your only alternative to a garden enclosed by a high fence.

Every year I plant a Sun Gold cherry tomato in a big faux clay pot right outside the back door. I love popping the deliciously warm bite-sized morsels into my mouth whenever I walk outside. There are some advantages to growing vegetables outside in a pot, and one is the proximity to the house. I can guarantee that any plants you pass by every day will get better care than those that are farther away and out of sight. Another big plus is that there will be few, if any, weeds to pull.

Almost any container will do as long as it's big enough for the *mature* plant (some roots can be bigger than the plant you see) and has good drainage. If you're growing very shallow-rooted veggies like lettuce, you can get by with half an inch or so of gravel at the bottom of 4 to 5 inches of soil. Otherwise, make sure your container has a good-sized hole or two in the bottom. It's easy enough to drill a hole in most planters if you need to. At least five hours is considered full sun in Colorado and much of the semiarid West. That's what most vegetables need, but you can grow leafy greens in part or dappled shade. Some sites at higher elevations may need more than five hours to warm things up enough for plants to grow well, especially warm-season vegetables.

Cover big holes with a pot shard or small rock before adding soil so the soil won't leak out when it drains, and don't let the container sit forever in a big saucer of water that doesn't drain. The idea is to provide consistent water for the plant but retain the oxygen in the soil by allowing it to drain so roots don't rot.

Since lightweight pots are easiest to handle and move around once they're planted, I like big plastic ones, though plain 5-gallon or bigger black nursery pots will work for many vegetables. I've seen prettier fiberglass and resin pots that look just like terra-cotta too. With little caddies on wheels, you can move containers into more or less sun or shade, or out of the way if you need to. You can always build simple planter boxes out of wood, but make them deep enough (12 to 24 inches or more) to accommodate the roots of the plants you want to grow.

There are many stunning pottery containers available from all over the world that can really show off your plants. I think it's wise to make sure they don't contain lead when you're planning to grow edibles in them. If your supplier can't assure you on this point, inexpensive lead testing kits are available at hardware stores or on the Internet.

Soil for Containers

Almost everyone advises to use soil-less mixes for containers so the growing medium won't compact, but you can't expect to grow healthy vegetables for months in this stuff. Since a large quantity of regular soil from your garden will compact in a container, it's best to make a special mix. You can start with a bagged mix, but make sure it's good-quality potting soil and add some additional ingredients to it. Many of the cheaper mixes are made from ground-up forest products, which usually means bark. They don't hold

water very well and often form a hard surface crust when they dry out. Some bagged mixes contain water-retaining crystals or gels. While these polymers can work well for ornamentals, I would avoid them for edibles since plants can take up the residues.

You want rich, fertile soil in your containers that will hold water but also drain well so the roots can get oxygen. Coconut fiber, or coir, is a great water-holding addition. It holds up better than sphagnum peat and is considered by most to be a more-renewable resource, though it leaches calcium and has no nutrient value, so you'll need to add some balanced organic fertilizer right from the start. Compost contains the nutrients that plants need and helps retain moisture. I add compost and a handful of kelp and alfalfa to container soil. Compost tea has an amazing beneficial effect on plants and helps to establish microbial soil life in containers too.

Speaking of compost tea, Roland Evans (the cheerful mountain gardener mentioned in chapter 3) grows everything under the sun at high altitude, including many vegetables in containers. As a side business, he sells his family's compost tea brewing kits and products (the line is called Organic Bountea). His brother John lives in Alaska, where he became famous for growing giant organic vegetables using Alaska Humisoil.

Watering Containers

Containers dry out a lot more quickly than garden beds, which means they will probably need watering once a day when it's hot. Sticking your finger down a few inches into the soil is the best way to tell for sure how dry it is. If it feels wet or damp, hold off. But if plants look wilty in the morning and the soil isn't wet or damp, they probably need a drink right away.

When watering containers with a hose, water slowly without its full force. Just

Roland Evans's Favorite Container Soil Recipe

4 parts coconut coir, peat moss, or reused soil from past containers

2 parts Humisoil and/or sieved garden compost

1 part sand (instead of vermiculite or perlite)

1 part garden soil if I feel like it (with worms)

Some SuperStart for Plants and a little Marine Mineral Magic (M3) for minerals and trace elements

A handful of alfalfa pellets if I have them

½ part ground organic charcoal (biochar), but it is hard to obtain cheaply, so it's okay to leave out

Mix everything well in a large container or wheelbarrow. Fill the planting containers to half an inch from the top and water until moist before planting (the soil level should go down at least half an inch).

as in the garden, slow infiltration is better. Remember to water the soil, instead of spraying the plant. Tomatoes especially will suffer if you get the leaves wet. Add mulch (grass clippings, dried-up fall leaves, even torn-up newspaper) around plants in

containers to conserve moisture and prevent a dry surface crust from forming.

Ollas are porous clay vessels that are becoming popular in the West. Once used by ancient peoples to hold and release water slowly to crops, they can be handy when you go away for the weekend. You bury one inside a pot and fill it to just overflowing every few days. Another watering device is made from a bottle with a special cone top that is pushed into the soil. There are also many self-watering containers available, as well as books and YouTube videos on how to make them yourself.

Many smaller vegetable varieties are bred specifically for container growing. I've tried Little Prince eggplant, Pot of Gold container chard, Garden Babies Butterhead lettuce, and Pizza My Heart peppers. Choose determinate tomatoes (they're smaller) and bush varieties of other vegetables.

But don't be limited by these and don't forget that herbs love containers too. My tarragon overwinters every year outside in the same pot, and the tasty, tangy tips are delicious in early salads. Basil is an old container standby (it benefits from afternoon shade in our region). Some herbs, like comfrey and many mints, grow so vigorously in the ground that confining them to containers can be prudent in small yards. If you group containers together, you can create a microclimate that shades the soil.

Chapter 7
Extending the Season

Row cover is a fantastic easy-to-use tool for western vegetable gardeners. Without blocking much sunlight, it warms the soil and air underneath a few crucial degrees, helping new plants get growing in cool weather. You can water right through it.

There is nothing more disheartening than an early frost that wipes out the vegetable garden in September, when the tomatoes, peppers, beans, and squash are loaded with ripe fruit. Except maybe May frosts that nip cherry, peach, and apple blossoms at their peak, or a hailstorm that pounds the entire garden to bits. These are some of the weather events that test western gardeners. The best strategy is to anticipate

and prepare for them in advance so your gardening morale won't be shattered.

A key phrase to describe our western climate is *fast changing*. It tends to be dry in the summer with lots of high-intensity UV sunlight, low humidity, few cloudy days, occasional (or in some areas, constant) intense wind, and some afternoon thunderstorms, usually in July, though they occur less regularly than they used to. Even on the plains it usually cools off comfortably at night because of our altitude, though hot spells in late June and July when it doesn't aren't uncommon.

Having said that, each growing season may be quite different than the last. Weather cycle data shows that we have both hot and dry and some cooler, wetter years within each decade. Global climate change projections call for warmer temperatures in North America as a whole, and hot, dry parts of the West may well get hotter and drier. Even an increase of a degree or two will have a big impact. But many western states or portions of states are located in a transition zone between the Southwest and the northern Rockies, and climatologists say that precipitation could either increase or decrease by 5 to 10 percent.

Gardening Strategies for Unpredictable Conditions
One gardening strategy involves planting a mix of varieties that prefer different conditions to cover various weather scenarios. Beyond the basic distinction between

cool-season crops like greens, peas, and brassicas, and warm-season crops like tomatoes, peppers, and squash, slow-bolting (i.e., slow to go to seed) vegetable varieties, like oakleaf lettuce, for example, remain tasty when others wilt or turn bitter in the heat. More drought-tolerant, heat-resistant varieties will thrive during our more typical hot, dry summers, while those that prefer cooler temperatures do better if we have a cooler growing season. Plant some of each and you'll have it covered. Most seed companies offer a lot of information about each variety on individual packets, in their catalogs, and on their websites.

If you purchase seeds specifically grown in and for higher altitudes and western climates, they will generally grow better here. This especially holds true for mountain gardeners with the shortest growing seasons. Very few seed companies have their own trial gardens anymore, and most now primarily *distribute* seeds, outsourcing their production to growers in a variety of places, including India and China. Seeds from local and regional companies that are actually grown locally may cost a little bit more, but packets of seeds are still an amazing bargain when you consider the huge return on your investment. Plus, many high-altitude seeds turn out to be adapted to extreme conditions, so they will often grow where it's hot and dry as well as in places with very cold winters and short growing seasons. If you learn to save your own seeds, as all gardeners used to do, they will become well adapted to your specific local conditions. Saving seeds is not difficult, just unfamiliar to most of us today (see chapter 12, Saving Seeds).

SITING THE GARDEN

Where your plants grow is important, especially at higher altitudes. The growing season is very short in the mountains, and though it may be cooler, the dry air and especially intense UV sunlight are hard on vegetable crops. Wind is usually an issue too, and since most native mountain soils are shallow, rocky, and lean, they dry out quickly. Making good use of shade and windbreaks can mean the difference between crop failure and success.

Many mountain gardeners swear by planting vegetable gardens on east- or north-facing slopes, which avoids hot afternoon sun exposure and follows the natural pattern of vegetation. On the other hand, warming up soil in the mountains is of primary importance, especially in the spring, so a south-facing bed against the house is a good bet for growing early in the season.

If you live on a small city or suburban lot or have a community garden plot, you won't have a lot of choice about where to site your garden, but if you do, pick the spot that gets the most sun. If you're planning your garden in the fall or winter, it's easy to forget where the summer sun will actually be and how much and where any trees will cast shade. Since you need at least five hours of sun to grow most vegetables in the West, make sure you consider the garden sun and shade conditions in May through August, not in December or January. Prune your trees if necessary to let in more light and use dappled, light shade areas for planting lettuce, basil, and other crops that tolerate or appreciate less sun.

You can create mini environments, or microclimates, that protect plants

When summer's heat arrives, a simple burlap lean-to will provide some shade for lettuce, basil, or new transplants that can't yet take the full-on western sun.

warming up and cooling down. It can be 80 degrees in May or September when the mercury suddenly drops and a blizzard arrives. But a foot of snow can disappear in a day when the sun comes out and warm chinook winds arrive.

A blanket of snow that covers cool-season plants will insulate them. It's the clear, frosty nights that are dangerous. But warm-season crops don't like the cold one bit and a sudden freeze usually puts an end to their growth or production, whether in spring or fall. By using season-extending techniques to take the edge off these temperature fluctuations, we can speed up growth in the spring and prolong growth and harvest in the fall.

When it comes to extending the season, our biggest western gardening advantage is our sunny climate. This benefit is huge and many more of us should be realizing it. By harnessing solar energy, we can provide some relatively simple and inexpensive structures and extend the growing season far more easily than our cool-climate gardening friends in New England or the Midwest. No wonder Colorado is a leader in alternative energy!

I'm not sure why, but almost all season-extending gardening structures in climates with cold winters are built above the ground. If we dig these into the ground, we can gain a significant amount of insulating benefit. Paired with our plentiful sunshine, this makes a winning combination.

There are many different possibilities for extending the growing season and the harvest. For example, Eliot Coleman, whose focus is year-round gardening in cold climates (he lives in Maine), has designed an

anywhere in the garden by warming the soil and surrounding air temperature when it's cold, and partially shading and sheltering them when it's hot and windy. This can be accomplished using existing plants (trees or shrubs) or structures (walls or fences) or by adding new ones. As the growing season progresses, you can also protect new seedlings by planting them in the shelter of more mature early vegetables, like pea vines. As the new crop becomes established, the spent pea vines come down.

USING OUR NATURAL ASSETS

We can be almost certain about two things: the sun will continue to shine nearly every day in our region, and temperatures will continue to fluctuate up and down a great deal in spring and fall, rather than gradually interesting system of moveable greenhouses on rails that can be easily moved back and forth by two people to cover different beds at different times of the year.

Here are some season-extending techniques and structures, many specifically for the West, that have worked very well for gardeners.

Row Cover

Using floating row cover is a highly effective and simple way to maximize plant growth by protecting them from cold, insects, and wind. A white polypropylene fabric that breathes, it generally comes in rolls 6 to 12 feet wide and 20 to 100 feet long, or longer for commercial agricultural use. It's also called Reemay and Agribon. You can sometimes buy small pieces from rolls at garden centers.

The downside is that, just like horticultural plastics used on hoophouses, it's a petroleum-based material that will continue to get more expensive, and, like other plastics, it eventually degrades and ends up in the landfill. Use it carefully and get as much use out of it as you can. Never burn it. A few

Row cover comes in various thicknesses. The thinnest is just right for giving young plants a boost of extra warmth in spring or fall. Thicker grades can protect mature plants from fall frosts but also keep cabbage worms alive.

companies now offer biodegradable plant starch–based mulch as an alternative to plastic mulch; maybe they'll come up with a similar plant-based row cover fabric.

You can use row cover on most plants without any supporting structure, holding it down along the edges with smooth rocks (they won't tear it) or sandbags (you can make your own) so it doesn't blow away. If you allow for some extra width when you lay it down, rolling up the extra fabric at one edge until you need it, you can unroll it later to accommodate plants as they grow taller. Row cover is especially good for protecting spring greens and root crops that don't require pollination by insects, like beets and carrots, or squash and cucumbers before they flower. Eventually all but the lightest weight will probably retain too much heat as temperatures warm up, and that's when you'll want to remove it. Some gardeners leave it on for a few weeks, others for months, depending on the weight, planting time, and conditions.

If you use row cover on a raised bed with a soil level that is a few inches below the top, you'll have some extra height for plants right from the start, but take care that any rough wood edges don't catch and tear the fabric. Stiff plastic, fiberglass, or bent metal conduit half hoops can be used to support row cover at a greater height. If you space the hoops a few feet apart you will still have easy access to the bed when you remove the cover. The advantage over plastic minitunnels is that you can remove or replace the cover very quickly and you can water through it. I've attached low hoops onto wooden raised beds with simple metal brackets, but stiff hollow plastic or metal conduit hoops can

be placed over pieces of rebar pounded into the ground, making them easier to remove and replace. A rounded hoop surface holds up row cover best in the wind, but in a pinch you can also drape row cover right over rebar without it catching and ripping by using tennis balls. Just cut a slit and place them on top of each piece of rebar. Secure row cover on the outside edges with boards, rocks, sandbags, or whatever you have on hand that works, but be mindful of our sudden, strong winds.

By placing 1-inch plastic irrigation pipe over pieces of rebar pounded into the ground at each end, you can create a simple framework for a removable plastic hoophouse, shade structure, or hail protector.

It comes in different grades, but most midweight row cover allows 70 to 85 percent of light to penetrate and protects plants down to about 28 degrees Fahrenheit. Use it in early spring and again when it turns cold

With a plastic hoophouse in a wind-protected spot, you can plant out earlier in the spring. Secure the plastic well, rolling the ends up around rocks or boards. Store it during the summer, and bring it out again for fall crops.

in the fall for a crop seeded in August. The lightest-weight row cover gives a degree or two of extra warmth or frost protection but allows 95 percent of light to pass through it. Row cover is also good for protecting crops from rabbits and insects like cucumber or squash bugs and borers in warm weather. But again, remove it as flowers form so pollinators can get at them—and at each other. Inside squash blossoms is where male squash bees often hang out and wait for females to arrive.

The thickest row cover, often called a frost blanket, can give up to 8 degrees of frost protection (down to 24 degrees Fahrenheit), but it only allows 50 percent light penetration. That's not as much of an issue in our high-UV climate as it is elsewhere. You can grow lettuce underneath it, but check on your plants to make sure they have enough light and aren't getting too warm. Frost blankets help strawberries and raspberries warm up earlier in the spring, resulting in heavier production. You can also very quickly use it to temporarily cover plants during light freezes.

The protection that midweight row cover gives plants makes a tremendous difference in speeding up spring plant growth of cool-weather crops like lettuce and other greens, onions, brassicas, and strawberries. It keeps warmth in when you need it, while allowing spring rain (or melting snow) to penetrate. If you plant early in March, you'll be eating fresh greens in April. Those extra 4 degrees will also help plants through light September and October frosts and keep your late summer planting of beets, carrots, and greens going strong. One Boulder farmer I know who has experimented with several methods says he has the best survival rate for overwintering fall-planted spinach, carrots, and turnips using floating row cover without any hoops or supports.

If you don't have row cover, you can also throw a sheet or light bedspread over tomatoes and other tender crops in the spring or fall when frost is predicted. If you use it on top of row cover, you'll have even greater protection.

PLASTIC MINITUNNELS

Structures can be multipurpose and versatile with a simple framework that can be covered and uncovered. You can cover framework hoops with plastic sheeting when it's cold, for example, then remove it and replace with lightweight row cover after it warms up. It's best to use UV-treated greenhouse plastic instead of the inexpensive rolls of plastic sheeting available in hardware stores, which doesn't last very long and ends up in the landfill more quickly. It comes in various thicknesses, or mils. Plastic tunnels create more warmth than row cover during the day, so you need to be mindful about ventilation whenever the sun is shining. You can't water through plastic, of course, but if you have a drip system or can roll up the front, this isn't a problem.

For an easy framework, you can use a length of stiff wire goat fencing, or other fencing, bent into a semicircle over your raised bed. It's an easy install, but make sure it's high enough so you can access your plants easily.

SMALL ROCK OR BRICK BEDS

Anyone who uses thick organic sheet mulching over the winter will find that their soil stays cool longer in the spring. And if you live in the mountains, warming the soil enough for plants to germinate in the spring takes ingenuity. Along with locating growing beds along a south-facing wall, small individual growing beds surrounded by rocks or bricks will also soak up and retain heat to warm soil and give plants a boost.

BLACK PLASTIC AND BIODEGRADABLE MULCH

Black plastic mulch will help warm and retain heat in the soil. You can buy it in rolls with preexisting holes or slits for planting.

Black plastic or biodegradable mulch has been used successfully to extend the growing season at higher altitudes by two to three weeks. On the plains, it can make a big difference for warm-season crops like peppers, eggplant, cucumbers, and melons.

There are also some biodegradable mulch films made from plant starch available now that are called biofilms; BioTelo is one brand name. Farmers can plough these back into soil at the end of the season. Though they cost more up front, biofilms eliminate the need for removal and disposal in landfills. In an experiment from the Horticulture Department of Cornell University, a CSA farm in La Jara, Colorado, at 8,000 feet reported a two to three week extension of their growing season, enabling them to grow peppers, eggplant, and cucumbers, by using biodegradable black mulch.

PLANT COVERS—
WATER TEEPEES AND CLOCHES

Another strategy for getting a jump on the growing season is to warm up the soil and airspace around individual plants. Wall o' Waters and similar water teepees with water-filled cells that surround plants do a great job. If you dig the holes and put up the water teepees a day or two before planting, your warm-season plants, especially, will have an easier transition into the garden. You can plant out tomatoes and peppers in April this way, and you'll be picking the fruit in early July. They can be a little bit awkward and floppy to set up by yourself, but with two people they're a snap. One gardener friend who lives where there are a lot of raccoons says he's been forced to discontinue using these teepees of water because the raccoons make a terrible mess of them. "They act like I've set up a miniature Water World just for them," he told me. Curious cats occasionally push them over too.

If you're so inclined and have a little storage space, hang onto your plastic jugs and larger plastic bottles instead of recycling them. You can use them to make your own (free) water teepees by filling them with water and encircling young plants. It isn't necessary to cap them—in fact, I find that at least flea beetles and aphids drown in the open jugs and cells of Wall o' Waters. You can also move them farther out as the plant grows. Dig them into the ground slightly.

At the turn of the century on French intensive farms, and in England during World War I, thousands of glass bell jars were used to cover individual plants. Labor was cheap (and voluntary for the war effort) so tending to them twice each day—propping them open for ventilation in the morning and closing them at night—wasn't a problem. British war workers grew lettuce in 250,000 bell jars for troops and civilians. It must have been a pretty sight, but it's hardly practical today,

Many western gardeners swear by Wall o' Waters or similar teepees with water-filled cells that surround and warm plants and soil. These speed up the growth and maturation process considerably for warm-season plants like tomatoes and peppers.

though you can find glass bell jars if you want to use them for their aesthetic value.

Mountain gardener Penn Parmenter refers to our ubiquitous plastic gallon milk or water jugs as "hideous American bell jars." She uses a lot of them in her garden for a week or two to help individual plants get started. Cut off the bottoms and bury them into the soil around young starts after planting and watering in. Don't forget to mulch thickly around the outside of the jug and be sure to remove the cap for ventilation.

COLD FRAMES

For fresh eating through the fall and into winter, and an early start to gardening in the spring, a cold frame is a simple and inexpensive way to go. This low-to-the-ground enclosure with a transparent roof that opens for ventilation and closes to retain heat, acts as a miniature greenhouse. You can easily build your own and even

A cold frame is another simple and inexpensive way to continue fresh eating through the fall and into winter or to provide a place to set out plants early in the spring. Ventilation is crucial, especially in our sunny climate.

download plans and instructions from the Internet. Face it south or southeast if at all possible and make sure the back is higher than the front so the "lights" (windows) on top slant toward the winter sun. Storm windows or reused/freecycled windows work well for the lights and are usually available wherever reused building materials are sold. Since tempered window glass can't be recycled, it's a great way to make use of old windows.

Build your bottomless frame to fit the lights using 2-inch-thick boards. You can also add 2-inch blueboard foam (a waterproof styrofoam used on concrete slabs) for more insulation. Ventilation is always crucial for cold frames, even more so in our climate. Unless you want to open them every morning and close them every night by

With straw bales, a few boards, and a few reused, lightweight, modular plastic panels, my friend Michael created an easy cold frame.

hand (which works fine for some people—a notched stick makes it easier), make sure you get automatic solar vents (roughly fifty dollars plus shipping), since cold frames can heat up quickly with all our western sunshine, no matter how cold it is. You can also use plastic gallon jugs filled with water inside cold frames as heat sinks for extra warmth at night. Snow is a good insulator, so a couple of cold days under a few inches of snow cover, without the sun shining through to warm up the bed, won't hurt your plants. The south-facing slope of the lights will help snow slide off as it warms, but several inches of heavy wet snow can break glass panes, so brush it off if more than 6 inches accumulates. A reflective insulated cover comes in handy when temperatures plummet—just remember to remove it during the day.

You can buy cold frame kits for a few hundred dollars, including the vent. These simple season extenders will enable you to enjoy scrumptious greens, carrots, radishes, beets, scallions, leeks, chard, and arugula all winter long if you plant early enough for plants to get established—on the plains in August and early September most years, in mid- to late July in the mountains. Eliot Coleman, author of *Four-Season Harvest*, has used cold frames under plastic tunnels in Maine, a place with much less sun than the West. That extra layer of plastic results in temperatures warm enough to grow and *maintain* cool-season vegetables confidently throughout the winter there, if they are started as early as late July or early August.

Every design I've seen is for aboveground cold frames, at least 12 inches high at the back and 8 inches at the front. But digging cold frames into the ground provides more insulation, and we have enough sunlight for it to work. If the box is deeper than 8 inches at the front (it will be 4 inches aboveground at the back), you start losing sunlight in the shade of the walls, so the box will need to be bigger (or the planting area inside smaller and centered) to compensate.

GREENHOUSES

I lust after my friends' greenhouses and some day soon I'll build one too. In the meantime, I've learned a few things about them. First of all, everyone I know says they look big when they're empty, but once they're full of plants, soil, watering cans, and other gardening paraphernalia, they wish they'd opted for a little more room to grow, so choose bigger rather than smaller if you have the space.

A two-door entrance to Mikl Brawner's below-ground greenhouse minimizes heat loss and keeps snow off the steps.

Mikl Brawner's Energy-Saving Greenhouse

When natural gas and propane were cheap, no one thought twice about putting a 4-inch gas line into a greenhouse. Now growers complain about the high cost of propane, but excuse it as the cost of doing business. Twenty-some years ago, I needed a greenhouse to grow nursery plants from seed, and I was inexperienced, frugal, and eco-logical. I looked around at heated greenhouses and decided mine wasn't going to have a gas line.

After researching, I decided on a design based on seat-of-the-pants logic that came from growing up in rural Iowa, two years in the peace corps, and the incredible power of the winter sun in Colorado. Aware that I didn't really know what I was doing, I built an experimental 12 x 24 foot greenhouse that has been in operation for nineteen years. As far as I know, it is the most efficient greenhouse in Colorado.

Brawner's energy-saving greenhouse is built 4 feet deep into the ground and has no windows on the well-insulated, cool north side. A perennial hop vine grows on the south side, providing cooling shade but dying back each fall to allow sun.

I built it 4 feet deep into the ground, because of the insulating and geothermal benefit. The perimeter and north side are well insulated, and there is ample solar heat storage. At 3 feet high, my south planting bench gets very little shade, and the entrance is only three steps down. The walls are 6-inch-thick poured cement, insulated with 2-inch blueboard foam—4 feet high (to ground level) on the south, east, and west sides, and 6 feet high (2 feet aboveground) on the north. The extra 2 feet on the north wall allows more vertical space above the north bed for plants and for solar heat storage as the sun strikes a row of 5-gallon buckets filled with water along the cement wall. The north planting bed, 5 x 20 x 3 feet deep, filled with soil, also acts as a heat sink, as does the earth floor.

Most greenhouses are entirely covered with glass or plastic, but the north side of mine is insulated instead of glazed. We use it primarily between January 1 and May 31, and the low winter sun never hits that side. Insulating the north side with 4-inch styrofoam substantially reduces nighttime heat loss, plus the south bench remains well lit even in high summer sun, so it seems foolish to trade heat loss for light. You couldn't do this on the East Coast, but you can in sunny Denver.

To minimize heat loss at the entrance, I built two doors: an outer, slanting cellar door and a vertical door at the bottom of the steps. The cellar door keeps snow out of the stairway and can be closed before opening the well-sealed inner door. A manual louvered vent in the east wall (as well as the door) lets in air for cooling, and there are two vents in the roof peak for cooling: a 12-inch square that exits into a wind turbine acting as a powerful exhaust fan, and a 6 x 2 foot hinged twin-wall polycarbonate vent. These solar vents operate without electricity. As conditions warm or cool, the paraffin expands or shrinks accordingly, opening or closing the vent.

At least two rotations of crops per year are possible because the inground depth keeps the greenhouse cooler in summer, and I grow hops over part of the south glazing for summer cooling. They die back to the ground in winter, leaving the glass unobstructed.

We start hardy perennials and vegetables from seed in January, and more-tender tomatoes, peppers, and basil in February and March. Tender tropical plants don't fare well in this greenhouse because nights are cool, but this results in plants that are tougher, more compact, stronger rooting, and less prone to pests and diseases—conditions that support growing plants organically.

Plants do very well in it, but people enjoy the space too. Winter visitors don't want to leave; it's cozy and earthy. If I built this greenhouse for home use, I would reserve a space for a small table and a couple of chairs for tea, fresh salads, conversation, the laptop, or just to chase away the winter blues.

Second, use solar energy for heat. We may have less water in the West, but sunlight is abundant. The sidebar on the previous page gives a simple solar-heated greenhouse design that nursery owner and sustainability pioneer Mikl Brawner came up with for the Colorado Front Range. He built his first greenhouse twenty-five years ago and has only occasionally added a small portable supplemental heater during extreme cold spells. He has grown tomatoes in it with no supplemental heat when outside temperatures were 0 degrees Fahrenheit and says he has never had to heat it more than five nights or two days in any one year. Others have adapted his basic design and improved on it for larger greenhouses. He generously agreed to share his design for this book so others can take advantage of our western sun and inground heat to create their own efficient solar greenhouses.

WIND, HAIL, AND SUN PROTECTION

While these aren't technically season extenders, protection from wind, hail, and, for some crops, hot summer sun can mean the difference between a garden that thrives versus one that barely survives, if at all.

Row cover provides pretty good wind protection for smaller plants especially, but a fence or screen in the right place can effectively shelter part of or the entire garden from drying winds, and it doesn't have to be a major project or expense. For example, Penn Parmenter simply plants part of her

A windbreak of wild plum or other shrubs can effectively shelter part or all of the vegetable garden during the growing season while feeding pollinators and providing fruit.

mountain garden in among stands of trees because they break up the wind.

· I bought a roll of 48-inch dark green plastic mesh fencing on Craigslist for fifteen dollars. Fastened with baling twine to T-posts on the southwest side of my garden, it makes a great windbreak and has held up fairly well for three years. By this I mean it hasn't blown off completely and flown away across the pasture, though sections have ripped through the twine periodically and needed to be replaced. I also used it to put up a 15-foot-long windscreen alongside my tomato plants, which I can easily walk around or remove at the end of the season.

You can use stronger wire fencing to support vertical growth of peas, squash, or beans, which will also block wind. A live hedgerow of Nanking cherries makes a good deciduous windscreen. They're tough and drought tolerant and don't get too tall; eight years after planting them as bare-root sticks, my tallest are under 6 feet with moderate to low watering. They're very pretty early spring bloomers, offering early nectar for bees as well as fruit for birds (the cherries are sweet but very small). Native golden currants can also work well as a windscreen, and they too provide fruit and support native pollinators. Another shrub to use in combination with these as a windscreen is blue mist spirea (*caryopteris*), which blooms late in the season, at the end of August where I live, providing food for all kinds of bees.

Simple structures can be versatile when used with various coverings for warmth, shade, or hail protection. Some savvy gardeners are creating raised beds with attached wood supports for screen or stronger hardware cloth

Mountain gardener Robyn Wallerich built these hail guards. After five years in her garden, they show no signs of needing replacement.

(sometimes with a layer of wire fencing underneath to make it even stronger), or fiberglass coverings to block hail. As any gardener who's been through a severe hailstorm can tell you, never underestimate the damaging power of hail. A heavy-duty storm hit the Denver/Arvada area at 10:30 in the evening in July 2009, smashing greenhouse panels, shredding plastic pots and plants, even shooting holes right through the trunks of small potted trees at local nurseries. Though you may not be able to prevent damage from a storm of that magnitude, you can certainly lessen the destructive effect of marble- to golfball-sized hail on your garden

Shade creates a comfortable microclimate for plants and gardeners. Shade cloth is versatile, attractive, removable, easy to work with, and comes in different colors and grades. Without it, my deck would be too hot for sitting comfortably outside.

with some protective coverings over your beds. You want material that's as strong as possible but also lets through as much light as possible. Screen or hardware cloth will also provide some shade for lettuce and other greens that prefer not to bake in hot summer sun.

I love shade cloth because it looks good and is so easy to work with. You can buy it in different colors (though basic, inexpensive black is attractive) and various gradients of shade. It doesn't fray when you cut it and you can fold over the edge and easily snap plastic grommets onto it with openings for easy tying onto posts, poles, or horizontal supports. This makes it easy to create one of the most important microclimates, a shady spot for the gardener and friends to sit and enjoy the garden.

Chapter 8
Beneficial Insects in the Garden

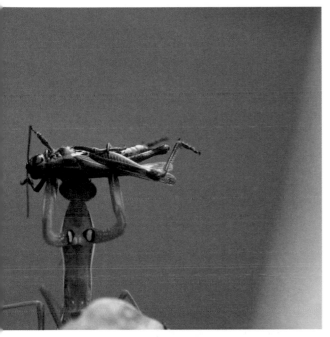

Adult European mantid feeding on red-legged grasshopper.
Note bull's-eye markings under forelegs.

Just as caterpillars transform into butterflies, other insects also go through several distinct life stages. Everyone recognizes a typical red ladybug (more correctly, a lady beetle) with black spots, but do you know what their eggs look like, or that they spend part of their life as larvae that resemble tiny alligators? Not only that, there are over 450 different species of lady beetles found in North America. Nearly all of these are beneficial insects that devour hundreds of aphids and other small insects per day, usually consuming more while in their larval stage than they do as adults. The two exceptions are the introduced Mexican bean beetle and the squash beetle, which eat plants instead of other insects.

Pesticide use has greatly reduced insect populations around the world, and this includes the beneficial ones that humans depend on far more than most of us realize. Too many of us have a conditioned response to recoil at the sight of insects or worse, kill them straight away, especially the unfamiliar ones.

The photos on these pages show the incredible diversity and life stages of some of the most common beneficial insects to help you recognize and support them.

Lady Beetle

Recently molted convergent lady beetle with pupa skins

Large lady beetle pupa

Two-spotted yellow lady beetle eggs next to larger, orange Colorado potato beetle eggs

Eye-spotted lady beetle

Two-spotted lady beetle pupa

Fourteen-spotted lady beetle adult

Large lady beetle larva

Seven-spotted lady beetle adults

Green Lacewing

"Aphid lion" larva eating

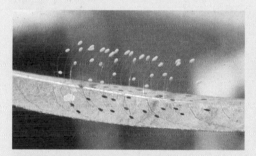

Green lacewing eggs

Larva and egg in colony of potato psyllids

Cocoon of pupal stage

Adult

European Mantid
(praying mantis)

Adult with wings and legs spread. Note typical eye markings on wing.

Egg case

Adult

Assassin Bug
(*Zelus* sp.)

Adult

Nymph feeding on elm leaf miner

Adult stage of this generalist insect predator

Eggs and nymph

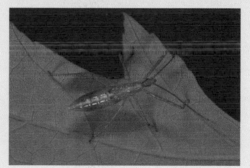

Nymph before last molt

Flower Fly and Syrphid Fly
(fairly obscure, and within an aphid colony)

Narcissus bulb fly

White egg near an aphid on a grass blade

Larval syrphid fly preying on aphids on a columbine plant

Rattail maggot larva

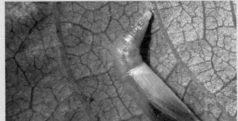

Flower fly pupa on a leaf

Adult syrphid fly

Flower fly larva on pine bud

Adult on white composite flower

Larva eating aphids

Hover fly

Tachinid Fly
(parasite of other insects)

Tachinid fly on white aster

Tachinid fly

Eggs on tomato hornworm

Tachinid fly eggs on squash bugs

Close-up of tachinid fly face

Dragonfly

You will probably find these ancient, goggle-eyed, biplane insects flitting about your garden, or anywhere near water, in mid- to late summer. They don't pollinate plants, and because they contribute little of known economic value dragonflies haven't received the study they deserve. They do hunt and consume huge numbers of mosquitoes, especially while in their wingless nymph stage, which they spend underwater in ponds and lakes. For this reason they are important to all of us, especially outdoor people like gardeners. Depending on the species, they can live for one to five years, but just a few weeks or months as sexually acrobatic, active adults. Their two pairs of independently operating wings make all kinds of astonishing maneuvers possible. Several fossils have been found of their early relatives with wingspans of 2½ feet, dating from 300 million years ago.

Chapter 9
Undesirables in the Garden:
Weeds, Wildlife, and Unwanted Insects

As gardeners in the Rocky Mountain West, we're fortunate to have fewer people and more available land than many other parts of the country. However, just like everywhere else, wild habitat that plants and animals once called home has shrunk considerably because of human activities. Open spaces have filled up with houses, roads, and large and small shopping centers, particularly along the Front Range. Cities buy up water rights and farms are developed; usually the only trace that remains is the name of the farmer on a street sign. The interface between the human concrete world (as my friend and former wildlife rehabilitator Vona Bates calls it) and the natural world now often occurs in gardens where there's some cover, water, and food for animals.

In fact, individual gardens and yards have become essential parts of a continuum that the very existence of many animals, especially insects, now depends on. Without insects to pollinate plants and provide the basic protein building block of the food chain, there wouldn't be any larger animals, including humans. A garden can be a welcome sanctuary for both humans and wild creatures, but this often requires a shift in attitude.

For one thing, most of us aren't used to accommodating any creatures other than our families and our pets—certainly not insects. For another, most urban and suburban environments are designed to create and maintain a human orderliness and neatness, replacing the natural diversity and ecological balance of wilder places. In most yards, there are a few species of plants with lawn grass predominating, fences for privacy and to keep the dogs in while keeping everything else out, and weapons—usually chemical—for exterminating any "pests." Interlopers, be they dandelions—the season's earliest important food for bees—or insects, are to be quickly eliminated. Low maintenance is said to be favored over complexity in the landscape, yet many hours are spent fertilizing, mowing, and keeping lawns weed free.

Weeds

Herbicides and Organic Gardening

Weeds proliferate wherever land is disturbed and where soil biology is lacking. Agricultural herbicide use has been rapidly increasing in the last decade with the rise of genetically modified, herbicide-tolerant (GMHT) crops, which were first introduced in the United States in 1996. These crops can be sprayed repeatedly with herbicide to kill the weeds that grow alongside them without being damaged themselves.

We're living in an herbicide-drenched world. Statistics from the USDA show a 46 percent increase in agricultural herbicide use between 2007 and 2008. In 2011, 94 percent of all soybeans, 72 percent of all corn, and 73 percent of all cotton grown in the United States were GMHT.

Lawns cover millions of acres of the United States. The US Fish and Wildlife Service reports that homeowners use up to ten times more chemical pesticides (insecticides and herbicides) per acre on lawns than farmers use on crops.

Selective and Nonselective Types

There are two basic groups of chemical herbicides: selective herbicides, which target specific types of plants (herbicides such as 2,4-D, the most commonly used for more than fifty years, MCPP, and Dicamba, which kill broadleaf plants but not grasses); and nonselective or broad-spectrum herbicides (such as glyphosate, the active ingredient in Roundup and the second most commonly used), which kill both broad- and narrow-leaved plants.

Nonselective herbicides kill plants in three ways: (1) on contact, knocking down all top growth without killing the roots of perennial plants; (2) systemically, by taking in the active ingredient through leaves and transporting it down to the roots; and (3) residually, by remaining in the soil to kill germinating seeds and shoots from perennial roots (also known as preemergents). Preemergents are commonly used in weed-and-feed lawn products, and atrazine is one of the most common ingredients.

Many gardeners and homeowners don't hesitate to use broadleaf herbicides to kill weeds or nonselective herbicides like Roundup to kill their lawn where they want a new garden because they are convenient and advertised as safe and quick to break down.

Safety

The vast majority of research studies on pesticides are industry sponsored. Manufacturers have made misleading safety claims in several instances, including for Roundup, which they retracted under legal pressure. Long-term, low-level, or cumulative exposures are rarely included in studies or required by the EPA. Products registered for nonfood use, on lawns, for example, are not evaluated for chronic health effects. There are independent scientific studies that link commonly used herbicides to birth defects or reproductive effects in animals and/or humans, to some types of cancer, and to Parkinson's disease. All except glyphosate and MCPP are known neurotoxins. Glyphosate is the most common cause of poisoning among landscape workers in California. Many questions remain about the health effects of herbicides.

New Compounds and Breakdown Time

Some of the compounds produced as pesticides break down are more toxic than the original active ingredients. The breakdown time for insecticides and herbicides varies from chemical to chemical and product to product. Most people have the perception that Roundup breaks down almost immediately, though the USDA's Agricultural Research Service has data showing that glyphosate has a half-life (the time it takes for half of the original amount to be gone) that varies from 2 to 174 days. The half-life of most forms of 2,4-D is 2 to 14 days, but one form (butoxyethyl ester) has a 186-day half-life.

INERT INGREDIENTS

In addition to the active ingredient, there are a number of inert ingredients that are not listed on labels but usually make up the vast majority (up to 99 percent or more) of any pesticide product. Some amplify the effects of the active ingredient and a few have been found to be more lethal. Roundup has twelve inert ingredients, one of which (POEA) was shown to kill human cells in a 2009 study.

ENVIRONMENTAL EFFECTS AND PERSISTENCE

In some cases, chemicals are found to be persistent in the environment and toxic at much lower concentrations years after they've been registered and approved for widespread use. All of the top ten most widely used pesticides and many more (both herbicides and insecticides) have been found in groundwater; atrazine is the most frequently found. Banned by the European Union, atrazine has been linked to several types of cancer and is a known endocrine disrupter, causing hermaphrodism in frogs at extremely low levels of exposure.

Soil was once thought to be a protective filter that stopped pesticides from reaching underground aquifers, but studies have shown that this is not the case, according to the USGS, which also points out that it can take many years after application for these chemicals to show up in groundwater. As they say on their website, "There's a hidden cost to the benefit we get from pesticides."

LABELING

Most edible and ornamental garden plants are sensitive to very low levels of herbicide damage. It is up to consumers to read labels carefully and use products accordingly. Some people mistakenly assume that if a little bit works, a larger amount must work even better, so they overuse these chemicals.

Most labels do not provide sufficient information or instruction regarding toxicity and risks, proper handling and disposal, potential to contaminate water, or effects on pollinators, fish, and wildlife. The information that is provided is displayed in tiny, hard-to-read type on the back of packages while catchy brand names such as Confront, Outlaw, Diablo, Weedmaster, and so forth are displayed much more prominently.

ORGANIC GARDENERS ARE AFFECTED

Because many organic gardeners rely heavily on organic manures and mulches to provide nutrients for plants, condition soil, and conserve moisture, they are disproportionately affected by herbicides. It is becoming essential for gardeners to be certain about their sources for manure, straw, grass clippings, and compost because it is increasingly difficult to find organic materials that haven't been treated, directly or indirectly, with herbicide.

Indirect herbicide contamination occurs in several ways: unintentional drifting to vegetation during application; mixing untreated material with herbicide-treated materials at composting facilities; or the addition of manure and urine from livestock that have consumed herbicide-treated forage to compost or planting mixes. Some herbicides can persist for weeks to years, and they are showing up in mulches, soil amendments, and even in some vermiculture products.

BANNED PESTICIDES ARE STILL AVAILABLE

Compounding this problem is the fact that herbicides and pesticides that have been banned for years for homeowner use are available for purchase by anyone through the Internet. A local organic grower I know lost hundreds of pepper plants to damage that local extension service employees believe pointed to a banned herbicide (one of the pyridine carboxylic acids.) It showed up in worm compost from a local supplier who had unknowingly used herbicide-treated materials in her vermiculture operation.

ALTERNATIVES TO CHEMICAL HERBICIDES

By destroying the soil food web and depleting the soil, conventional chemical-dependent agriculture actually creates huge weed problems, then spends a lot of money and labor trying to control them. Overhead and flood irrigation methods spread weeds too. Expensive genetically modified herbicide-resistant crops are developed as a solution, but they have high hidden costs, leaving behind contaminated surface- and groundwater and herbicide-resistant superweeds.

Technological fixes like more-precise water- and nutrient-delivery systems on more-expensive tractors with advanced GPS systems may wow large-scale farmers, but they still don't build soil or sustain life. Whether it's giant farms of GM soybeans and corn or large collective acreages of chemical-intensive green lawns, there is no system

---

A Test for Chemical Herbicides

Here is a simple test for the presence of herbicides that takes a few weeks:

- Plant three pea or bean seeds or one small tomato start in each of five or six small pots using a half-and-half mixture of a trusted commercial soil mix and the amendment you want to test (manure, compost, grass clippings, and so forth).
- Plant a second group (this is the control) using just the commercial mix, and keep the two groups separate so water draining from the test group pots won't mix with the control group.
- Grow plants for two to three weeks, until there are at least three sets of true leaves on the plants. For tomatoes, extend the growing test for seven weeks as they take longer to show damage.
- If the control plants all grow normally and the pots with amendment don't (either they don't germinate or the leaves look deformed), you can assume your amendments are contaminated with herbicide.
- If all the plants grow normally, you can probably assume your amendment is fine.

Source: Jeanine Davis, Sue Ellen Johnson, and Katie Jennings, "Herbicide Carryover in Hay, Manure, Compost and Grass Clippings: Caution to Hay Producers, Livestock Owners, Farmers, and Home Gardeners," North Carolina Cooperative Extension, 2010, www.ces.ncsu.edu/fletcher/programs/ncorganic/special-pubs/herbicide_carryover.pdf.

Weed-Prevention Strategies for Gardeners

Weeds are either annuals, which produce large amounts of seed every year and then die, or perennials, which produce a more-modest amount of seed but come back every year and regenerate quickly if damaged. While both are very competitive, annuals favor disturbance. They are the first to move in and cover bare ground, and first to emerge when soil has been tilled.

When growing vegetables there are several weed prevention strategies:

- Do not rototill the soil regularly or at all—at least not more than once.
- Cover bare soil with thick mulch year-round to smother weeds, prevent weed seeds from germinating, and to conserve moisture for vegetable plants.
- If your garden is large enough, plant cover crops like buckwheat that can outcompete and suppress weeds.
- Use drip irrigation for watering at the soil or plant-root level instead of overhead sprinklers, which promote weed germination.
- Mow weed patches regularly and always before they go to seed. Pull weeds or use a hoe in the garden to dislodge them when they're small. Stirrup hoes are very effective.
- A mulch of ryegrass on the soil surface inhibits weed seed germination because it contains generous amounts of allelopathic chemicals, which effectively suppress weeds for a month or two. (When rye is tilled in, the effect is lost.)
- Keep removing the top growth of persistent weeds like bindweed to deprive the roots of energy. Also plant rotations with tall, shade-producing crops like sunflowers since bindweed doesn't do well in shade. Chickens and goats eat and can eventually destroy bindweed. Be patient and don't expect a quick fix or complete eradication. (Chemical herbicides won't do this either.)
- Studies show that plastic mulches can be effective for reducing weeds and warming soil, though they eventually end up in landfills. Green and brown plastic were shown to work better than black or clear plastic.
- Though not feasible in home gardens, a roller/crimper is an effective no-till machine for weeds on organic farms.

Organic Herbicides

- Use corn gluten meal as a preemergent herbicide. Typical application is 40 pounds per 1,000 square feet.
- Use vinegar-based (acetic acid) herbicides. Those that also contain citrus or citric acid work especially well. Effective concentrations of vinegar are above 5 percent (the percentage in household vinegar) and up to 20 or 30 percent. Handle with care, since these concentrations can burn skin or damage eyes. Use for spot spraying once weeds have emerged and in fall when plants' energy is returning to the roots. Check Organic Materials Review Institute listings for these products. Cornell University has tested several and found them effective.
- Essential oils like clove, mint, and thyme are reported to kill broadleaf weeds and grasses. They can be mixed with vinegar formulations.
- A propane flame torch effectively kills weeds and weed seeds (unlike Roundup), but it can be expensive and time consuming depending on the situation. Use with a 3-foot extender to avoid bending over, never use on a windy day, have a hose and bucket ready in case of flare-ups, and use great care to avoid adjoining vegetation, especially around trees.

Gardeners need not contribute to herbicide use. It isn't difficult to stay on top of weeds by pulling them when they're small (especially when the ground is still moist after a rain) or using a hoe occasionally to knock them down, using thick mulch to suppress their growth and stop seeds from germinating, and keeping any surrounding weedy patches mowed. Many weeds contain valuable minerals, so compost them as long as they haven't set seed.

more out of balance and less sustainable long-term than the monocultures of today. They are destroying the diversity of life on millions of acres of land, especially in North America, where they are most widely grown.

Biodiversity creates stable ecosystems. There are methods available right now that can turn things around on a large scale. Permaculture remediation programs are proving successful on some of the most worn-out, ruined land in the world.

Retiring the chemicals, replacing at least some of the lawn with vegetables, herbs, flowers, and shrubs, and including some native plants in the landscape will benefit all animals, from butterflies and bees to humans and their pets. (Today, according to the National Canine Cancer Foundation, one out of every three dogs is affected by cancer. Studies have shown a significant increase in risk for the most common type of bladder cancer among dogs exposed to lawns or gardens treated with the most commonly used broadleaf herbicides, such as 2,4-D.)

Until very recently, most of us had completely lost sight of soil as a web of life that supports plant growth. Healthy soil or dirt is loaded with microbes and fungi that make nutrients available to plant roots, as well as worms and many other critters that continually aerate and enrich the soil. These are the most important fauna in any garden. The guiding principle of feeding the soil instead of the plants really means feeding the multitude of diverse soil life creatures, most of which aren't visible. They in turn nourish the plants.

Western gardeners who use organic matter and mulch to build soil with a healthy population of soil life have very few pest problems. All the soil microbes and critters maintain a balanced environment in which pests and diseases do not thrive. Predators keep the "bad bugs" in check. According to Dr. Elaine Ingram, world-renowned soil biology researcher and founder of Soil Foodweb Inc., healthy soil biology enhances all of the following:

- disease protection
- nutrient retention and carbon sequestration
- nutrient availability
- decomposition of toxins
- improved soil structure that holds more water and oxygen
- improved plant root health
- decrease in amount of water required by plants
- increased yields, better flavor, nutrient density, and shelf life of food
- decrease in weeds

Studies show that synthetic nitrogen fertilizers make plants *more attractive to pests.* Chemical fertilizers will certainly grow plants and make grass green, but by artificially propping them up at the expense of soil life and by depleting the soil over time. Most are overapplied and end up leaching into groundwater. Microbe-nourishing materials, such as beneficial mycorrhizal fungi, brewed compost teas, and humic acid, on the other hand, will literally make your soil come alive, and your plants will grow more vigorously. Organic mulches help keep soil from drying out and blowing away while holding in the moisture that worms and microbes need.

Let's say you've made the switch to gardening without chemicals and you're welcoming pollinating insects into your garden by adding plants with flowers they like. You generally embrace the idea of sharing your outdoor space with other critters and are pleased to be doing your part to support the diversity of biological life. Gardening *with* nature is always interesting, but your relationship to wildlife may not always be as harmonious as some would lead you to believe.

Nature is anything but dull, so once you've accepted the challenge of peaceful coexistence, be prepared to be surprised, delighted, and sometimes tested and frustrated by who and what shows up. Unless you're a saint, you probably won't take kindly to sharing all the fruits of your labor with all of God's creatures. Whether it's javelinas in Tuscon or bears in Boulder, every part of the country has special wildlife challenges. And there are also the ubiquitous raccoons, deer, squirrels, and rabbits that have proliferated wherever food is plentiful and predators are lacking —in other words, wherever a lot of humans live.

WILDLIFE

In general it's the rodents (that also carry diseases like plague) and the deer that do the most damage to gardens. Animals like skunks, raccoons, foxes, and raptors will keep the rodent and insect population down. Foxes are especially valuable because they do this without stealing your fruit or vegetables. Here is some helpful information about these critters that can sometimes try even the most enlightened gardener's patience. Keep in mind that the animals that wander into our yards are just looking for the basics: food, water, and shelter.

RACCOONS

Raccoons repeatedly came into my house through the cat door. When I lived on the creek, the locals were huge, almost as big as bears, and made a terrible screechy racket at night out back up in the willows. Once in a while I found a dead squirrel out there that appeared to have died from raccoon-induced fright. Being omnivores, the coons will eat almost anything, plant or animal.

I only grew sweet corn twice and then gave up because raccoons beat me to it the night before I planned to pick, as if they could read my mind. I decided growing my own corn in town wasn't worth the aggravation.

One afternoon when our Italian plum tree was bursting with ripe fruit, a Boy Scout neighbor came by selling something to raise money for his troop. The next morning, the tree was stripped bare. My first thought was that Colin, the Scout whose wares I'd declined to purchase, must have come back with a friend or two and picked all the plums. I cringe to think of it now, but I was so peeved that I called his mother to ask, as tactfully as I could, if she thought her son might have accomplished this. Terribly offended by the suggestion, she told me that Colin doesn't like plums and if he did he would certainly never steal them. It was the raccoons, of course, though I had no idea they were capable of such a stealthy feat. We hadn't heard one chirrup all night.

Though I've never seen a raccoon at my current, more rural home and garden on the plains, I know they're around, so I've been hesitant to grow corn. I also don't want them to show up and discover my grapes, which I share, somewhat begrudgingly, with just birds so far. My neighbor leaves dry food

Backyard Chickens and Wildlife

Chickens have become extremely popular with gardeners for many reasons: they eat insects, help create wonderfully rich, well-composted soil when they're managed well, produce tasty eggs, and they are endearing to have around—people really love their hens. If you ever have a chance to see Mark Lewis's 2000 film, *The Natural History of the Chicken*, don't miss it.

This bi-level coop allows chickens to scratch in the dirt during the day and move up to roost at night. Difficult to knock over, it uses sturdy hardware cloth, instead of chicken wire, that flares at the bottom to deter predators.

So many gardeners want to keep backyard chickens today that city ordinances outlawing the practice are being challenged, and some are changing to allow them. I even read an article recently in *MaryJanesFarm* magazine about keeping chickens inside the house—with diapers! I like hens, but indoor chickens are way over the top in my opinion. This got me thinking that most new gardeners probably have little if any direct experience with chickens and might benefit from some straight talk in relation to wildlife.

Most wild predators, especially raccoons, skunks, and owls, come looking for chickens at night, often a few hours after sundown or before sunrise, but hungry foxes and coyotes may also show up during the day if no humans are around and will often stake out a coop for days, watching for an opening.

My neighbor once came home to discover a raccoon attempting to drown one of her hens in a tub of water that she'd left out for her dog, which turned out to be scared of raccoons. With their opposable thumbs and dexterous little hands, raccoons are also adept at catching hold of chickens through any small opening in a fence and attempting to pull them through it. The end result is a bloody mess. Raccoons often kill multiple chickens in a frenzy of bloodlust, ripping open their necks to eat them. They go after eggs too.

Some dogs (huskies are notorious killers of poultry) will do the same, but often mutilate them severely without eating anything. Most dogs, but not all, can be trained not to kill your chickens, though training them not to kill a neighbor's can be more difficult. Foxes and raccoons will dig or climb to the top of a coop in search of entry. They usually break in, grab a hen (or two), kill it, and run off to eat it elsewhere, returning later for another. Skunks will dig in wherever they can and usually go after eggs, but they sometimes kill a hen too. I have occasionally found a neighbor's beheaded chicken in my pasture accompanied by a strong eau de skunk, although I may have found the kill of an owl, which usually eats the head and neck and sometimes leaves a heap of defecated whitewash next to the carcass.

In a sardonic moment, my daughter once told me that having animals has taught her a lot, especially about violence and death. If you want to keep chickens, you need to understand that they are a magnet for predators that really, really want to tear them apart and devour them. So whether you live in the city or the country, and especially if you have children who will definitely not enjoy the gruesome aftermath of a wild visitor, make sure your chicken coop is predator-proof from top to bottom. And be careful about letting chickens range free in your absence.

outside for stray cats, which attracts the raccoons. One recently found its way into her fenced-in chicken coop, grabbed one of her hens, and was attempting to drown it in a big bowl of water when she managed to run it off. The clawed-up, traumatized hen survived, but just for a day.

The best way I know to keep raccoons away from corn or grapes is a secure fence with a hot wire on top, which can be solar powered or electric. They'll screech in protest if they touch it, or out of frustration if they don't; it usually works. I've read that a wire fence should be erected on top of a section of fence that's fixed flat on the ground to stop them from digging under, but in my experience they will more easily climb right over any tall fence without an electric wire at the top. Raccoons love to go fishing in ponds and water features too, so if you have one with fish, beware.

There is a motion-sensing scarecrow made by Contech that emits a burst of water to scare animals away that is very effective because it also trains animals to stay away. What a fabulous idea! You just need to make sure it won't spray your tomatoes and other plants that don't like wet leaves, especially at night. Outdoor lighting with motion sensors is sometimes effective too.

SQUIRRELS

There were so many squirrels in town that I quit bothering with window boxes or container gardens because they always dug them all up, even the flowers. Far fewer squirrels survive in rural plains areas because there are fewer trees and more predators—coyotes, foxes, snakes, skunks, raccoons, and raptors—to keep them in check. Dogs,

some cats, raccoons, and cars are their main threat in urban areas. They can pivot 180 degrees on their feet for quick getaway maneuvers and will sometimes lose their tail to a predator. This enables them to escape, but a new one doesn't grow back.

Squirrels can be extremely destructive in the vegetable garden, digging up lots of seedlings. Carrots and sunflowers often don't stand a chance. I had an early apple tree that squirrels frolicked in, taking a bite or two out of every apple, then dropping them on the ground. They'll bite into cucumbers and tomatoes, sometimes just for the moisture. Because their sense of smell is so keen, organic repellants with hot pepper sprayed on plants can work well to deter them, whereas these won't stop birds at all. Some say blood meal and repellants with predator urine work, others say they don't. My experience isn't conclusive.

Longstanding feuds between squirrel lovers (and feeders) and squirrel loathers aren't uncommon. I once met a university professor who admitted to relocating 89 raccoons (a terrible solution for rural residents on the receiving end) and 116 squirrels in Havahart traps over two years from his yard in town—and somehow still found time to garden. You're not going to get rid of squirrels in an urban area no matter how many you relocate. Squirrel-proof your house so they can't get inside the attic or elsewhere and nest, don't feed birds if you have a squirrel problem, and try pepper sprays and repellants on the plants.

FOXES

I've read that foxes have become the most successful urban predators. It's startling to see a beautiful red fox trotting through a Denver neighborhood. Their favorite food is rabbit, so I'm assuming that's what beheaded our pet (and urban manure provider) Lima Bean. When I called the City of Boulder's wildlife officer to ask his opinion, I was amazed to hear him suggest kids and satanic rituals. He must have just moved here from out of state.

Besides rabbits, foxes mostly eat mice and other small rodents, insects, birds and bird eggs, unsecured chickens, birdseed, a little bit of fruit if they're very hungry, small amounts of corn, and occasionally domestic cats. They've also been known to play games with cats. Though they are more adept climbers than you might imagine, a fox probably wouldn't harvest an entire fruit tree, much less make it a family outing as raccoons do. In Aesop's fable, the fox gave up on those out-of-reach grapes pretty quickly.

A female fox may make a den under a structure in the spring to have her kits, but otherwise they sleep curled up outside. Foxes usually won't bother the garden much, but occasionally they'll dig or rummage around looking for food. Playful kits have been known to almost stumble into gardeners while chasing each other around.

To keep chickens secure, use heavy gauge or welded wire instead of chicken wire to completely enclose them, and bury it a foot deep.

Deer and Elk

I consider myself very fortunate because deer never visit my plains garden. When I lived in Boulder, they blithely leapt over our 6-foot fence and bedded down in the grass in the corner of the yard, eating all my tulips and much of the vegetable garden every year. When I put the house up for sale, the buyers said it was the fawn trotting out from under the blue spruce that sealed the deal. Magical moment, but I doubt they were gardeners.

While some city folks are thrilled at the opportunity to spot even a common mule deer, they are the bane of gardeners in the foothills and in the mountains, where gardening is plenty daunting even without the wildlife. Mountain people choose to brave wilder, more extreme conditions, but many give up on gardening or don't even try because of all the deer and elk, moles, and gophers. Those who persevere are more likely than the rest of us to own a gun.

Penn and Cord Parmenter are tenacious, innovative gardeners who live in the Wet Mountains, near Westcliffe, Colorado, and grow huge quantities of food at 8,120 feet, including sweet corn and tomatoes, to feed themselves and their three boys. They refer to deer as mountain rodents and have enclosed their large gardens with a secure 10-foot wire fence (entered through a beautiful wrought iron gate, hand-forged by Cord, a blacksmith). From all accounts, a fence this tall is a necessary first step for successful mountain gardening—a fence plus attitude, something many mountain people possess. When I first visited the Parmenters they had just returned from their annual elk hunt, on horseback over a snowy mountain pass in the Sangre de Cristo range. They came back spiritually enlivened but empty-handed and resigned to no winter meat. But the following day, Cord shot an elk that appeared a few hundred yards from their house. You won't find many catch-and-release mousetraps in a mountain cabin.

Penn and Cord Parmenter's 10-foot fence with hand-forged iron gate effectively excludes deer ("mountain rodents") from their very tempting and productive vegetable garden.

BEARS

Every fall, bears need to fatten up on vast quantities of fruit, seeds, and nuts before they retreat to hibernate for the winter. Sometimes, especially during drought years, after a fire, or where subdivisions have encroached on their natural habitat, the natural pickin's can be slim so bears wander into mountain neighborhoods or head down to the foothills and plains in search of food. They may know of a favorite grapevine or berry patch that they return to every year. Or, they may find unsecured garbage cans and bird feeders, which emboldens them to look further. They are clever opportunists, and if they don't fear humans or are hungry enough, they will figure out how to enter unlocked homes (they are especially good at opening lever-action door handles) or garages with freezers or refrigerators looking for food. This isn't a pleasant wildlife-watching opportunity for the homeowners, and it almost always ends fatally for the bear.

Like other large wildlife, bears sometimes follow the river courses from the mountains out to the plains and show up in neighborhoods. A resident of Hygiene, the tiny plains town nearest to me, phoned in a story to the local newspaper last year (with photos to prove it) about a cow/bear interaction in which Apple the cow ran off a bear that was planning on eating the ripening apples on Apple's favorite tree.

Bears' love of honey is legendary, but even more it is the larvae or bee brood, a rich source of protein, that they're after. If hives are near a garden, even better! Once bears get a taste for brood and honey, they will likely continue to raid the beeyard, so it's best to take a preventative approach. Proper location and siting, plus solar- or electric-charged fences are the best deterrent. The CSU Extension has a good fact sheet called Managing Bear Damage to Beehives.

Skunks

Where I now live on the plains there are still lots of predators: raptors of all kinds, coyotes, foxes, and even a few elusive mountain lions. It's a tough neighborhood for domestic cats and, as I mentioned, there are not many squirrels. We do have skunks, which can decimate honeybees if they can get close to a hive, steal eggs and kill chickens, and, as I was dismayed to discover, dig up the corpses of buried pets, the ranker the better, to roll in.

They apparently like to return to the same den each year, and you can tell if they've been in the garden by the small trenches they dig at an angle looking for grubs and earthworms. At least one (though you rarely have just one skunk) always found a way in under my renovated garden shed each spring, emitting a distinctly skunky musk that emanated up from under the floorboards. The shed sits on 8 x 8 inch timbers. It's hard to find much to say that's positive about skunks, but they do eat great quantities of grasshoppers, grubs, and wasps, plus I hear they are a favorite dish of the great horned owl (a majestic creature that also lives out here).

Over several years I tried all the recommended remedies to outwit and evict skunks and all worked temporarily: playing a radio loudly in the shed (a good deterrent when their status is still "visitor" and hasn't yet become "resident"), ammonia-soaked rags attached to a stick or mothballs in pantyhose shoved in under the shed, which the skunks always managed to shove back out. Covering their hole with large rocks never works because skunks are such skilled and speedy diggers that they make a new hole in no time or simply dig around and under the rock. Aside from trapping and relocating, having their scent glands removed and making pets out of them, or killing them—all solutions that don't interest me—secure fencing, visualization, and prayer were the only remaining options I could come up with. I decided to try all three simultaneously.

Before you fence skunks out, you need to make sure they have exited from under your porch or shed and don't have young babies, which are typically born in May or June, weaned after eight weeks, and are extremely cute. Since they are mostly nocturnal (though I have seen babies out exploring in the afternoon), you can get your fencing in place during the day, except for the area near their hole. I admit that I only got as far as purchasing and cutting the fencing, so I haven't personally tested the instructions below from the CSU Extension and other credible sources, though they make perfect sense to me:

• Dig a trench 10 inches deep and 8 inches wide
• Go down to the bottom of the trench with the wire fencing and then extend

it out horizontally 8 inches in an L shape toward you and away from your structure

- Cover the fencing and fill in the trench. When the skunks dig down and keep hitting the fencing, they eventually give up.
- To evict them during the day, if necessary, so you can finish up your fencing, use a cayenne-pepper spray all around their den and a few inches inside the hole (they might reciprocate and spray you if you go deeper). Or try the loud radio, ammonia-soaked rags, or mothballs inside pantyhose. Much-less-smelly mothballs are manufactured today and are easier to find, but for this job, that's not what you want.
- Or you can wait until it's dark, when the skunks will go out on their own. If you put flour around their entrance hole in the afternoon, then check it at night for footprints with a flashlight, you'll be able to tell if they're outside. Once you know they've exited, you can finish filling in and putting the last bit of fencing around their hole before they return. Adding some motion-sensor lights will also help deter them from returning.

Winter visitors leave their prints in the snow.

After several years of grappling with my skunk problem, the ones that took up residence under my shed have departed and haven't come back for two years, despite not having fencing in place to exclude them. I don't know why—maybe it was those other two options. In any case, the experience demonstrated the virtue of patience. They never really harmed us, and it costs hundreds of dollars to have skunks removed (and killed). A few days ago I saw five cute babies outside my barn. I left the radio on inside and have since heard through the grapevine that my neighbor now has baby skunks. I plan to get the fencing in place right away to be on the safe side.

RABBITS

We have a lot of bunnies. Until recently I was one of the few people in the neighborhood without dogs or cats, so I guess they considered my place a safe zone. The adults pretend they're invisible and only dash off when I come within a few feet. So far they haven't done much damage except burrowing temporarily in my mounded-up potato beds, probably because there is a lot of pasture grass and clover around to keep them well fed, and the predators keep their numbers down. I protect the trunks of all my trees, especially young ones and all fruit trees, with inexpensive plastic mesh guards that I got from our local soil conservation service. For trees like mulberries that they especially like, I use heavier wire mesh. Our new cat is helping to keep the population in check by catching and eating the babies during the few hours I let her outside while I'm gardening nearby. It's not pleasant to witness, but we do seem to have an endless supply.

The trick to fencing out rabbits is the same as for skunks: bury fencing 10 inches or more deep and then bring it out horizontally in an L shape. I've also protected some individual plants and very small beds by encircling them with thorny rose clippings, which soft-pawed creatures avoid. But thorns get in my way too, especially when the wind blows them around.

Some commercial repellants work. There's a gooey, sticky one called Deer Vic that you put on sticks around the garden and hang in trees that my friend Eve tells me did the trick when rabbits became a big problem at her nursery in Boulder, but it's really messy and smells nasty. Various gardeners I know use hot pepper and garlic sprays on vegetable plants or scatter blood meal or grated soap around. As is usually the case, it depends on your situation. Some gardeners swear by their dogs, terriers in particular. The Contech ScareCrow, which emits a burst of water when it detects an animal, can work well to scare off rabbits and skunks.

BIRDS

Birds and fruit—cherries and grapes in particular—are my biggest challenge. I love birds, feed them, and plant for them, and we have a lot of different species that visit. When my fifteen-year-old daughter and I first moved here from town, she used to complain that the birds sang too loudly in the morning. But many species are struggling. They have a difficult time keeping young nestlings and fledglings safe from roaming cats (the statistics on cats killing songbirds are shocking, which has led me to keep my cats mostly indoors), plus spring storms always seem to blow a few nests out of trees, cruelly scattering featherless babies on the ground.

But robin redbreast, especially, is my fruit nemesis. There is plenty else to eat out here, including a long hedgerow of Nanking cherries with small sweet fruit that they supposedly love, but robins are a fruit bird and will go after strawberries and larger cherries relentlessly. When the grapes ripen, the blue jays join in.

It's easy enough to make a low chicken-wire enclosure for strawberries, and I've even deterred robins by draping lightweight white row cover around on temporary fence posts that stick in the ground—a spontaneous, temporary fix that worked better than I expected. The lightweight stuff billows in even a light breeze and seems to scare

Keeping birds off of strawberries is a must. Low chicken-wire enclosures or even casually laid fencing a few inches above the bed will work.

them off. That gave me the idea to wrap some around my cherry trees as the cherries ripen, securing it with clothespins. It works pretty well, until the wind comes up, and it's only needed for a couple of weeks.

You can also purchase bird netting. But in my experience, unless you have poles or a structure of some kind that keeps the netting off the tree, the typical ½- to ¾-inch netting available at hardware and home-improvement stores or online can create as much of a problem as it solves. Birds always get snagged in it, and then you have to catch them while they're desperately flailing around and cut them free, and often the tangled net has injured them. Shiny metallic strips or wind ornaments that dance even in light breezes will keep birds at bay to some extent, and the iridescent types work the best. Scarecrows help a little and if you want to get elaborate about it, there are even some with metallic strips attached that move periodically to scare birds.

Tighter-weave netting that birds can't get stuck in is a much better solution if you're planning to put it right on the tree. Light shade cloth could even work. Grapes can be more problematic to cover because they grow so large and wander so far. In early summer, I put a shade cloth covering on the top of my open deck where grapes grow up on the east side. I use it for shade, not to keep the birds away, but it ends up preventing many of them, though not all, from swooping in on all sides to eat the grapes. I love shade cloth! It comes in different gradients (20 percent shade, 30 percent, and so forth), in nonfraying rolls. You can cut it to the size you want and easily punch plastic grommets into the corners and edges for easy tying onto deck rafters or posts—wherever you want to create some light shade. It's very versatile and easy to work with, and I like the simple, breezy look of it too.

SNAKES

It's illegal to kill snakes in Colorado. They are extremely important for keeping rodents under control and almost always beneficial to humans. Nevertheless, plenty are killed. One summer I had a couple of strapping young cowboys help me load hay. When they noticed a sleepy 4-foot bullsnake, they had to catch it, but it hissed at them and tried to strike (if all you had to defend yourself was a mouth, you would too) and struggled to get away. Unfortunately their reaction was to kill it immediately, and they didn't stop talking about it all day. I think they expected me to be pleased instead of appalled.

A garter snake is the only one you'll probably ever encounter in your yard. It stays slender, rarely grows longer than 3 feet, and likes to live near water, which is why it is attracted to irrigated gardens. Domestic cats are significant predators of snakes and will sometimes bring them into the house unharmed if you have a cat door. The plains garter snake has a bright yellow or orange stripe from its head to its tail along the middle of its back. Quite a few are captured for human pets since they are gentle, though a garter snake may try to bite if you pick it up, and they sometimes emit a foul odor as a defense mechanism. If you come upon one, it will usually slither quickly away.

Garter snakes eat insects, slugs, worms, toads, frogs, fish, and mice, swallowing them whole and alive. If they've just eaten, they will be more sluggish. I had the rare opportunity to watch one vomit when a friend decided to demonstrate how friendly his was by picking it up and stroking it until it finally lifted its head, opened its jaws, and regurgitated the meal it had been working on for hours. That cleared the room.

TOADS

Toads are my favorite garden critters and we have a lot of them. They can tolerate drier environments than frogs, burrowing underground to escape cold and hot, dry conditions. They usually appear in the pasture when we irrigate, in the garden, or around the outside of the house near the water outlets and in the window wells, where they sometimes get stranded. After finding a few dried corpses in there, I started leaving boards for escape bridges so they can hop out. The larger ones often take up residence in a flowerpot, startling me when they emerge as I'm watering or investigating the decline of the potted plant. The tiny ones hop around wherever there's moisture. My friend Trudy had them all over her basement one wet spring. In a shady spot, I leave a few small clay pots overturned and propped up on one side to give toads some shade and a big shallow saucer with some water and rocks in it. Toads eat lots of pest insects in the garden, including slugs. Like all amphibians, they are very sensitive to chemicals. If you have them, it's a sign of a healthy environment.

UNWANTED INSECTS

In addition to animals, damaging insects sometimes show up in gardens in large numbers due to weather, a lack of healthy beneficial predators, or other conditions that upset the balance and overwhelm the system.

Here are some strategies to prevent population explosions of unwanted insects and, in case they persist, some effective, nontoxic, organic controls for common garden pests.

PEST INSECT PREVENTION AND ORGANIC CONTROLS

- Create environmental conditions that specific vegetable plants like, such as their preferred delivery of water, sun exposure, planting temperatures, and wind protection. Pests usually attack tender young or weak plants.
- Provide nectar sources for beneficial insects that prey on pests. Sunflowers, buckwheat, yarrow, cosmos, spearmint, sweet alyssum, and plants in the carrot family (dill, fennel, anise, Queen Anne's lace, chervil) are good nectar sources for small parasitic wasps that prey on many garden pests, especially caterpillars.
- Rotate crop families (nightshades, brassicas, and so forth) to different parts of the garden each year to confuse overwintering pests. Rotate susceptible crops with nonsusceptible ones. (With healthy soil microbe populations, rotation becomes less crucial.)
- Use flowers or other vegetables to interplant so specific crops aren't so easily visible, especially against a bare-soil background.
- Plant sacrificial trap crops, like Chinese mustard and radishes, that pest insects prefer near susceptible vegetables. This gives the vegetables time to mature and become strong enough to resist pests.
- Use lightweight row cover to protect young seedlings and susceptible plants from pests.

- Use companion planting techniques to grow compatible vegetables that support each other close together.
- Use compost tea as a foliar spray and soil drench to strengthen plants and increase helpful microbe populations. This works to prevent blight in potatoes and other crops.
- Kelp and nettle tea both improve the overall health of plants and promote healthy root growth. Use either as a foliar spray or as a soil amendment.
- Use botanical and soap-based products as a last resort. They also kill beneficial insects, including predators and parasites that maintain a healthy balance in the garden. Products like neem oil can be very effective but usually don't kill on contact; it may take a week or two to see results. Always read and follow directions on labels. Using soap sprays in hot sun can burn leaves, so use early or late in the day.
- Diatomaceous earth powder is a mineral product made of the skeletal remains of diatoms. Its microscopic sharp edges pierce small insects and dry them out. It feels like a fine powder to us and is made of natural minerals, but still take care not to breathe it in. Use carefully and specifically as it also kills earthworms and beneficial insects, and it doesn't break down in the environment.
- Solarization can work well in warm, dry climates as a pasteurization process to fumigate soil and destroy pests in severe outbreak conditions. Prepare the area for planting first to avoid stirring up soil pests later, and add drip irrigation buried at least an inch deep to prevent sun damage. Add compost and mustard plant

1904 Ernest Haekel print of microscopic diatoms shows their elaborately beautiful shells. Diatomaceous earth from ground shells has tiny sharp edges that cut the bodies and legs of insects.

residue (to fumigate soil), moisten well, and cover with clear, UV-protected plastic (which holds up better and can be reused) for four to six weeks, depending on weather, day length, and the quality of the plastic mulch.

NONTOXIC CONTROLS FOR SOME COMMON GARDEN PESTS AND DISEASES
Aphids

There are approximately four thousand species of aphids with varying life cycles and hosts. Females of many species can reproduce without mating, which results in population explosions. Outbreaks often subside without human intervention if the environment is healthy for beneficial insects.

- Garlic and garlic oil sprays
- Nettle spray
- Diatomaceous earth
- Diluted soapy water spray (Dr. Bronners eucalyptus or castile soap—1 tablespoon per gallon of water)

Army Cutworms
(caterpillar stage of the miller moth)

- Army cutworms are not usually a problem in gardens mulched year-round. They like to lay eggs in dense weeds.
- If cutworms are cutting off seedlings at the soil level (they forage at night), create collars around the stems of plants to deter them. Use cut sections of cardboard rolls from paper towels or toilet paper and push down into soil, or use plastic or aluminum foil collars.

Cabbage Worms, Tomato Hornworms, and Other Caterpillars

- Wasps and parasitic wasps attack and eat many caterpillars including cabbage worms, so tolerate them and provide nectar plants (see earlier). If you plant them, they will come.
- Inspect the leaves and stems of all brassicas (broccoli, cabbage, kale, Brussels sprouts, collards) and handpick any well-camouflaged green cabbage worms and destroy the pale yellow eggs on the back of leaves. Wear lightweight gloves if you're squeamish. Handpick the big striped hornworms from tomatoes.
- *Bacillus thuringiensis* (Bt)—available in spray, dust, or granular form. Follow label instructions.
- Garlic spray
- Diatomaceous earth

Earwigs

These introduced insects are active at night and mostly eat other insects like aphids and mites. Occasionally they damage soft plant tissues and proliferate to become a nuisance.

- Trap them in moist rolled-up newspaper, moist corrugated cardboard, or a bowl with vegetable oil, keeping it an inch or more below the top so they can't crawl out. Replace traps every few days.

Flea Beetles

Tiny black flea beetles attack brassicas and members of the nightshade family, like tomatoes and eggplant, especially in the spring. Cool-weather crops are more susceptible to attacks if planted out in hot weather, while warm-weather crops like tomatoes and eggplant that struggle in cool conditions are more vulnerable in cool weather. As the plants become larger and stronger they usually outlast the flea beetles. The following have also worked effectively:

- Row cover, if applied early enough, before beetles are flying
- Replanting or reseeding a week or two later if seedlings are attacked
- Interplanting radishes or Chinese mustard as a trap crop
- White and yellow sticky traps
- Entomopathic nematodes applied to soil
- Garlic, onion, or mint sprays
- Diatomaceous earth
- Diluted soap sprays, especially Dr. Bronner's eucalyptus

Grasshoppers

- There are many different species and a few feed just on weeds. Grasshoppers lay their eggs in dry soil and most hatch in mid- to late spring. Cold, wet weather will harm young grasshoppers, though very dry springs will also reduce the vegetation they depend on. They are difficult to control because they're highly mobile. Populations naturally fluctuate from year to year. Control is best directed at young grasshoppers in May, or early June at higher altitudes.
- Ducks may be the best grasshopper predators, but chickens, guinea hens, turkeys, cats, skunks, coyotes, toads, many birds, snakes, spiders, robber flies, and praying mantids also consume a lot of them. (Poultry will also damage garden plants.)
- Row cover will keep them off plants.
- *Nosema locustae* (sold as NOLO Bait or Semaspore) is a parasite that kills young grasshoppers when they ingest it. Mix with bran meal or purchase it premixed. Keep it refrigerated since it's perishable. Kills some species quickly and is slow acting (a few weeks) in others.

Mexican Bean Beetles

- Handpick the yellow-to-coppery-brown spotted lady beetles on bean plants adults, elongated larva, and the yellow egg clusters—when they first appear and put in a bucket of soapy water.
- Diatomaceous earth powder or soap spray

Powdery Mildew and Fungal Diseases

- GreenCure is an environmentally safe product made of potassium bicarbonate that works well and quickly.
- Milk spray, diluted to 5 or 10 percent

Undesirables in the Garden

Fungal Preventatives
- Horseradish tea spray
- Kelp spray
- Apple cider vinegar spray

Slugs
- Slugs like moist, humid conditions and are active at night.
- Reduce crowding of plants, and use trellises for plant foliage to create better air circulation around plants.
- Use drip or soaker hoses to water and avoid overwatering.
- Trap them with bowls of beer, sugar water, and yeast mixture.
- It's usually recommended to avoid organic mulches like straw and grass clippings, but slugs are not a problem in my thick hay mulch, probably because it's difficult for them to travel through it.

Squash Bugs
(brown, flat, shieldlike bodies)
- Pull mulch back from around base of plants if you have these insects.
- Diatomaceous earth

Tomato Spotted Wilt Virus (dark spots on leaves and yellow spots and rings on fruit, spread by thrips), Fusarium Fungi, and Verticillium Fungi
- Virus protective spray of ½ teaspoon antitranspirant (Cloudcover, Wiltpruf), 8 ounces skim or prepared powdered milk (provides calcium), 1 gallon water
- Don't crowd plants or get the leaves wet when watering.
- Pull out and destroy affected plants.
- Don't plant tomatoes in the same spot for three years if you have these diseases.

Helpful Online Resources
- ATTRA's National Sustainable Agriculture Information Service and Resource Guide to Organic & Sustainable Vegetable Production
- Organic Materials Review Institute (omri.org)
- Golden Harvest Organics (ghorganics.com)

Chapter 10
Water

An irrigation ditch and weir at the USDA Cheyenne Horticulture Station. When funding for the station was eliminated in the 1950s, most of the fruit trees were bulldozed and irrigation water was shut off permanently. A few survive today.

*W*ater resource scarcity continually
defines and redefines the West...It is
inescapably vulnerable to drought.
—Western Governors Drought
Task Force, October 1996

HOW WESTERN
WATER LAW SYSTEMS WORK

Though almost any place can have dry spells, water shortages, and drought at one time or another, these are a regular part of the natural cycle in the semiarid western United States, and water laws reflect this. The system for surface water rights in the West is based on priority and "beneficial use" as laid out in the doctrine of prior appropriation of water laws.

The underlying principles of the doctrine originated in the gold-mining camps of California, where there often wasn't enough water for all the miners to wash their placer deposits. Whenever this occurred, they applied the same rule used for gold claims: first in time, first in right.

Because of the dry climate, topography, and other practical concerns, adoption of the existing water law system of the wetter eastern states, where all property owners have an equal right to the "reasonable use" of surface waters, was opposed for the West. As a result, surface waters don't belong to western landowners, even if a stream runs through their property. Instead, the rights are appropriated for the exclusive use of those who first acquired them through diverting and using the water. Whenever stream flow isn't enough to meet the demand of all the water users, priority is given to senior users who came first rather than sharing it equally among all users. And western water rights must be used; they can't simply be held for investment purposes or speculation. "Use it or lose it," as the saying goes.

Beneficial use isn't precisely defined but it includes irrigation, mining, industry, general municipal use, domestic use, and aesthetic use like landscaping or raising fish in ponds, though most states don't allow an individual appropriation solely for aesthetic use. Maintaining in-stream flows for eco-system health, fish and wildlife, and/or recreation is a recent addition. Efficiency of use is also considered so water isn't wasted. Because water is a limited resource, water rights and use can become extremely contentious, especially during times of drought.

Each state has developed its own specific system of water rights, which makes cooperation between them difficult, though there are interstate and international compacts. The federal government also has considerable power over water, especially any navigable bodies of water. It can and increasingly does act as a regulator to prevent pollution or waste, to protect public rights to navigation and recreation, or to promote the public interest.

Because the federal government was exceedingly generous in providing water to settlers who were encouraged to explore, use, and develop the land and resources of the West for mining, cattle ranching, and farming, the federal reserved water rights doctrine was set up. It reserved the rights to unappropriated water for occasions when the United States needed it for a federal purpose. In 1963, for example, it was used to set aside Colorado River water for Indian reservations, national forests, and recreational and wildlife areas. The state of Arizona sued to challenge the use, but lost.

WATER FOR GROWING TOWNS AND CITIES

Recurring water shortages due to the climate is only a part of the overall issue. The increasing environmental, economic, and social costs associated with keeping clean water flowing to our growing western population centers is central. Large water diversion projects to pipe water from wetter regions are regularly proposed.

Most western residents and businesses have a contractual right to receive water from their local municipal government or a private water supplier that holds the actual water rights used to supply their customers. Growing cities and towns have increasingly bought up water rights from farmers, which they often lease back to them in various types of agreements and arrangements. Some cities structure their rates to provide an incentive for conserving. Others offer rebates or tax incentives, or mandate Xeriscape or other water-conserving methods for home landscapes. Many new towns and developments that didn't acquire water until recently are struggling to maintain adequate supplies and find solutions for the future.

GROUNDWATER

Irrigation for agriculture is by far the biggest use of groundwater and surface water in all the western states. Increasingly, domestic water users in the West are also relying on groundwater in deep basin aquifers, which is regulated to varying degrees in different states. In Colorado, for example, Douglas, Elbert, and Park counties, ranked as the first, third, and fourth fastest growing counties in the United States just a few years ago, all rely on the Denver Basin aquifer. Like many other aquifers, this large deepwater basin is considered nonrenewable because surface recharge from precipitation is negligible.

In central Arizona, where the water table dropped significantly from municipal pumping, Colorado River water is pumped deep underground to artificially recharge

Water rights are based on priority and "beneficial use" in the West. Property owners in wetter eastern states have an equal right to "reasonable use" of surface waters; in the West those who first acquired and used them retain exclusive use.

Saudi Arabia is one of the most arid countries in the world, it managed, amazingly, to become self-sufficient in wheat production in a few years. Within thirty years, however, the aquifers were depleted. The country is again dependent on grain imports, and there is a lot less drinking water.

In some places, including the San Luis Valley in southern Colorado, groundwater contains a high concentration of salts leached from agricultural irrigation with surface water. Mining, uranium and radium milling, the oil and gas industry (both production processes and leaking petroleum tanks), and toxic-waste disposal have also degraded groundwater quality. There are Superfund sites all over the West, and billions of dollars have been spent to clean them up. In addition, household pesticides, lawn chemicals, auto-related chemicals (antifreeze, oil, and the like), and even pharmaceutical drugs make their way into streams and groundwater.

Today there is greater awareness of environmental issues like water quality. However, many western urban and suburban residents still use the majority of their domestic treated water on chemical-intensive lawns without thinking much about it. And though some may consider growing food gardens to be a better use for domestic water, there is no distinction as far as water providers are concerned.

groundwater. The practice of recharging aquifers is occurring in other parts of the West now too.

For a cautionary tale we might look at Saudi Arabia. In the 1970s, the country began using its oil-drilling technology to tap deep underground water from aquifers and using it to grow wheat. Even though

COLLECTING AND HARVESTING WATER

In Arizona and New Mexico, both rainwater harvesting and gray-water collection for landscape use are now widely practiced, and in some places mandated for new developments. Rainwater harvesting became legal in Utah in May 2010. Colorado still has the most restrictive laws, but even here things are beginning to change. Capturing and storing rainwater was illegal in Colorado for over a hundred years. Based on a ground-breaking 2007 study that showed that 97 percent of the precipitation that fell either evaporated from the ground or was used by vegetation instead of ever reaching a stream, an exception was enacted for rural residents who are not connected to a municipal or commercial water supply and who obtain a permit.

There are also many opportunities to shape our landscapes so they retain water naturally. Instead of designing properties so all the water runs off onto pavement and streets into storm drains, a practice which has increased the severity of urban flooding and the pollution of streams, we can make them more permeable so rain and snow soak in to water our plants. And we can also direct water from roofs and gutters to gardens while it rains.

DESIGN LANDSCAPES TO RETAIN WATER

This is the backdrop against which many of us garden in Colorado and the West. Food gardening may be a more productive use of resources than maintaining a green lawn, but it is still water intensive. We need to do any and everything we can as gardeners to conserve and stretch our clean water resources, which we tend to forget are also shared by other creatures. Here are some ways we can do this.

Much of the technique involved in reshaping our landscapes so they hold onto water on-site is common sense. The trouble is, most of us have become so far removed from natural systems that we don't recognize common sense anymore. Demonstrating my own lack of it, for example, I once asked prolific gardener, seed collector, and retired horticulture professor Jim Ells if it isn't terribly difficult to collect your own seed. "Oh yes, terribly difficult," he replied, amused. "The weight of all that seed!"

The first step, as permaculturists always advise, is to observe how and where water now pools and moves through your property whenever it rains, and where snow collects and runs off as it melts. Go outside and take a look around. Consider gravity and where you might want to direct the water or create a new garden to take advantage of the existing flow.

Brad Lancaster wrote the three-volume *Rainwater Harvesting for Drylands and Beyond*, which offers lots of specific detail on almost every aspect of capturing rainwater in landscapes. He discusses the three S's: Slow the water, Spread it, and Sink it (let it sink in). You can use rocks, terracing, berms, swales (shallow troughs that carry water), bowl-shaped depressions of various sizes with flat, mulched bottoms for planting holes, and even permeable paving materials instead of solid concrete driveways to accomplish this.

There are also lots of ways to direct and move water around. I learned the hard way that it's difficult to flood irrigate a flat pasture with ditch water, so I've become adept at using rolls of soft plastic tubing to direct it. My neighbor installed a French drain that collects the rainwater from all the gutters on his house into an underground channel that slopes gently down to his garden, a few hundred feet beyond the house.

A few years ago, an enterprising couple invented the Drought Buster, an inexpensive hard plastic attachment that fits over the end of a typical gutter downspout and tapers to a plastic fitting where you can attach an ordinary garden hose. It also has an overflow escape for heavier flows. I bought three and use them to direct water from downspouts to trees and gardens. You can find them at rainstonellc.com.

All of us have the ability to get creative and design something that works for our particular situation or landscape or to locate someone who can help us. I sometimes become frustrated by my lack of expertise with tools and hardware, but I find that employees at hardware stores, especially the remaining independent ones, can be very helpful.

LESSONS FROM ANCIENT FARMERS

Gary Nabhan is director of the Center for Sustainable Environments at Northern Arizona University, a founder of Native Seeds/SEARCH and the Renewing America's Food Traditions campaign, and the author of twenty books. I heard him speak last winter on Arabs in the Americas who came as slaves and refugees escaping persecution during the Spanish Inquisition. Later they became "camel whisperers," guiding Camel Corps caravans from Texas to California, and they brought their knowledge of ancient water harvesting, sustainable irrigation, and building-cooling techniques to American desert oases, transforming them from groves of wild palms to date, olive, fig, and pomegranate orchards where anise, cumin, and coriander grew in the understory.

On his website, Nabhan offers twelve lessons on water conservation from traditional farmers of the Colorado Plateau.

The practices in these lessons from ancient farmers who successfully grew food in arid environments with much less water than conventional farmers today are still relevant, and in some cases still used by Hopi and Navajo people. Many of the methods, like sunken waffle gardens in protected microenvironments and "planting sensitive understory crops beneath the canopies of shade-bearing trees" echo through permaculture principles of water harvesting and planting.

His lesson to plant deeply where subsurface moisture persists was of special interest to me because of a story we ran in *Colorado Gardener* about Bessie White, an eighty-year-old gardener who plants seeds many inches deeper than usually recommended. "Sometimes it takes a while," she said, "but they come up." And as Nabhan explains, some varieties of corn and beans grown by the Hopi and Navajo can be planted a foot deep in sandy loams, where there are reserves of soil moisture. Nabhan says they are adapted to have "both rapid-growing roots and extended mesocotyls that allow the seedlings to 'dig' up through the sand mulch to reach light."

OTHER PRACTICES TO CONSERVE WATER IN THE GARDEN, ESPECIALLY DURING DROUGHT
BUILD SOIL WITH GOOD TILTH AND MULCH YEAR-ROUND

As with most everything in gardening, the place to start is in the dirt. Use organic amendments to build soil that will retain moisture while also providing the oxygen and drainage that plants need. Vegetable plants don't like to sit in hard, caked soil. If you don't use thick mulch in your garden, buy a hoe and keep it sharp so you can cultivate (loosen) any crusty, caked soil around your plants an inch or two deep if it dries out. This would also be a good opportunity to scratch in some extra compost as you cultivate. Breaking up crusted soil will allow rain or irrigation water to soak in more easily. A stirrup hoe is an excellent and inexpensive tool for both cultivating and weeding.

Vegetable plants also detest constantly soggy, boggy soil, no matter how hot and dry it is. You will rarely if ever encounter naturally soggy soil here, but I mention it because a first-year gardener I know created it artificially, thinking he was doing his plants a big favor.

Since I grow hay and have lots of it around, I like to keep a thick layer of hay mulch on my garden year-round, which almost completely eliminates the need for hoeing and weeding (see chapter 6, Creating the Vegetable Garden). You can also use straw, leaves, or a combination, or an inch or two of compost if hay is hard to come by, though compost dries out and vanishes pretty quickly when used as a surface mulch.

PLANT LESS DENSELY

It's often recommended to plant gardens densely in raised beds, usually because of space constraints. It can almost become a competition to pack as many plants as possible into a small growing area to see how much you can produce. While dense plantings do shade the soil, overcrowding taxes plants and forces them to compete with each other. It works as long as you load on the water and nutrients, but over time it's just that same old paradigm of maximizing production and yield (because we can) without

much thought about conserving water or giving anything back to the soil that sustains us.

Transpiration of water up through plant roots, stems, and leaves dries out soil more quickly and more deeply than evaporation from the surface of the ground. It used to be common practice for farmers and gardeners to create a dust mulch by breaking up the top few inches of the ground with a hoe to interrupt the upward movement of water in soil and its inevitable evaporation.

You can actually cut back on plant density without reducing yields as much as you think. After gardening for several decades, Steve Solomon, author of *Gardening When It Counts*, *Gardening West of the Cascades*, and the online publication *Gardening Without Irrigation*, began to notice how much plant density affects soil moisture. He says, "In most cases having a plant density one-eighth of that recommended by intensive gardening advocates will result in a yield about half as great as on closely planted raised beds." Be sure to remove weeds when they're small too, since they compete very successfully for water.

USE DRIP IRRIGATION TO DELIVER WATER

Drip irrigation will deliver a slow, steady trickle of water right to the plants at the soil surface. Drip is widely available and not terribly difficult to install. Think of it as similar to LEGOs, with interchangeable parts and pieces that you can build into a custom design for your garden. Overhead watering with sprinklers is the least efficient method of delivering water. It increases weed germination, and the water often evaporates in our dry air before it reaches plant roots. Sprinkling plant leaves also increases the chances of disease, especially for plants in

Chard on a drip line. Drip irrigation under mulch is the most effective way to water vegetables in the semiarid West. It delivers the moisture right where it's needed, keeping plant leaves dry and healthy.

the nightshade family, like tomatoes, that don't like to get their leaves wet.

Use a timer to make sure your drip system doesn't run for hours and hours. It's easy to forget and leave water running if your system is manual.

If overhead sprinklers are your only choice, water early in the morning or when it's cloudy, while evaporation rates are still low and leaves have a chance to dry off before it cools off at night. Avoid overhead watering on windy days because you will lose almost all of it through evaporation. If you chose to use mulch thickly, as I do, sprinklers on top won't deliver enough

water to your plants through the mulch, but drip irrigation or soaker hoses underneath the mulch will do the job.

When it's hot and dry it can be tempting to overwater your garden. This oversaturation will fill up all of the air pockets in the soil, depriving plant roots of needed oxygen and making it more difficult for them to grow. Some plants, like squash, will wilt regularly in the heat of the afternoon and revive as it cools off at night. If a plant still appears limp in the morning, water right away, but if it has perked up, wait. Don't drown your plants!

Given limited water, most say it's better to water plants thoroughly every few days to encourage deeper rooting than to water lightly and superficially every day and encourage shallow roots. But a few gardeners I know swear by using a drip system every day for a short time for some vegetables so soil never dries out completely. If you do the math correctly, this doesn't use any more water overall as long as the system is on a timer or very carefully monitored so you don't accidentally leave the water running. (I know from experience that this can easily happen.) Don't forget to actually check the soil an inch or two down to find out if it's dry. It if holds together when you squeeze it, there is adequate moisture in it. Thick mulch really helps keep moisture in.

If you just have a few small manageable beds, you may choose to hand water. Experienced gardeners know this, but if you're hand watering—even if you're in a hurry—don't torture your plants by using the hose at full blast. This not only removes oxygen from the soil but it can uproot and destroy young plants or wash the soil away from the base of mature plants, exposing the roots. Turn down the pressure or get an attachment for the end of your hose so you can apply the water in a spray or fountain instead of a strong blast that washes away soil. Water at the soil level instead of getting leaves wet.

For a large plot, you'll find that hand watering is extremely time consuming and wish you'd sprung for drip. With a drip system, you can still walk leisurely around your garden with a cup of morning coffee while the water is circulating and, if you add an automatic timer, you can even leave town without enlisting or employing someone to water for you.

Drip irrigation line in enclosed raised beds. Mulching around the perimeter of raised beds will help hold in moisture.

To Conserve Water, Don't Use Raised Beds
If conserving water is your primary goal, or if there are watering restrictions in times of drought, don't use enclosed raised beds. I know—they are extremely popular right now. You can build them inexpensively and quickly, they look neat and well defined, plus, lumber—especially cedar—lasts for many years without rotting in our dry climate.

But in effect, raised beds are a lot like giant containers. They dry out more quickly than inground gardens, and during very dry years that's a problem.

It may be that you have no choice. For example, you may be creating raised beds on top of asphalt, or maybe you live in the mountains with extremely rocky soil and lots of deer. But if one of your goals really is to save water, skip the boxes or figure out a way to insulate them so they don't dry out.

Prepare Beds Ahead of Time
Waiting until spring to prepare vegetable beds

can be risky, especially in a wet year. If you encounter rain or wet snows, it will be very difficult to work clay soils without removing all the oxygen in them, so you will need to wait until it dries out to amend and prepare the beds, which can delay planting. If you have prepared the beds months ahead of time, they'll be all ready to receive spring moisture. Timing can be everything in a garden.

More Water-conserving Tips

- Planting vegetables in blocks instead of rows and using other plants or fences as windbreaks will save on water. As in any type of garden, it's always best to group plants with similar water needs together.
- Plants need moisture the most when they're germinating, during their first weeks of growth, during flowering and fruiting, as well as right after transplanting, when a little temporary shelter will help them adjust too.
- Add mycorrhizae to your soil or use it in liquid form to water plants. It extends plants' root surfaces, increasing their ability to locate and take in moisture. An organic fertilizer that contains mycorrhizae is ideal, since good nutrition helps plants retain water.

Garden Hoses

It has come to light recently that many garden hoses leach lead and other chemicals into water that sits inside the hose. There is usually a label in very small print that says: **WARNING: This product contains a chemical that causes cancer, birth defects, or other reproductive harm.**
Even those labeled Safe for Drinking leach tiny amounts of lead into water that sits in a hose, and those without the safe labeling leach ten to one hundred times the allowable levels of lead. Lead is used in the process of manufacturing brass hose fittings and as a stabilizer in PVC.

Always make sure that any garden hoses, soaker hoses, and black pipe used for irrigating are labeled Safe for Drinking. Flush sitting water out of garden hoses before drinking and before watering edibles. Lead-free, safe-for-drinking hoses are often sold as marine or recreational vehicle (RV) hoses.

Chapter 11
What to Grow

Abbondonza Farm's booth at the Boulder, Colorado, farmers' market. The farm also harvests and sells its own locally adapted vegetable seeds.

You can really grow almost any vegetable in most parts of the semiarid West depending on how much effort you want to put into it. Some will be easier in hotter years and places, others in cooler years and places.

In our climate, there are two distinct categories of vegetables to grow. Cool-season veggies like greens, broccoli, and onions will germinate and grow in cool soil, and most will withstand late spring and early fall freezes that aren't too severe. Because of our higher elevations and drier continental climate, the temperature usually cools off significantly at night, which cool-season vegetables really like, along with our high intensity light. They grow especially well near the foothills and in the mountains. On the plains of the Front Range, and wherever else the growing season is long enough, there are also two distinct growing seasons for cool-season veggies: spring and fall.

Warm-season vegetables are easier to grow in the warmer parts of the region and at lower altitudes, or in a warmer-than-usual growing season. Since warm-season vegetables need warm air and soil, cooler nights can make it difficult for them to get growing early enough to set fruit that ripens before the first frost arrives. This is especially true for many of the tasty heirloom varieties that ripen late in the season. In bigger cities like Denver where concrete predominates, and in Phoenix where all the swimming pools create heat sinks, it cools off less at night because the heat is retained. This makes it easier to grow tomatoes, peppers, eggplants, and melons, which need the warmth to give a delicious yield.

Soil makes a difference too. There are some sandy, loamy old river-bottom soils in pockets on the plains and in the mountains, which make growing many vegetables and some particular varieties a lot easier. Much-maligned clay soil is heavier and more difficult to work with, but it contains a lot of nutrients and holds water. When it's lightened up by adding lots of organic matter, clay soil is a great growing medium.

COOL-SEASON VEGETABLES

Though many people wait until May to start a garden and plant everything all at once, you can seed greens, beets, broccoli, onions, and other cool-season crops in the garden in mid-March, even if it's snowing, and be eating some of these veggies before other folks even begin to plant. If you prepare your garden in the fall, you'll be ready to plant as soon as spring moisture arrives, and if you seed greens every three weeks or so you'll have an ongoing fresh harvest, at least until the intense summer heat sets in.

Spring snows give seeds and plants the moisture they need to germinate and grow, and they actually provide insulation. Freezes are more likely when skies clear; once the cloud cover disappears, temperatures can drop quickly. Unless conditions are rainy, water seeds twice a day with a fine spray until they germinate. Once they're up, you can give young plants some added protection from the elements and the flea beetles by covering the bed with a layer of lightweight floating row cover (see chapter 7, Extending the Season). This will speed up their growth considerably.

You can also start cool-season vegetable seeds indoors under lights or in a sunny window, or you can buy starts from reputable garden centers, farm stands, or other growers. Sometimes commercial starts are pumped up with a lot of chemical fertilizers.

They look great when you buy them, but if you don't keep up with the chemical regimen they fail to thrive, so be aware of what you're buying. Plants that have been growing indoors in a warm environment need to adjust, or harden off, before they go in the garden, so put them outside during the day and inside at night for several days before planting, and make sure to water them every day since plastic packs dry out very quickly.

Many helpful garden products are readily available today. A soak or root dip of compost tea, liquid mycorrhizae, and/or kelp before planting will help seedlings become strongly established, though this isn't necessary. Biodynamic gardeners like to use a brew made from comfrey and/or stinging nettles for watering and foliar spraying young plants. If you feed the soil microbes, they will protect and feed your plants.

Plant in late afternoon if possible, especially when days are sunny and warm. Water in carefully, without using the full force of the hose, and mulch around the plants with dried leaves, straw, hay flakes, and/or compost. Floating row cover will protect the plants from bright sun and drying winds while they adjust to their new environment.

June 1 is a target date for direct seeding and planting out seedlings of cold-tolerant crops at 8,000 feet. The mountain gardeners I know recommend varieties that will mature in 90 days or less so they have enough time to produce a crop in the short frost-free mountain growing season.

On the plains, you can grow a second crop of many cool-season vegetables planted in the summer for harvesting in the fall. In fact, without the early spring menace of flea beetles, some grow even better in the fall, especially Asian greens. Plant a second round of lettuce, arugula, spinach, chard, mustards, and other greens, plus carrots, beets, and scallions in mid- to late July or August, depending on the crop and the weather. Their growth will speed up as days and nights cool off. Get out the row cover again if temperatures dip. A cold frame will extend your growing season even more.

WARM-SEASON VEGETABLES

Though it's very tempting, don't even think about planting warm-weather crops outside before mid- to late May if you live on the Front Range plains or anywhere else with an average last frost date in mid-May unless you have special protection for them. Warm-weather crops include tomatoes, peppers, eggplants, beans, squash, pumpkins, cucumbers, corn, melons, and tender herbs like basil. Check *average* last frost dates for your specific area with the understanding that this date is less of a guarantee with our seesawing spring than it is in climates with a more gradual warm-up. An average date is determined by taking the mean of all the last frost dates on record for the area.

In the mountains, some experienced high-altitude gardeners manage quite well with warm-season crops like tomatoes and sweet corn. The trick is to plant varieties that are adapted to mountain conditions, with short seasons and cooler temperatures, and to use techniques to warm the soil, retain heat at night, and extend the season of growth. Season extenders take on a whole new meaning when your frost-free growing season is only 70–90 days long. Cucumbers and summer squash are a good bet because they mature in a short season (around 60

days). And both potatoes and summer squash will tolerate cooler nights as a trade-off for high-intensity UV light during the day.

In many seed catalogs, the Days to Maturity listing often begins with the transplanting date, not the sowing date, so understand what you're getting. A variety that requires 90 days from the time the seed germinates has a shorter growing season than one that takes 90 days from transplanting.

Grouping plants in the cool- and warm-season vegetable categories listed below is a simple and practical approach for western gardeners, especially beginners. But since plant classification and practical gardening categories are sometimes at odds, there are gray areas. For example, melons are cucurbits (Cucurbitaceae family) along with squash and cucumbers, but because they are sweet most of us consider them fruits, so they are listed here as such. Plants commonly and informally referred to as "nightshades" (in the family Solanaceae) include the warm-season tomato, eggplant, and pepper, as well as the potato, which grows best as a cool-season crop. And almost all familiar garden beans are warm-season crops, but the fava bean, or broad bean, prefers the same conditions as peas.

It's important for vegetable gardeners to know basic plant families because pests and diseases often affect specific plant families and can remain in the soil through the winter. This is why it is advised not to grow brassicas or nightshades in the same spot year after year. Moving plant families around in the garden, known as rotation, is one of the organic gardener's best preventative tools.

Varieties and Cultivars

Before commercial seeds became available, all home gardeners used to save seeds, selecting from plants that thrived and produced well in their gardens and passing them along to others. But as seed companies captured the market, they came to favor seeds they could sell nationally, to more people. As a one-variety-fits-all seed industry developed, the overall number of varieties plummeted and pass-along seeds that are adapted to specific local conditions almost disappeared.

Seed Savers Exchange began in 1975 as a nonprofit dedicated to saving and sharing heirloom seeds, and other similar efforts and organizations followed. Today, much home-garden-seed growing is outsourced to growers in China, India, and elsewhere, but a few smaller seed companies still produce regionally adapted seeds in their own trial gardens or contract with local growers. Some small farms are also beginning to produce and sell their own seed locally. Regional adaptability can be especially important when growing in more extreme conditions, like in the mountains or during drought.

This is not to say that mainstream hybrid varieties aren't any good, or that vegetable seeds from other parts of the world won't grow well. Some, like Asian greens, grow extremely well on the high plains, especially in the fall.

But seed from plants that have been grown locally or regionally are already adapted. It's also great to have the option to save our own seeds instead of buying them. Hybrids don't allow us to do that with predictable results because their offspring don't "come true," meaning they don't have the same characteristics as the parent plant.

Hybrids are created by crossing two plant varieties, either in nature (squash do this readily) or by humans wanting to create a new plant that combines traits from both parent plants. Since most of the food-plant breeding in the United States is done for commercial purposes, selected hybrid traits often relate to being tough enough to hold up under large-scale planting, harvesting, and shipping instead of home garden quality traits like flavor.

Open-pollinated plant varieties are not hybrids, although they probably were sometime in the past. They have become stable, meaning that each plant generation is identical to its parent and we can harvest their seeds to plant again with confidence. This can be a money saver and allow you to preserve varieties that do extremely well in your area. Seed companies follow fashion and often drop the older varieties when new ones appear.

Adaptation is an ongoing life process for plants and people. Like it or not, believe it or not, the world is always changing and the planet seems to be warming. A stagnant, extremely limited supply of seed varieties doesn't serve us and runs contrary to the overwhelming abundance in nature. Of the commercial vegetable varieties available in 1903, 96 percent are now extinct. Let's keep the gene pool vibrant and diverse in our home gardens.

Before buying seed, look through catalogs (most are now online) and read the information on preferred growing conditions, length of growing season, and disease resistance for specific varieties and cultivars. Check with local gardener friends to see what grows well for them, but don't be afraid to research and experiment—all good gardeners do. Grow what you like to eat, but be willing to expand your palate. Seek out locally and regionally grown seeds, and start saving some of your own for next year, choosing the specific plants that fare best in your garden.

I mention some specific varieties and cultivars below that either I or trusted gardeners and farmers I know have grown. This is by no means an exhaustive list and in some cases opinions conflict, which may be due to soil, location, microclimates, conditions in a given year, or any number of factors, including the suitability and economics of growing for farmers' markets or CSA members. In our region, there can be much variability from location to location (even when they're relatively close), from year to year, garden to garden, and also in the philosophy and priorities of the gardeners. It might not make economic sense for a small-market farmer to grow the sweet but smaller, flatter Cipollini onions that are so good for roasting, for example, but a home gardener doesn't have the same constraints. So by all means, try the ones mentioned here, but do a little research and choose for yourself. Your only limitation may be having enough space and water to grow everything you like.

When you're planning and planting your garden, don't get too carried away, especially if you're a beginner. Keep in mind that you will need to harvest and cook or store all the food you're growing, and this can take a lot of time at the end of the gardening season for the vast majority of us who have other full-time jobs. If you can pass the baton to your mate or a housemate who loves to can and cook, count your blessings.

And keep your local food bank in mind; those in need will really benefit from your excess.

By summer's end the bounty that you've been able to grow in what many consider a very tough climate will amaze you. In fact, you'll probably be ready for a nice break as the inevitable Halloween storm moves in. In a few months, the seed catalogs arrive!

COOL-SEASON VEGETABLES
(OP indicates open-pollinated)
GREENS
Plants are the only self-nourishing life-forms on the planet, able to convert sunlight into energy-rich food molecules for themselves and for all the rest of us. Leafy greens are nutrient powerhouses, loaded with vitamins, minerals, and phytochemicals, including antioxidants that boost the immune system and do wonders for our health and vitality. If more of us grew and ate more greens, we'd be a healthier nation, instead of quarreling so much about healthcare.

Greens grow exceptionally well during the spring and fall in our intensely bright western sunlight and cool nights. Most don't ever bolt in the mountain garden, so you can grow them all summer if you plant in succession every few weeks. Lettuce is the most familiar green, but others are far more nutritious and tasty, especially when young and tender, so expand your palate to include them.

Arugula is a spicy, nutty green that's easy to grow. As the season progresses and temperatures warm, the bite of arugula becomes stronger. The most familiar annual variety is known as rocket or roquette arugula (*Eruca*

Amaranth and arugula. Cooked amaranth leaves are eaten in many countries because they contain so many vitamins and minerals.

sativa). It grows up to 3 feet tall and flowers early, but the white flowers are also tasty. It grows well in spring and is exceptional in the fall, plus it often self-sows. Astro is an early, heat-tolerant selection. Ice-Bred has great cold tolerance and especially rich flavor. The lower-growing Sylvetta or Italian Rustic arugula (*Diplotaxis muralis*) is a perennial in the mustard family. With narrower leaves and a delicious but sharp taste, it flowers later and holds up better in warm temperatures. This one has naturalized around my gardens so I pull most out, leaving a couple of small ones for picking. Johnny's Selected Seeds carries Discovery, a selection with "a hint of sweetness."

If you chop off arugula about 2 inches above the ground when it starts to form flower buds, it will produce tasty new growth all season long. You can also foil flea beetles in the spring if you sow arugula seeds repeatedly; plants sown just two weeks after a first crop that is under attack may completely escape the tiny beetles' onslaught.

Don't overlook **beet greens**. They're wonderful fresh and raw in salads when young and tender, and steamed or braised like chard when they're bigger. They contain even more vitamins and minerals than beet roots. Some OP varieties with especially good greens are Crosby's Egyptian, Sweetheart, Lutz Green Leaf (a winter keeper type), and Bull's Blood (tender red foliage).

Claytonia (miner's lettuce or winter purslane) is a low-growing, plump, juicy, nutritious green that will grow even in deep shade in the mountains. A very hardy salad green, it tolerates moderate frost and is easy to grow but needs consistent moisture.

Cress (peppergrass) adds some spice and crunch to a salad and grows rapidly in cool weather. It can be ready to eat 10 days after planting. Trim it so it keeps coming. Though I love and have tried to grow watercress on the plains, I've found it difficult. I've read that you need a stream or sunny bog with clean water (it easily picks up contaminants). But Bill McDorman of Seeds Trust (seeds for high altitudes) says it's surprisingly easy in the garden if kept moist. So if you love it and have the water, give their watercress seed a try, especially in the mountains. You can also grow it as a water plant in water-tight containers.

Lettuce is easy to grow from seed or transplants and has good frost tolerance down to about 26 degrees. Using row cover will speed up growth a lot in cold weather. Lettuce grows on the plains in sun, part shade (afternoon), or dappled shade, and since it's shallow rooted (about 4 inches), it does well in containers.

There are several types and dozens of varieties to choose from, plus some mixes, most with 40-to-60-day growing seasons. Plant a little every few weeks to keep fresh salad greens coming, and choose slow-bolting or heat-tolerant varieties later in the season if you live on the plains. Most crisphead or iceberg types take longer (70–80 days), plus they're boring and less nutritious, though

A mix of cut-and-come-again greens grows in a whiskey barrel, conveniently located near the kitchen door for easy snipping.

I do like Webb's Wonderful (65–70 days). You're better off planting batavian, loose-leaf, romaine (or cos), and butterhead types.

Batavians (a.k.a. summer crisps) are the most heat-resistant lettuces, germinating well in warm weather, and are also very cold tolerant. Pablo forms, big, beautiful, wine red heads that are loose and crisp. It's one of the last to bolt and stays sweet to the end. Anuenue (Hawaiian for "rainbow") comes into its own later in the summer, when other lettuces are about done, and never turns bitter.

Loose-leaf types don't form heads, so they work well for cut-and-come-again growing as long as you don't snip into the center crown. They're good in containers too. Just give the plants a haircut or keep picking the outer leaves. Amish Deer Tongue, Black-Seeded Simpson, Salad Bowl, Oakleaf (slow to bolt), and the mesclun blend that's available in many supermarkets are all loose-leaf lettuces. Another one, Red Sails, set sail all over my garden one year,

Green Deer Tongue (or Matchless) lettuce, an heirloom dating back to the 1740s, is slow to bolt and has a rich, nutty flavor that doesn't turn bitter.

producing lots of volunteers that held up valiantly through summer heat the next year.

The most nutritious lettuces are the romaines (also called cos) with double the vitamins A and C. Two that are good for cutting and tolerating heat are Craquerelle du Midi, a French romaine, and Freckles, an unusual speckled variety. I've also enjoyed growing and eating Crisp Mint.

The butterheads have small loose heads and tender, succulent leaves. Boston and Bibb are the most well-known varieties. Tennis Ball, with small tight rosettes and a slippery texture, was one of the most popular at the beginning of the twentieth century. I like Yugoslavian Red and Marvel of Four Seasons, a crisp French heirloom known to grow well in a variety of different conditions, and which Penn Parmenter also grows at 8,120 feet. Penn's other favorites are Merlot (a loose-leaf with beautiful dark red frilly leaves), Cimmaron (a crisp red romaine that dates back to the 1700s), and a unique specialty Bibb-romaine type known as Winter Density.

Lettuce seed is very easy to collect and save (see chapter 11, Saving Seeds).

Mâche, or **corn salad**, is a nutritious European green high in vitamin C with a delicious and delicate buttery flavor. It grows in a small rosette form. Large-seeded varieties remain flavorful in the heat, while small-seeded varieties prefer it cool to cold and moist. Mâche is a good green for the mountains—Dutch Broad Leaved will even overwinter there, yet it also has some heat tolerance. Eliot Coleman says he has harvested mâche frozen solid and it thaws perfectly, without turning to mush, so it's at the top of his cold-hardy list.

Spicy **mustard greens** like cool weather and sun. The taste gets very strong when it's hot or when the soil dries out. They're easy to grow if sown in spring or late summer for a fall crop, and they're loaded with vitamins, minerals, and antioxidants. As with most greens, use the young, tender leaves raw and the mature leaves for cooking.

Asian cultivars in the mustard family grow very well in Colorado at all altitudes. On the plains and in the foothills they do especially well as a fall crop. **Komatsuna**, or **Japanese mustard spinach**, has thick, glossy, calcium-rich leaves that are tasty raw or cooked. Both heat and cold tolerant, it rarely bolts. For continuing growth, cut off and use the outer leaves instead of cutting the entire plant. The stems can be used like celery. **Mizuna** is a mild, peppery Japanese mustard green with jagged leaves, less spicy than arugula. Its name means "water vegetable," and its stalks are really juicy. It's a vigorous and rapid grower (14–20 days) and very cold tolerant. Keep cutting for a continuous crop. Penn Parmenter calls mizuna free food because once you plant it, you'll always have it. Especially in the mountains, it self-sows readily, even coming up in gravel driveways. **Tatsoi**, or **totsoi**, is a mild, peppery-flavored Japanese mustard green. The small, spoon-shaped emerald green leaves form a rosette and have a creamy taste. Extremely cold tolerant, it can be harvested from under snow.

Garden **orach** (*Atriplex hortensis*), or **mountain spinach**, was once cultivated but has been gradually replaced by spinach (*Spinacia oleracea*), its close relative. Now it's making a comeback since it's colorful, vigorous, and easy to grow. It tolerates drought, alkaline and poor soils, and moderate frost, and it's packed with vitamins, including three times the vitamin C in spinach.

Raab, or **broccoli raab**, **rapa**, or **rapini**, is a tasty Asian green in the mustard family often described as having green turniplike leaves. I grow Even'Star American Rapa from Fedco Seeds with leaves that are more blue-green and taste sweet. Its yellow flowers taste good too. The leaves surround a small cluster of buds that resembles a small, loose head of broccoli. I find it irresistible raw and fresh from the garden. It has good staying power during the summer, and it's easy to collect the seedpods for sowing next year. It often self-sows. When the leaves of Even'Star get wet, they appear just as distinctly silvery as the jewelweed (*Impatiens capensis*) we used to hold underwater as kids in Pennsylvania to watch the leaves turn silver.

Spinach grows quickly and beautifully for gardeners in the Front Range foothills and plains in the early spring, but as soon as the days get hot it usually bolts and turns bitter. It's a good crop for the mountains and high desert with cool nights. Direct seed, mulch it, don't allow the soil to dry out, and give it some late-afternoon shade if you can. Plant again as summer cools off for a fall crop. Gardeners with sandier soil seem to prefer Tyee, those with more clay, Bloomsdale Long-Standing. Also try Regiment (top pick in CSU's spinach trials), Melody, Space, and Giant Noble. In addition to several vitamins and minerals, spinach contains a substantial amount of protein.

Swiss chard, in the beet family (Chenopodiaceae), holds up throughout the growing season. As long as it doesn't dry out too much, this deep-rooted vegetable can handle short dry spells better than many others. Sometimes it even overwinters in my

For a hefty dose of phytonutrients, eat small chard leaves raw. As they get bigger, steam and add balsamic vinegar or butter.

mulched garden. White-stemmed cultivars taste tenderest to me, and Fordhook Giant is one that performs really well in unpredictable climates. But others have beautiful deep red or yellow stems. Rainbow Mix, Northern Lights (OP), and Bright Lights (a.k.a. Five Color Silverbeet) have a colorful mix of yellow, orange, and red stems.

Harvest the outer leaves and it will keep producing. Delicious raw or steamed when still small, chard is loaded with phytonutrients. The entire stem is edible and tasty. Since the cooking liquid contains a lot of nutrients, save it to use in soups. Argentata is an heirloom with large deep-green savoyed leaves and a mild taste. Baby chard greens are silvery and good in salads. Chickens absolutely love chard, so toss them a few leaves too.

Chicories
Escarole, **endive**, and **radicchio** are chicories, very cold-hardy greens though they can't take frozen soil. Just like kale, their taste improves after frost because they convert starch in their cells into sugar, which acts like antifreeze and remains in their leaves after temperatures warm up. Radicchio is a red-leafed, white-veined leaf chicory, beloved by Italians, that usually heads up in late summer. I confess to having a provincial palate, having never really appreciated its bitter, spicy taste, but maybe what I ate hadn't been through any taste-improving frosts. It's the absolute favorite of some Italian American gardener friends, and I hear the taste is even better when roasted or grilled.

Escarole and endive have a somewhat bitter taste, but both are loaded with vitamins

Prized in Italy, distinctly bitter radicchio comes in at least fourteen varieties. The rosette above eventually forms a more upright head.

and minerals and make a good cleansing tonic. The young inner leaves are paler, less bitter, and tender enough for salads. Both are good in many hot dishes, and braising brings out their best flavor. Escarole is great in bean soups. Curly endive is a feathery, spicy green also known as frisée.

Like other bitters, the chicories have medicinal properties, especially for eliminating internal parasites.

Alliums
Allium seed has a shorter shelf life than other vegetables. Though I have grown onions from seed that's a few years old, germination can be very spotty, so fresh seed is always best.

Chives are the only allium native to both the Old and New Worlds. They're very easy to grow as perennials and pretty, with their big purple blooms that bees adore.

While they are green and tender, remove and feast on garlic scapes or curls—flower stalk shoots that form before bulbs mature.

or shoots, that develop on hard-necked varieties are tasty too. These scapes need to be cut off anyway in the spring so the bulbs will grow large.

Elephant garlic isn't a true garlic, but a type of leek with really big cloves and a milder taste. In the best conditions, bulbs can grow 3–5 inches in diameter.

Garlic chives are very easy to grow. The leaves are flat instead of hollow like regular chives and grow about 12–18 inches tall. Both leaves and flowers are edible, and they have a mild garlic taste. Keep harvesting by cutting the leaves so new growth will continue. The flowers are tasty and very pretty in salads or as a garnish.

Undesirable insects don't like the plants, so it's good almost anywhere in the garden.

Plant **garlic** in the fall, preferably in October, for some good growth before winter, and harvest it in July. Keep it in a cool dry place and save enough, including your biggest bulbs, for planting. There are hundreds of varieties in several colors and many heirlooms with stories behind them. Soft-necked types keep longer than hard-necked. Use soft-necked types for garlic braids.

Plant individual bulbs a few inches deep in soil that's well-amended with compost, water over the winter, and mulch to keep moisture in. I plant throughout the garden and around the perimeter of some beds for pest confusion, as well as close to roses (along with smaller garlic chives, which are also delicious and easy to grow).

Early spring green garlic trimmings are delicious in stir-fry, and the curlicue scapes,

Leeks have their own distinctive taste and are delicious in soups and stir-fry. Short-season leeks (70–120 days) are generally smaller and less hardy, but good in high-altitude climates. They generally take the heat

Leeks are a delicious and nourishing alternative to onions. Slice very thin and sauté or make wonderful soup.

What to Grow 145

and the cold. Seed them inside in February to set out in early April on the plains; seed in January at higher altitudes. (Don't make the silly mistake I once did by planting seeds of bulb crops like leeks and onions in net-enclosed Jiffy peat plugs that expand when watered. The netting doesn't disintegrate and really cramps their growth.)

Trim off the tops of the leaves to strengthen them before planting out. Poke a 1½-to-2-inch-diameter hole in the soil about 6–8 inches deep with a dibble, if you have one (it is precisely the right tool for this job), or a fat stick or rake handle if you don't. Put the seedling in the hole, then lift it up so the roots are spread out and down, and the bottom of the first green leaf is level with the soil. Fill in carefully with soil and press firmly around the plant so the leeks are held in place. Water in well, but slowly. The stalk you just covered up will become the tasty white part of the leek. Some people plant in trenches instead or mound up soil as the leeks grow, but I never have. It isn't necessary with short-season types.

When you harvest leeks in the fall or winter but don't plan to eat them right away, leave the soil on the roots and store in a cold place where they won't freeze. Packing them together in a bucket with a little soil works well. Be sure to harvest overwintered leeks well before the spring equinox, in March, or they will bolt.

King Richard (84 days) is a good summer leek—mild and tasty, long and slender. It's hardy to about 20 degrees, especially if you mulch it. Siegfried Frost is even hardier. A small grower in Idaho crossed the two to produce King Sieg (84 days), which has nice fat stems and may overwinter here. Blue

Solaize (100–120 days) is a French heirloom hardy enough to overwinter for spring harvest. Some others are Lancelot (90–100 days, good as a fall crop) and American Flag (95–130 days).

Growing **onions** can be confusing and difficult. Onion bulb formation is affected by temperature, light intensity, and the amount of light and darkness. Bulb growth begins and leaf growth stops when the balance of daylight and darkness reaches a certain point, which depends on the type of onion. Onions are classified as short day (12 hours of daylight), medium day or day neutral (12–14 hours of daylight), and long day (15–16 hours of daylight).

To get large bulb onions in cold-winter climates in northern latitudes, gardeners can grow long-day or medium-day types from sets. These are the small round bulbs produced after one year of growth by these two types of onions. They go dormant and

Like other alliums, onions in flower attract bees galore.

Blooming chives are a bee magnet and one of the easiest culinary plants to grow.

United States. Long- and intermediate-day sets won't produce globe onions in southern warm-winter areas. But all types of onions can be harvested and eaten as scallions. White Lisbon is a scallion type that has grown well for me.

Scallions are a very reliable long-season crop if you don't pull them up by the root, but harvest just the aboveground green leaf. Removing the flower bud also keeps the plant growing better, or in summer you can cut the plant down to about 2 inches above the soil and it will immediately send up new green shoots. Scallions will yield tasty green onions from spring right through the winter if they are heavily mulched for the cold season. Even when the leaves freeze they can be added to cooked dishes.

You can also purchase medium- and long-day onion plants in the spring. They'll keep up to three weeks before you plant them.

The other, more-economical option is to plant medium- or long-day onion seed. On the northern Colorado plains this means mid-March to mid-April, or starting inside in February for transplanting in April. At 8,100 feet, Penn Parmenter plants all her alliums in a greenhouse in January for planting out in early June.

Most commercial OP varieties of onions have given way to hybrids. As Steve Solomon says in *Gardening When It Counts*, most of the classic OP types have "degenerated into something nonproductive," so he cautions not to buy cheap onion seed.

Try the following long-day winter storage types from seed: Copra, Cortland Storage, and Early Yellow Globe (yellow); Mambo, Red Bull, and Southport Red Globe (red); Bedfordshire Champion, Sierra

die to the ground, are harvested in late summer/early fall, and are sold as sets that keep well for six to seven months. Planted in the spring in northern cold-winter areas, the sets will mature into full-grown globe onions that store well over the winter if kept cool and dry, with good air circulation.

Short-day onions won't produce sets at all because they don't go dormant. Grow this type if you live in the southwestern

Blanca, and Snow White (white). Two good onions for shorter storage are Ailsa Craig (100 days from transplant, good storage for a sweet onion) and Walla Walla (115 days from transplant). Candy, Red Candy Apple, and Superstar White are very sweet day-neutrals that get nice and big when grown from transplants in the spring. Red Candy Apple is described as sweet enough to eat like an apple. The sweeter onions don't keep as long as sharper-tasting types, so eat these first.

Onions like well-amended, well-drained soil. Space plants 3–4 inches apart, and thin seedlings to this distance when they have several leaves. Onions don't like crowding or competition from weeds. Mulch and don't worry if bulbs develop on top of the ground. As the tops begin to fall over toward the end of the summer, stop watering. When most of the leaves have fallen over, pull the onions, breaking off the roots, but leave them to cure on the ground for a week or two. Bring them in if a freeze, rain, or snow is forecast. When they're dry, cut off all the leaves and store in a cool dry place.

Egyptian Walking Onions form small bulblets in clusters on top of stems as well as small bulbs underground. Usually you eat the bulbs and plant the bulblets—or they plant themselves, wandering into new locations in your garden. They thrive in the mountains, moist or dry, and are always reliable. Multiplier onion bulbs divide into smaller bulbs that will keep multiplying if you don't harvest them.

If you like **shallots,** be sure to grow some of these too, especially considering how expensive they are in the grocery store and how well they grow in our climate. They're sweeter than onions. Plant seeds inside in February for transplanting in early April, or plant bulbs in October, just like garlic. Shallots are multipliers that always divide into clusters. They help with scab if planted under apple trees.

Brassicas (or Crucifers)

All the brassicas (also called crucifers) are extremely nutritious and have been linked to cancer prevention. Most people don't realize that the leaves are also flavorful and packed with healthy vitamins and minerals. While waiting for the heads to form, you can harvest some and use them much like cabbage leaves in stir-fry and soups. Just don't strip the plant—it needs leaves to photosynthesize.

Brassicas are very good crops for our climate, though tiny black flea beetles sometimes attack the young plants with a vengeance in the spring. Using row cover right after planting will usually prevent this problem. Once the plants get bigger and stronger, they're usually able to withstand the onslaught until the beetles vanish. Rotate the brassicas to a different part of the garden every year (for four years, if possible) so the overwintering beetles won't find their hosts so easily. Spinosad is derived from a rare soil bacterium and is sometimes recommended for severe flea beetle outbreaks, even by Rodale, but it's very toxic to bees until it dries completely, so I would avoid it. Pesticides that are toxic to bees, even organic ones like Spinosad, have a caution on the label that states, "Do not apply this product when bees are active." This is easier said than done since honeybees fly whenever the temperature is above 50 degrees, from early morning until late afternoon. Some native bees fly even earlier and at cooler temperatures.

All brassica leaves, including mustard greens, broccoli, collards, brussels sprouts, and kale, are linked to good health and cancer prevention.

White cabbage moths always seem to flutter around the brassicas, and sometimes the green worms that hatch from their eggs eat holes in the leaves, but in a home garden, who really cares? European paper wasps have colonized the Colorado Front Range and usually take care of any cabbage moth worms before they do much damage (and, unfortunately, most of the other caterpillars that would otherwise become butterflies and moths). If you have a severe problem, a dusting of the soil bacteria Bt (*Bacillus thuringiensis*) will kill them.

Broccoli has grown well in every one of my Colorado gardens. It loves our high-altitude climate. As long as you plant it to mature when the temperature isn't too hot, and as long as the soil is well amended and doesn't dry out, broccoli is a winner on the plains and in the mountains. My own always seems more delicious than any I've bought. If you've never been wild about broccoli, this is one vegetable that may win you over when you grow it in your garden; just don't overcook it until it's mushy and flavorless.

I start seed for transplants inside in February for planting out in early to mid-April. I also direct seed in the garden in early to mid-March and add row cover, which helps warm things up. Depending on the weather and the flea beetles, which go after tender young plants, one or another variety will outperform the others, usually temporarily, which also usually staggers the harvest of big heads. I've also put in transplants in late June to early July for a fall crop, though the plants barely grow until temperatures cool off in August or September.

When the weather turns and stays very

hot for several weeks, many broccoli varieties will lose their sweetness and acquire a strong taste. When that happens, parboil for a few minutes to improve it. Growth slows down in hot weather, but picks up again as nights get cooler, when broccoli's fresh sweet taste also returns.

Don't make the beginner's mistake I once did by pulling up the plants after you pick the main head, thinking the harvest is over. The small, delicious side shoots will keep coming for a month or more. If some heads or side shoots flower, cut them off to encourage more production, but if you don't get around to it, bees love the yellow flowers.

Hybrid varieties include Early Dividend (45 days, 8-inch heads, extra early, lots of side shoots), Pacman (57 days, 8-inch heads, big yields, side shoots, and less likely to bolt than others), Premium Crop (58 days, 9-inch heads, long lasting on the plant), Windsor (56–75 days, cold and more heat tolerant than many), Fiesta (65–80 days, sweet, adaptable to cold and heat), Waltham (65 days, many side shoots), and Arcadia (70 days, smaller plant, 5-inch purplish green heads, crisp and flavorful). Two Italian OP heirlooms that produce a lot of side shoots are DeCicco (50–65 days, with smaller, taller heads) and Calabrese (60–90 days).

Brussels sprouts are impressive plants that take a little longer to grow (90–110 days). They don't like heat but are very cold tolerant. It's not a short-season crop yet it's perfect for the mountains, so transplant starts into fertile, rich soil as soon as possible in late spring to early summer. On the plains it's best as a fall-harvested crop. I've had the best success direct seeding in early May or planting out starts in early June (if it isn't too hot) to mature in late August to early September. When I've planted them earlier, the sprouts start to develop but get loose and don't hold up as well through summer heat.

Plant stems down half an inch or so and don't crowd the plants. The leaves will start to turn yellow as the sprouts mature. Harvest from the bottom up by twisting sprouts off little by little instead of all at once, so the smaller, upper sprouts will continue to grow. If you remove the bud or sprout at the top as the lower sprouts on the stalk start to develop, you'll end up with fewer but larger sprouts sooner. Brussels sprouts get leafy and loose and can also get aphids if they dry out or aren't harvested soon enough. A strong spray of water will help, or garlic or hot pepper sprays, or neem oil if the infestation is severe. Soaking sprouts in salt water helps remove the bugs after picking. The sweetest sprouts develop when the weather gets cold and frosty in the fall. They're excellent paired with sweet potatoes. This year I'm trying an OP red variety called Falstaff, which has smaller sprouts than the green hybrids but is said to be tasty and able to mature in cold climates.

Cabbage is a very cold-tolerant crop when mature, but the young plants need some frost protection. It doesn't like heat and is best grown as a fall crop on the plains. Remove competing weeds, and don't crowd the plants. Cabbage benefits from steady watering (like drip irrigation) and mulch, which keeps soil cooler. Heavy watering followed by drying out can cause cabbage to crack. It grows well in the mountains, and crisp mountain cabbages make incredible

If you want big heads, give cauliflower plenty of room and nutrient-rich soil.

in the fall. If you don't tie the leaves up over the heads of most types to protect them from the sun, they get ricey (grainy and dark) instead of snowy white. Snow Crown is a self-blanching variety, which stays white without covering the heads. While mature plants survive hard frosts, young plants need frost protection. Instead of a nicely formed, contained head, cauliflower will button and form small exposed curds if it's deficient in nitrogen or crowded so its growth is cramped. Yet, in good soil with adequate, even moisture, a snowy head of cauliflower is glorious. My friend Jeff wrote a poem to his 14-incher with giant winged leaves, calling it the condor of the garden.

My friends at Stonebridge Farm start Snow Crown (50–60 days), Candid Charm (65 days), and the purple Graffiti (80–90 days) in a greenhouse in mid-March for planting out at the end of April or beginning of May under row cover to avoid flea beetles. Carefully transplant starts and plant the stems deeply, up to the bottom leaves. If you

coleslaw. Cabbage juice is a well-known healer for stomach ulcers. Members of the cabbage family contain indoles (phytochemicals) that ward off cell changes that lead to colon, stomach, and breast cancers.

Some varieties to try include Golden and Red Acre (76 days), Early Market Copenhagen (heirloom, 68 days), and Mammoth Red Rock (heirloom, 100 days). Early Mountain Wakefield (65 days) has a tight, cone-shaped head, which means that bugs have a more difficult time finding their way in.

Cauliflower has been much more difficult and tricky for me, though some people grow it very well in our region. It has a weak root system and needs well-amended, fertile soil and frequent watering. Regularly adding some fresh compost around the plants (often called side dressing) helps. Cauliflower generally doesn't like hot weather, especially for forming heads, so most grow it to mature

Many varieties of cauliflower need to be protected from the sun by tying the leaves up around the heads.

What to Grow 151

want large heads, give each plant plenty of space. There are also orange varieties and a cone-shaped lime green hybrid called Veronica with spiraling pointy florets (sometimes called broccoflower, or Romanesco broccoli or cauliflower). High-altitude seed company Seeds Trust recommends Early Snowball (65 days) as the best OP variety for home gardens at higher elevations.

Chinese cabbage comes in two types. Bok choy (or pak choi or taisai) is the leafy type with delicious white stalks and dark green

Napa-type Chinese cabbages grow well in the mountains all season and as a fall crop on the plains and foothills.

crinkly leaves. There are twenty varieties available in Hong Kong, with the smaller-leaf types like baby bok choy preferred. It's cold hardy to just under 30 degrees and loves cool weather. It does especially well in the mountains and on the plains near the foothills in the fall. Penn Parmenter says Joi Choi "outshines them all" in her garden at 8,120 feet.

The heading or Napa type (pe-tsai) do well in the foothills and plains as a fall crop. But in the mountains, Napa cabbage is one of the most glorious high-yielding vegetables. Penn says they grow it all season, getting three crops (sometimes four) to one crop of head cabbage, and her favorite variety is Optiko.

Collards tolerate heat better than other cool-season greens. A traditional southern and African American dish, they have a somewhat bitter taste. I know gardeners who prefer these cholesterol-lowering,

Immune-system-boosting collards tolerate heat better than other greens. Frost improves the flavor; overcooking brings out an unpleasant taste.

immune-system-boosting greens to all others and munch on the young leaves just picked and raw. I haven't yet acquired the taste for cooked collards, preferring kale, a close relative. But since overcooking brings out an unpleasant taste, that may be the reason. The flavor improves with cold-weather fall frosts. Some varieties to try include Blue Max (68 days), Champion (OP, 74 days with good frost tolerance), and Georgia Southern (OP, 75 days).

Kale is a very cold-tolerant loose-leaf cabbage that tastes sweeter after a few fall freezes, but also holds up well in heat. Most require moderate water. It can usually be harvested through Thanksgiving, sometimes until Christmas. Aphids sometimes inhabit kale leaves in late summer. Wash them off

Purple-stemmed kale

with a direct stream of water from the hose, or remove infested leaves and feed them to your chickens as a treat.

Lacinato or dinosaur kale has long, narrow, deep blue-green savoyed (crinkled) leaves and matures in 50–60 days. Pick leaves from the bottom up. Red Russian, with red veins, also does well in both heat and cold. Johnny's carries a strain with purple veins and especially tender leaves (*Brassica napus pabularia*). Redbor (50 days) is a vigorous magenta ruffled kale. Other types have leaves that are green, red, or purple, and curly or frilly. Seeds Trust carries a dwarf blue-green Siberian and they say, "Mark in fall to facilitate finding delicate fresh greens in waist-deep snow."

Kohlrabi (50–60 days) is an oddball but crisp and delicious brassica with a sweet, nutty taste that also seems to do better in the fall. It's good raw or cooked. Harvest when the aboveground bulb (really a bulbous

Smooth-leaf, ribbed lacinato or dinosaur kale

Kohlrabi tastes great raw or cooked.

greenhouses, celery isn't harvested until late summer or fall at lower altitudes. The difficulty is that it doesn't like hot, dry weather, but doesn't grow quickly enough to mature while it's still cool.

At higher altitudes it's a completely different story. Mountain gardeners report great success growing celery. Penn Parmenter recommends Golden and especially Red Venture, which she says is "tough as nails—in the good way."

Celery needs fertile soil with lots of organic matter and good tilth so its weak taproot can easily penetrate. Add some organic fertilizer every few weeks. Celery also needs water more often than just about any other vegetable, so add an extra drip emitter or two, or plant it where you can regularly spray it with the hose. If you like to double-dig, celery will certainly benefit, but no-till sheet mulchers can grow it too.

To harvest, cut off individual stalks or the entire plant just under the soil line.

Celeriac is grown for its edible root, which tastes like celery. It takes a little longer to mature, but growing requirements are the same.

A much easier herb to grow on the plains is **cutting celery** or **leaf celery**. The stalk isn't edible, but the leaves will give you the celery flavor you want for soups and sauces. The young leaves are the mildest.

stem) is 2–3 inches across, before it gets woody. They will keep in the garden well after frost. Early Purple Vienna (60 days) is offered by Great Harvest Organics in Fort Collins and is beautiful grown with flowers.

CELERY AND CELERIAC

The gardeners I know who manage to grow **celery** consistently and well on the plains (and I'm not one of them) have sandy loam and plenty of water. Their celery doesn't taste much like the mild, light green, usually blanched celery you buy in stores; it's darker, richer, strongly flavored, usually more fibrous, and makes the best soups and soup stocks.

Celery takes a long time and a lot of care on the plains. Good-quality seed and varieties matched to growing conditions make a big difference. Started in March inside

FAVA BEANS

Fava beans (*Vicia faba*), or **broad beans**, are an ancient food eaten for centuries in many countries all over the world. They came to the New World with early Spanish settlers who grew them in cool, high deserts in North and South America. Unlike true beans, which require long days and warm soil to germinate and grow, favas are a cool-season legume seeded in the garden in early spring like peas, though they take roughly two weeks longer to mature.

While favas prefer loamy soil, they're adaptable and one of the few vegetables that will tolerate salty soils. Soak seeds before planting. Plants grow to about 3 feet high.

Windsor is an old English variety that takes 75–85 days. The 6-inch pods are filled with large plump beans that can be used fresh or dry. Aquadulce (90 days) can take much colder temperatures, down to 15 degrees.

They're best when young and pale green, and preparing them is relatively labor intensive. The easiest way to eat the beans is to harvest them when they're small and cook them in the pod. In Latin America they're popular fried, salted, and spiced as a snack. For dry beans, they are left to mature and are shelled before cooking. The bean's skin is often removed, too, which is relatively tedious.

Favas contain lots of nutrients and are especially rich in L-dopa, so they've been used to treat patients with Parkinson's disease. They are also poisonous to some people, more men than women, who have a genetic condition called favism.

Peas

Plant peas outside early, before any other vegetable, as soon as soil reaches 40 degrees. This is usually in March on the plains and April to early June at higher altitudes. Alternatively, you can sprout pea seeds indoors, grow them to about an inch or two high, and plant out with lots of mulch. Give them plenty of moisture. It can take a while (weeks) for peas to germinate, depending on conditions.

Fresh **garden or shelling peas** are exquisitely delicious, but shelling them takes work. If they haven't grown before in your garden, you can inoculate the soil with the nitrogen-fixing bacteria that helps them grow (available from seed catalogs and local garden centers). Most shelling peas grow 15–30 inches tall, with a few on taller vines. Maestro, Wando, and Little Marvel are favorites of Larry Stebbins, a well-known organic vegetable grower who runs Pikes Peak Urban Gardens in Colorado Springs.

Snow peas, with crisp edible pods, often grow well in spring and again in fall on the plains, planted in late July. Oregon Sugar Pod II (68 days) and Dwarf Grey Sugar (60 days) grow about 2 feet tall and don't need staking. Golden Sweet is an heirloom from India (65 days). Ho Lan Dow (65 days) is a sweet, crisp Korean bush type that does well in containers and doesn't need staking.

Snap peas have both edible peas and pods. Sugar Daddy (68 days) is a heavy-yielding favorite.

Root Crops

Beets provide a sweet, succulent, nutritious root and tasty greens too. They are a blood-building, detoxifying, cancer-fighting food. Baby beets are especially tender.

Beets like our bright light and cool nights but can also take some heat, so they do well in both spring and fall and become sweeter with freezing nights. Like other root crops, they prefer sandy soil but do fine in amended clay soil. Thin them (and eat the thinnings) and pull all surrounding weeds. Beets will keep growing without getting tough as long as they have room. They are frost hardy and can be left in the soil over the winter, especially if mulched. Early Wonder is reliably tasty at 48 days. Others are 55–65 days, including Detroit (good for canning, great greens), Golden (a little sweeter than red beets), Chioggia (concentric red and white circles when cut), Bull's Blood (hate the name, grown for tender red tops, but the 2-to-3-inch beets are nice too), and Red Ace. Beet greens are loaded with vitamins and minerals and are delicious steamed or braised. Eat the baby leaves raw in salads.

Growing **carrots** that taste great and are well shaped (though misshaped ones can be surprising, fun, and risqué) requires loose soil with good tilth and that's not too potent. In clay soil that's fertile and well

Colorful carrots at the farmers' market. They aren't just orange anymore.

amended with compost and lots of manure, carrots may not produce so well. Sometimes they get hairy and develop forks. They like plenty of organic matter that lightens up the clay but not too much nitrogen, so ease up on manure in the carrot bed. Sandy loam is perfect if you've got it. Raised beds work very well for growing carrots.

Even though they are considered a cool-weather crop, carrot seed can be very slow to germinate, especially in cold weather. Plant twice as deeply as recommended to hold in more moisture. Planting less densely means less thinning, but it's a very fine seed so some gardeners combine it with a little sand to make sowing easier. Carrots like sun but will tolerate some shade.

Chantenay carrots are sweet, crunchy, fat heirlooms, originally from France. Shorter than other carrots but bigger around (up to 3 inches in diameter), they used to have a yellow core until red-core varieties were introduced eighty years ago. Chantenays are good keepers.

The Nantes-type carrot, originally from the Atlantic Coast of France, is a medium-sized cylindrical carrot with rounded tip and top, known for its tender sweetness. Scarlet Nantes (65 days) is good fresh or stored and great for juicing. Yaya (60 days) is one of the best tasting: a sweet, crisp, crunchy, 6-inch orange carrot that holds well in the ground for several weeks. The small, round Tonda di Parigi (55 days, harvested at 1½ inches long) is an easy one for clay soil. Mokum (65 days) is very crisp and grows to 6–8 inches, or it can be harvested as a baby carrot.

The Danvers carrot, developed in Connecticut, tapers to a point at the tip and is known for tolerating heavy soils better than other types. Kuroda Chantenay (70 days, from Japan) will grow in poor soil, though it does better in good soil.

The longer Imperator carrot is the type most frequently sold in American supermarkets.

Carrots come in several colors. Dragon (70–90 days) and Purple Haze and Cosmic Purple (both 73 days and may be the same variety) have purple skin with orange inside and a sweet, slightly spicy taste. These purples are the most similar to the original carrots, first cultivated in Afghanistan in the seventh century. Burpee has a mix of purple, red, orange, and yellow carrots called Kaleidoscope (75–80 days). Seeds Trust carries Carnival Clown (90 days), a unique mix of multicolored carrots (including pink) developed by ThunderfooT (that *is* the correct spelling), a seedsman from northern Arizona who has been breeding for diversity and nutrition for twenty years.

If you hold off on watering for several days before harvesting, many carrots will concentrate their sweetness. But watering immediately before harvesting makes them easier to pull. I find that under thick hay mulch, carrots will keep well into the winter and can be pulled as needed. The greens are also edible and loaded with many healthy nutrients, including a lot of potassium, but they taste very strong.

Florence fennel, or **bulb fennel**, or **finocchio** (*Foeniculum vulgare azoricum*), is a delicious, mild anise-flavored bulb with a crunchy texture similar to celery that can be chopped up and eaten raw in a salad, roasted, or used like an onion or leek in soups and stir-fry. It becomes even milder when cooked. All parts of the plant are edible, though it's a different plant than the fennel grown for its fragrant seed (and offered as a digestive aid

after eating at Asian and Indian restaurants), though it was developed from it. I've grown Zefa Fino (65 days) in containers, since the seed packet warns that no other garden vegetable likes its company. It's a heavy feeder that likes our bright sun and cool nights.

Potatoes. When I traveled to Peru a few years ago to visit my daughter, we took the bus from Arequipa, in the south, to Cabanaconde, the end of the line at the top of the Colca Canyon, where the condors live. Late in the day, a few miles out from town, the bus stopped in a couple of spots to pick up sunbaked Peruvians, mostly woman, with thick, shiny blue-black hair who stashed huge sacks of potatoes and their shovels in the luggage compartment below, then climbed onboard, usually with a baby or two tucked into their bright clothing. If they were lucky, the bus wasn't filled with tourists and they found a seat; otherwise they stood.

In the little groceries we saw the the huge sacks, each one open at the top to display snowy white, pink, purple, red, brown, or golden yellow potatoes, round or oblong, from peanut-sized to small- and medium-sized. I've read that one Peruvian valley might have over a hundred different cultivars.

A few days later, as we headed back to the city early in the morning, the bus stopped to let off several Peruvian women, each with a shovel and an empty sack or two. As the bus roared off, we watched them climb the steep hillside for a day of digging and tried to envision them dragging such heavy sacks of potatoes down the hillside to the road.

In 1536, as the Spanish battled and eventually conquered the Inca in Peru, they brought the potato back to Europe. Since

Peru is close to the equator, the potato was adapted to a different day length and climate, and it didn't yield much. Eventually it was bred to become a better crop, but since breeding had begun with just a few varieties, the potato was not genetically diverse and was vulnerable to disease. In 1845, late blight destroyed the entire crop in Ireland, causing the Irish potato famine.

Today there are many varieties of potatoes available to plant in home gardens—at least sixty—and they are much more delicious with a much higher protein content than the big starchy russets that most of us grew up eating as fries and bakers. Many are loaded with high-potency antioxidants called anthocyanidins, which have been shown to strengthen the immune system and reduce age-related memory loss and the risk of some major diseases.

Potatoes like our high altitude with intense UV sunlight, much like their native Peru. They grow best in sandy, well-drained soil with a lot of organic matter and minerals, but not too much potassium, which produces higher starch and lower protein content. Most Front Range soil is clay and already contains a good amount of potassium, but if you build your soil and microbe population by adding compost and other organic amendments over time, it will balance itself out so don't worry about it.

Always buy "certified seed potatoes." There is no such thing as a "certified disease-free" seed potato, according to Paul New of White Mountain Farm in Mosca, Colorado, who grows a lot of organic potatoes. Because they are susceptible to dozens of diseases, and because they are grown in a concentrated way, no one can guarantee

disease-free potatoes. To prevent blight, New sprays the leaves with a concoction of compost tea, kelp, and fish emulsion.

Where rotting is an issue, it's recommended to chit seed potatoes by laying them out in a brightly lit room, but not in direct sun, for several weeks so the sprouts are already growing before planting. This is much less of an issue in our climate, but do it if you want. Seed potatoes don't look any different than regular potatoes. When you cut the larger ones up for planting, make sure each piece has at least two eyes or sprouts and is as big as a golf ball or bigger. Handle them carefully as the sprouts can break off. Let the cuts callous over to cure for a few days before planting.

To avoid disease, plant potatoes where other nightshades (tomatoes, tomatillos, peppers, eggplants) or raspberries haven't been growing for three or four years, and don't let any volunteer potatoes from previous years grow. Depending on the weather, plant on the plains around March 15 to May 1 (I've had some success planting even later too, but the harvested potatoes are smaller), mid-May to early June in the mountains. The leaves can be nipped by a hard frost, which will set back growth but usually won't kill them. If you're preparing a new bed in the spring, do it when soil isn't wet. Loosen the soil deeply with a fork so compost can sift down to the lower soil levels; this helps potato roots. Mix straw into the soil to keep it loose.

The traditional way to grow potatoes is to hill them. After planting the pieces 4 inches deep with sprouts facing up in a trench that's about 12 inches wide or in the middle of a 3- to 4-foot-wide raised bed, cover them up carefully. Space them about 12–18 inches apart, or more if dry conditions are a concern. As the stem and leaves grow at least 4 inches aboveground, mound up soil, or straw and soil, covering a quarter of the new growth. Keep mounding up soil and straw over another quarter of the new growth every week or two. This mound is where the potatoes will grow. Water consistently.

For those with less time and, like me, less inclination to follow through on the hilling, you can try the easy sheet-mulcher's method. Plant potatoes several inches deep and cover them with a thick layer of hay mulch (you want 6–8 inches minimum after it has settled). Hay comes in flakes, which you can partially pull apart, but don't spend a lot of time pulling them completely apart; partial flakes are fine because you want a thick layer. The Parmenters grow potatoes this way and point out that the plants are strong enough to push right up through the mulch, often causing a hay cone to erupt before they break through. The thick mulch also helps to hold up the young plants and protect them from wind. When the plants grow taller, add more mulch. The potatoes will grow in the dark layers. The key to mulching with hay in a vegetable garden is to lay it on thick. If green hay grass starts growing, your mulch isn't thick enough. Ruth Stout didn't even "plant" potatoes—she just threw the pieces on the ground and covered them up with thick hay.

As the flowers form aboveground on the plant, the underground tubers begin to form too, and it's especially important to keep the plants watered at this stage. Water less later, after the potatoes have formed.

Harvest with a fork to prevent cutting into the potatoes. Potatoes mature in 65–120 days, depending on the variety. They turn green and semipoisonous if they grow in sunlight near the soil's surface, so discard these or cut out the green part. Store long term at about 40 degrees after curing for a few days at 50–60 degrees; they will also store well for a while if left in the ground.

Radishes sprout fast and grow quickly. They like cool weather and, like most root crops, light loamy soil. At their best they have a crisp, tasty bite that's not excessively spicy. They don't like crowding, so thin them and pull any weeds; if you don't, they may not even develop. In hot weather, radishes get pithy and bolt. The good news is that if they do, you can eat the seedpods; they're crunchy and tasty. French Breakfast (24–28 days) is mild, cylindrical, and red and white. Easter Egg (25–30 days) is mild and a mix of colors. Botanical Interests carries a Rat Tail radish (40–50 days) that produces crisp, mildly spicy beanlike pods aboveground, even in hot weather, instead of edible roots. The larger Asian or daikon types are also delicious. You can plant them in May and again in late July on the plains (or 7–8 weeks before the average first fall frost). Seeds Trust likes Miyashige (50 days) for higher elevations.

Grow **rutabagas** like turnips for fall harvest. They're bigger—big enough for the Irish and Scots to carve for jack-o'-lanterns, though earthier and scarier than our cheerful pumpkins. They originated as a cross between the cabbage and the turnip, are considered a brassica, and have edible leaves as well as roots. I haven't eaten or grown these, but they are usually mashed with potatoes and/or carrots, onions, and butter.

Friends report they are delicious in a veg-etarian stew or curry.

Turnips grow well as a fall crop in our region, planted 8–10 weeks before first frost. These are vegetables that most of us didn't grow up eating, unless we had farmer or hippie parents, but they really are delicious so give them a try. Grown in the spring, they often taste stronger and sometimes bolt before they get big enough, depending on the weather. Japanese Haku-rei turnips (38 days, from Johnny's) are smooth, white, and crisp, sweet, and deli-cious raw. Cooking enhances their natural sweetness. Scarlet Queen (43 days) tastes and looks more like a big, crisp, mild rad-ish and has very tasty greens. Turnip greens are considered one of the world's healthiest foods, loaded with calcium and vitamins A, C, and K, among other healthy things. Purple Top White Globe (50 days) is a large sweet turnip with lots of greens, Seven Top is for greens only, and White Egg is sweet, mild, and a good keeper.

Warm-Season Vegetables
Beans
Beans are edible legumes. Grown for centu-ries by many different Native peoples in the Americas, they are a traditional food in the southwestern United States and throughout Central and South America. Many evolved in our high, dry conditions and intense sun-light. There are several types: bush, pole, snap (which used to be called string beans until the strings were bred out of them), runner, lima, and dry, and there is some overlap in these categories. All these beans grow in warm soil and won't tolerate frost.

They like full sun and soil with plenty of organic matter, but not too heavy on the nitrogen since they are nitrogen fixers. Beans take in nitrogen from the air and, through symbiotic bacteria in nodules in their root systems, convert it into nitrogen compounds for their own nourishment. These remain in the soil for other plants when the bean plants die.

There is no point to planting beans in soil cooler than 60 degrees. Wait until about a week after the average last frost date. They will only germinate when days are long and soil temperatures are warm. If we have a cool, late spring, germination can be spotty. If that happens, just sow again once the soil warms, or try a different variety. The gour-met tender French varieties often struggle in our climate. If you have a greenhouse, you can start beans in early May and transplant them outside when they're about 3 inches tall in the first week of June. That's what Barbara Miller of Boulder does, and then tucks them in with thick hay mulch. Plenti-ful pine needles also make good mulch.

Beans need consistent moisture at the roots, especially during flowering, and they are sensitive to salinity in soil and water. They also need phosphorous, which can be less available in *very* alkaline soils. This isn't usually a problem in organic gardens that have been well amended with compost and manure, but bone meal is a good slow-release source of phosphorous. Some gar-deners inoculate soil for beans with nitrate-forming bacteria sold in many catalogs and local garden centers, but the bacteria will also be there naturally if you've been build-ing your soil over time by adding manure and compost.

Bush beans mature more quickly than pole beans (climbers), but since they have smaller root systems they dry out faster. They also mature all at once. I don't have as abundant a source of water as some gardeners I know and since snap beans are thirsty plants, I like to soak seeds overnight, plant them every 6 inches and thin to 12 inches or more apart, in rows about 30 inches apart. This is more than usually recommended, but makes sense to me in our drier climate. Dense plantings require more water (and nutrients) as plants compete with each other. Cutworms can be a problem but less so in warm soil. Help protect seedlings until they grow larger with a temporary collar pushed into the soil around them (slices from the cardboard core of a paper towel or toilet paper roll work well).

Bush beans don't need any support. Jade (60 days) and Provider (50 days) are two prolific green varieties that grow very well. Golden Rocky (50 days) is bright yellow and tolerates cold better than most. Royalty Purple (55 days) is delicious raw, plus it germinates in cooler soils, tolerates light shade, and isn't bothered by Mexican bean beetles.

Limas grow both as bush and pole types. They like soil temperatures even warmer than snap beans, plus the plants are bigger and need more room. Most varieties mature in 65–75 days.

Snap pole beans take longer to get growing but are even more prolific producers than the bush varieties, over a more-extended period. Keep picking to keep vines productive. Pole beans produce more and use less ground space in the garden than bush beans. They need strong supports or trellises. Nylon mesh stretched between tall

The bright red flowers of Scarlet Runner beans attract hummingbirds. (Bottom) Pole (climbing) beans take longer to mature than bush varieties but are very prolific and don't dry out as fast.

posts works well, or tall wire fencing. Some people like to use the teepee approach, with tall poles lashed together at the top.

Rattlesnake pole beans (65 days) are considered drought tolerant because they can survive on monsoon rains in the Southwest. As green beans they are tender, dark green, and streaked with purple, or they can be left to mature and eaten as dry beans. Kentucky Wonder pole beans (67 days) are an old-fashioned high-yielding string bean variety, which some say still taste better than the stringless.

Runner beans like Scarlet Runner and Painted Lady (80 days, sometimes grown just for their pretty flowers) prefer cooler temperatures than other beans. They are native to Mexico but won't set fruit above 90 degrees. Relatively weak as seedlings (make sure soil is well prepared and loose so they can easily push through), the vines grow rapidly and vigorously; they need a tall fence or support. The pod is edible if picked very young, but most people grow them just for the beans, eaten raw or cooked. They can be harvested at fava bean size (7–8 inches) and cooked as shelling beans, or you can let them ripen until hard for dry beans in winter dishes. That's three harvests from the same plant. But the very best reason to plant runner beans is to give hummingbirds a good reason to visit your garden. They love the vivid flowers. Runner beans twine clockwise while all other beans twine counterclockwise. Keep this in mind when providing support.

Many gardeners skip growing dry beans because they take up needed garden space and are so readily and inexpensively available. But like most other home garden–grown crops, they taste much better than store bought. Most dry beans can be eaten early as green or yellow beans. When they rattle in their pods, they're ready to harvest as dried beans. Coco Bianco (62 days) is an Italian heirloom bush type that is most flavorful as a dried bean. One of the most beautiful (and great for baking and soups) is the Calypso with black-and-white yin and yang markings.

An adventurous gardener friend grew a variety of Asian long bean this year, intrigued by their picture and description in a catalog. Long beans are colorful and *very* long: 18–36 inches. She found the taste lacking, but they make great hair for a scarecrow.

CUCURBITS—CUCUMBERS, SUMMER SQUASH, WINTER SQUASH

There's no point in trying to get a jump on the season by planting warm-season crops in cool spring conditions. But once the soil has warmed to 60–65 degrees, they will germinate quickly and amaze you with rapid, vigorous growth. Pumpkins and winter squash need a long, warm growing season, but there are some early varieties. Summer squash and cucumbers mature in a shorter season.

You can use season-extending techniques to warm up the soil, and especially if you live at high altitude with a short growing season, this is a very good idea. Row cover, raised beds made of rocks, water teepees, plastic jugs and mulch, mini hoophouses, and black plastic mulch can all be used to good advantage. Since the soil in hills warms up and drains faster, this can be a good way to plant cucurbits. But hills also dry out faster, so using black plastic mulch on hills helps to retain moisture and heat. The sheet mulcher's all-purpose thick hay mulch works well for these crops too, just make sure the soil has warmed before you plant.

Some vegetables, the cucurbits in particular, grow better and stronger from seed. They don't like their roots disturbed so, as transplants, they struggle; plant them carefully with as little root disturbance as possible. Though most pull out of the transplant shock that sets in after planting, seeded plants can overtake a transplanted young cucurbit in short order. Bioactive compost teas and kelp sprays will help transplants acclimate. For areas with short growing seasons, transplants may be your best bet, though fast-maturing varieties will grow and produce from seed. On the plains, plant zucchini and winter squash first. When these come up and start growing, plant cucumbers. As these are growing, seed melons, which need the most warmth of all.

But sometimes things don't progress as planned. One year, rabbits ate every squash seedling that came up in my garden—two plantings' worth. Fortunately, I had also put in two zucchini plants that a friend practically forced on me. Though they sat there for almost three weeks without growing at all, they finally took off and provided me with the only homegrown summer squash of the season.

To foil the rabbits and overcome dry conditions and cold mountain temperatures, Penn Parmenter suggests capping each planted hill with a cloche and pulling some dirt and thick hay mulch up around the bottom so it won't blow away. This helps the plant germinate and become strong until it's time to remove the cloche. At 8,100 feet, Penn says that whenever possible she plants both seeds and transplants and waits to see who wins.

All the cucurbits like soil that drains well. Sandy loam is ideal, but you can grow them in any well-amended soil with good tilth and good drainage. If you're concerned about soil fertility, put some composted manure in the planting holes or add a cup of blood meal and a cup of bone meal for every 100 square feet (or a quarter cup of each per every 25 square feet).

Cucumbers are easy to grow from seed once the soil warms up. Transplants sometimes don't do as well because the young stems are so susceptible to damping off, especially in chilly weather. But Barbara Miller, a test grower for *Organic Gardening* magazine, grows her cucumbers from seed in a greenhouse in May, where they all germinate. She plants them outside at about 3 inches tall in early June. This way the cutworms don't eat them, which is what happens when she plants from seed outside. If you don't have a greenhouse, but do have a

Spacemaster cucumber is a prolific producer in a small space.

Cucumbers on vertical bamboo support structures produce more, save valuable garden space on the ground, and stay healthier.

sunny window and/or grow lights in a warm room, you can do the same. Some fresh air and a spray of chamomile tea or liquid kelp help strengthen the young stems and prevent damping off. Moving the plants outside on nice days for some fresh air is also helpful.

Cucumbers have an extensive but shallow root system. Water them consistently at the base of the plant, without getting the leaves wet, but don't ever let them stand in wet soil. If you've amended well, this won't be an issue because the soil will drain. Mulch to regulate moisture after the soil is warm. I use hay, but black plastic or weed barrier mulch helps keep the soil warm too.

In most years, cucumbers do very well in our climate. They're heavy feeders and most will produce better on fences or trellises than sprawling on the ground. This saves space in the garden and also provides a healthier growing environment. Cucumbers are natural climbers but you may have to weave their tendrils onto supporting twine or tie them up to get started. Try a dwarf bush type if you have a small growing space. Spacemaster was a prolific producer and the favorite of several friends in Boulder last year. At higher altitudes, cucumber plants need cover at night.

There are slicing and/or pickling, burpless, and some specialty types. Boothby's Blonde, Marketmore, Poona Kheera, and Diva (doesn't need pollination) are some recommended varieties. The rounded Lemon cucumber (58 days) is better adapted to dry conditions and lower soil fertility than others. Sweet and prolific, it has thin, edible skin; harvest while still pale, not bright, yellow. Golden Harvest Organics carries a miniature white heirloom cucumber. The plant stays small, works well in containers, and has a big yield of crisp, sweet, 3-inch cukes good for fresh eating or pickling. Cool Breeze (45 days) is a very early hybrid that's prolific, great for sweet pickles or fresh eating, and doesn't require cross-pollination.

Asian cucumbers grow up to 18 inches long, are crisp and delicious, and have a small seed cavity. Orient Express is very tasty and prolific. Pickle them when small for crisp results. The Armenians grow up to 36 inches long, are very heat tolerant, plus they don't need a pollinator. Technically, these are melons that taste like cucumbers. There are lots of other varieties to try (Baker Creek Heirloom Seeds lists thirty-eight).

Keep on top of harvesting so the plants continue to produce, and cut the fruit rather than pulling or twisting it off to prevent damaging the vine.

Cucumbers have a rejuvenating and cleansing effect on the body, and they contain silica, a trace mineral that strengthens connective tissue. Used externally, they sooth the skin, including sunburn and puffy eyes.

Squash

There are four species of squash: *Cucurbita maxima* (hubbard, buttercup, kabocha, banana, some pumpkins), *Cucurbita mixta* (cushaw pumpkin), *Cucurbita moschata* (butternut), and *Cucurbita pepo* (most have ribbed fruit, pentagonal stems with prickly spines—most pumpkins, acorn squash, spaghetti, delicata, summer squash,

crooknecks, pattypans, scallops, zucchini). You can also harvest squash blossoms, which are delicious but highly perishable and must be used right away; morning is the best time, before the flowers close up. The female blossoms develop into the fruits at the end of thick buds, but the male flowers on longer, thin stems can be harvested without reducing your squash harvest. Using floating row cover can speed up maturation by a week or two, but be sure to remove it as flowers start to form. Depending on required days to maturity, both winter and summer squash are good plants for the mountains. They don't mind the cool nights and they love the intense high-altitude sun.

Summer squash is native to North America and it grows very well in the West. It matures in a shorter season than winter squash, has a thinner, edible skin, and doesn't store well. Wait until after the last frost, when the soil is warm, to plant seeds. In very cold areas, use black plastic or weed barrier mulch and low rock walls to warm the soil. All squash like full sun, consistent moisture, and warm soil well-amended with compost.

Zucchini is an easy, very productive vegetable plant that makes even beginner gardeners feel successful. One or two plants are all you'll need, but plant a few extra seeds and thin out all but the most vigorous. Give each plant plenty of room, at least a 4-foot-diameter circle. Keep picking zucchinis when they're about 6–12 inches long, but if you miss one and it morphs into a big lunker, which can happen quickly, it's still good—not as tough and inedible as usually described. Pick it right away and put it in the

Heirloom winter squash: warty pink Galeux d'Eysines, blue-gray
Jarrahdale, and orange-pink Banana Jumbo.

shade where it will keep outside for a few weeks without taking over your refrigerator. One friend of mine even prefers the big ones because the seeds contain lots of protein. Make soup, bread, casseroles, and Mr. and Mrs. Zucchini Head for the kids. Line up some recipes ahead of time so you'll know what to do with your bounty. Juicing is always an option for extra produce.

Costata Romanesca (62 days) is an Italian heirloom. Cocozelle, Black Beauty, and Grey Zucchini (excellent flavor and good keeper) all mature in 53 days. My friends at the Zweck Farm, one of the oldest

family-owned organic farms in Colorado, say striped zucchini grows the best for them. Magda is a sweet, nutty-tasting Lebanese squash that resembles a short, pale green zucchini with more of a teardrop shape.

In *Gardening When It Counts,* Steve Solomon says many OP squash varieties degenerated as hybrids came to dominate seed catalogs, but Yellow Crookneck (58 days) is the exception. It's a great-tasting summer squash and a prolific yielder. Many of the hybrids may yield more, but they don't taste any better. Do we really need higher yields from summer squash?

Some consider Benning's Green Tint (55 days, pattypan) the best-tasting summer squash. White Bush Scallop (49 days) has a delicate nutty flavor, is high in vitamins and minerals, and is easy to grow. The pattypans are best harvested when small (3–4 inches) and tender.

Winter squash and pumpkins. There are so many varieties of squash in so many colors, shapes, sizes, and textures that you would be hard-pressed to grow them all over the course of a lifetime. Their lush, prolific vines and leaves wouldn't mind taking over the entire garden. A volunteer squash plant sprouted one summer in an already-planted garden bed of mine. Though I usually remove these because I read that squash cross freely within their species and usually produce inferior offspring, this one was so dynamic and healthy that I left it alone. Without any special attention, it sent out 15-foot vines in several directions and yielded nine nutty, sweet, delicious dark green kabocha squashes. I had never grown or eaten these before, so the seed wouldn't have been in my compost. Where it came from is still a mystery.

Heavy-duty trellises or fences that allow winter squash (or melons) to grow vertically and off the ground are a good solution to the space issue. One gardener I know lets them climb through her trees and festoon the branches with hanging squash lanterns. The stem always holds the weight of the fruit. Apparently, they need all that growth and photosynthesis to produce fruit, so don't prune the vines.

There are also some more-compact growers like Sweet Dumpling, Bush Buttercup, and Table King Bush Acorn. Sunshine is a hybrid orange kabocha-type winter squash that also stays fairly compact, forming a lush mound of green. Earlier in the season, in its immature form, its fruits can be eaten as delicious summer squash. Hopi Blue Ballet is a Native American semibush type with a vine that grows 3–5 feet. The plants each bear two fruits weighing 4–6 pounds, with a blue-gray exterior and sweet, fiberless deep orange flesh.

There are some other Native American squash varieties that my friends grow successfully, including Hopi Orange (90–110 days). It has beautiful, bright orange, round, flattened 10-to-15-pound fruits with yellow-orange flesh and good squash bug resistance.

I like the warty French Galeux d'Eysines, with smooth, sweet orange flesh. Then there's the Pink Banana Jumbo and several delicious hubbards in many sizes, shapes, and colors, including the elongated blue-gray Pikes Peak or Sibley.

Winter squash can usually withstand light fall frosts, especially if you use row cover. When harvesting, make sure to cut off each squash with a knife and leave a couple of inches of stem attached, otherwise it won't store well. If the stem breaks off, cook and eat the squash soon. Ideal storage conditions are 50–55 degrees and dry. A cool basement usually works. Most winter squash except delicata, acorn, and sweet dumpling benefit from curing, which means keeping them at about 70 degrees for ten days or so before moving them to a cooler spot.

The best culinary pumpkins have firm flesh and a sweet taste: Small Sugar, Winter Luxury, Cheese, Golden Cushaw, Jarrahdale (a gray-blue Australian) and Rouge vif d'Etampes (Cinderella). Lady Godiva is a good thin-skinned variety for highly nutritious pumpkin seeds.

Growing giant pumpkins has become a cult hobby, as told by Susan Warren in *Backyard Giants*. Joe Jutras from Rhode Island holds the world record at 1,689 pounds. Colorado isn't too far behind, though, with a new state record of 1,306 pounds set in 2010 by Pete Mohr of Longmont. There's nothing culinary about these pumpkins.

GLOBE ARTICHOKES

Globe artichokes can be fun to grow. A member of the thistle family, they have gorgeous soft purple flowers that bees adore. In my opinion, they are one of the best-tasting vegetables, though just getting to their succulent flesh involves patience. Growing them requires a fair amount of space and effort for a pretty small return, if you only look at it quantitatively.

Green Globe, the variety usually grown in Colorado as an annual, sometimes doesn't bud and bloom until the second year. Since artichokes don't reliably overwinter in many

Green Globe artichokes

Artichokes like a rich, loamy, warm soil and need a fairly long frost-free growing season of 85–95 days. Plant 4 feet apart. If the season is very hot, they can get tough. Don't delay harvest or the succulent heart will become a spiny choke.

Cardoon, a wilder thistle relative, is a favorite in Europe, though there is a small surge in popularity among gardeners in the United States who love a challenge. Preparing the stems for eating is especially labor intensive. According to my Italian American friend who grows it, carefully wrapping each mature stem with brown paper, cardoon is way more trouble than most Americans are willing to put up with. But it makes a spectacular statement in the garden with its massive presence and lovely purple flowers that bees of all sorts will visit. Just don't let it go to seed or you will have a cardoon plantation in no time.

parts of the semiarid West, the secret is to start them from seed every year in February and then convince them that they've been through a miniwinter and are in their second year. Exposing them to cold temperatures in this way, so they will flower and develop fruit, is called vernalization. The way to do it is to grow them in pots from seed. Soak the seeds first or germinate on moist paper towels, and sow some extra since about 20 percent won't come true. When they've developed into sturdy little plants with at least two leaves, move them to a cold, wind-free place where the temperature won't dip below freezing, though low 30s is okay. Up against a wall on the east side of the house can work, and you might need a warmer backup location where you can move the pots in case you have a spring cold snap.

The variety Imperial Star is said to produce more viable buds in the first year, which eliminates the need to trick the plant. The purple variety Violetta is tasty but has low yields.

Cardoon is closely related to artichokes. To soften and blanch the thick, edible stalks, wrap in brown paper three to four weeks before harvest.

NIGHTSHADES

The nightshade or Solanaceae family includes the most familiar American garden plant—the tomato—as well as peppers, eggplants, tomatillos, and potatoes (see cool-season vegetables). The family is also well known for various potent alkaloids, including the capsaicin in hot peppers, the nicotine in tobacco, and the powerful and potentially highly toxic tropanes in belladonna (deadly nightshade) and datura (jimsonweed).

Eggplant, or **aubergine** (as they say in the clothing catalogs), likes growing conditions very similar to peppers: fertile soil with a lot of organic matter, warm soil, warm air (optimally 80 degrees), full sun, and warm nights. Eggplants need a consistent supply of water, especially during flowering. As is true pretty much across the board, the better your soil the more it will retain water and oxygen and nutrients for your plants, the less you'll need to keep pouring on the water. Mulching after the soil is warm helps to regulate moisture.

Start from seed inside in early March, and plant in warm soil at the end of May on the plains or after the average last frost date. If soil is still cold, they will just sit there and refuse to grow. Cover plants with lightweight row cover to warm them up, especially at night. Black plastic or black weed barrier used as mulch helps warm up the soil. Water teepees work great for just a few plants (though they cost nearly five dollars each now).

Swallow (51 days), Millionaire (54 days), and Ichiban (58 days) are three dark purple Asian varieties with long slender fruit appearing before some other varieties are even flowering. Slim Jim (OP, 70 days) is a smaller, 6-inch elongated type. Kamo (60 days) is a Japanese heirloom. Black King (79 days) is a vigorous, high-yielding hybrid from Japan with 7-inch oval fruits. Rosa Bianca is an Italian heirloom, teardrop shaped with rose-lilac streaks. It can be grown in a 5-gallon container and it tastes great. Since the flowers are pretty and the fruit is stunning, put that container in a hot, sunny, prominent spot for all to see.

I once grew shiny orange rounded Turkish eggplants that were visually stunning but bitter because I let them go too long. They're best for eating when picked just slightly orange with some green striping, but I let mine turn brilliant orange-red, sacrificing taste for beauty. Peeling, quartering, and salting eggplant before cooking removes the bitter taste.

Harvest eggplants when still glossy, and cut them instead of pulling or twisting them off.

Chuck Rozanski of Jay Hill Farm has grown **peppers** in the Boulder/Denver area for more than twenty-five years and says, "Growing peppers in Colorado is neither easy nor impossible." He recommends starting with the easiest—sweet bell peppers and Anaheims, the standard chili relleno type—and growing your own seedlings under lights in an equal mix of topsoil, sphagnum peat moss, and vermiculite. This organic growing medium has enough nutrients without all of the artificial nitrogen and phosphorus that are in most commercial mixes (enough to produce little drug addict plants, says Rozanski, which is why they look so big and green when you buy them,

Peppers benefit from extra warmth (row cover, water teepees) when nights are cool, especially when they finally start producing in the fall.

in with very lightweight row cover (which allows in more light than heavier grades) to keep temperatures warmer for a week or two or until temperatures and the soil warm up. Water teepees work well if you're just growing a few plants. I grow peppers in big tractor tires, which hold in heat at the soil level pretty well. A little extra warmth and protection are also useful in the fall when the peppers are finally producing heavily, nights are cooling off, and frost is always possible. A number of gardeners I know put down black plastic as a soil-warming mulch around peppers and other warm-season crops like melons and squash; Rozanski prefers black weed barrier fabric because it allows water and air to pass through and keeps soil from blowing away during dry, windy winters.

Always check the soil before watering pepper plants. They don't need as much as other vegetables and, like squash, they sometimes wilt during the heat of the day, even when they don't need water, and then perk up when the sun sets. I use thick hay mulch almost everywhere in the garden. I pull it away from pepper plants so the soil warms up faster, and then replace it to help regulate moisture.

Rozanski grows more exotic peppers too, and at one time had over a hundred varieties before tomato spotted wilt disease wiped them all out in one season. He now plants the exotics in 2-gallon pots outside and moves them indoors under grow lights in the fall, first giving each one a bath with insecticidal soap.

Another great pepper to try is Jimmy Nardello (76 days), a thin-walled heirloom from southern Italy that's listed on Slow Foods' Ark of Taste. It's sweet raw and

but so often fail after planting). If you can't start your own from seed, buy starts from a reputable grower so you know what you're getting. They grow perfectly well without the chemicals.

You need to get them off to a quick and healthy start because we have cool nights and a relatively short growing season for peppers. As with other vegetables, if you've built organic soil that's alive with microbial life, you'll be giving them just what they need in the way of nutrients. But if you haven't, you can fill raised beds with purchased topsoil and add some extra bone meal or greensand for the phosphate peppers need to fruit well.

When you plant out pepper starts after the danger of frost has passed, tuck them delicious fried or stuffed with cheese and roasted. Many sweet bell peppers, including the miniatures, and less commonly grown brown chocolate bells do well here, though mine are often smaller than the ones market farmers seem to grow. Try Flavorburst for an especially good-tasting golden sweet pepper. Pinot Noir produces large, thick-walled, gorgeous purple peppers that are sweetly spicy but not hot over a long period until frost. An equally beautiful variety for containers is Gusto Purple, with 2-inch pointed hot peppers. Usually, the hotter the pepper variety, the more it will tolerate cool, wet weather.

Tomatillos (*Physalis ixocarpa* and *P. philadelphica*) are sprawling heat-loving plants in the nightshade family, native to Mesoamerica. Start them from seed indoors about four weeks before the average last frost and transplant in the garden at the same time as tomatoes. They like the same growing conditions as their tomato, pepper, and eggplant relatives, warm soil and sunshine, though they're better at handling less water. The fruit grows inside papery hanging lantern husks, and it's ripe when it fills the husk or splits it. Typical wire tomato cages work better for tomatillo plants than they do for heavier tomato plants, but you can let them just run free and spread if you have the room. It's not unusual to have volunteers come up in subsequent years after planting them.

Botanical Interests carries Toma Verde, which grows 3–6 feet high, with green fruits. Purple de Milpa has a sharp but sweeter taste than other varieties and stores better. The ripe fruits are about 2–3 inches in diameter, depending on the variety,

and are great in Mexican dishes and salsa. Remove the husk and rinse before using. Expect a big yield from each plant.

Everyone seems to loves growing **tomatoes**, but like other warm-season vegetables, success depends on timing, the weather, and the varieties you choose. Planting in well-amended healthy soil that's rich in humus and compost is a given. Three or four tomato plants are usually enough for fresh eating for a small family, but plant more if you plan to put up sauce, salsa, or the like. I usually plant too many—more than I'm able to process—but I always factor in that one of my tomato plants may succumb to some type of wilt or disease, in which case I just pull it out and dispose of it with no regrets (but not in the compost pile, where it could spread disease).

Tomatoes are not an especially easy vegetable to grow in our climate because of our cool nights and drying winds. In 2010, everyone complained that theirs tasted bland, but no one knows why. Tomatoes need some fussing over, so don't be discouraged if it takes a little while to get the hang of growing them. If you create a microclimate by warming the soil, blocking the wind, and staking them well, tomatoes will often reward you. Consistent watering is also crucial and, in order to avoid a condition known as blossom end rot, where the bottoms of the tomatoes turn brown, drip irrigation is the easiest way to accomplish this. Then again, this condition could be caused by a calcium deficiency. It's always something. If you don't have drip lines on your tomatoes, make sure you water at the soil level and keep water from the sprinkler or the hose off the leaves to avoid diseases.

Water teepees were designed for growing tomatoes, but they will help any warm-season vegetable get off to a great start. Set them up a few days before planting to warm up the soil. You can also use plastic gallon jugs, which are free. First cut off the bottoms, remove the caps, and push them down into the soil where you plan to plant, mulching around them to make sure they won't blow away. After warming the soil for a few days, remove them one by one and plant a tomato inside, then replace the jug. Water teepees perform like Cadillacs, plastic jugs like Volkswagens.

It's easy to grow your own tomatoes indoors from seed under lights. The hardest part may be deciding which varieties you want to grow. Most heirlooms taste better but ripen later than hybrids. I grow a couple of cherry tomatoes to tide me over since they always ripen first. Some good choices are Sungold (57 days, orange-yellow, always very sweet, reliable, and early) and Pop-In (60–65 days, red, teardrop shape). Black Cherry (75 days) is also very tasty but it's not early. Galina (59 days, yellow Siberian) is very productive at higher altitudes and when the weather cools. Study seed catalogs for descriptions in late fall or early winter so you can decide and order seeds in plenty of time for sowing indoors, and before companies run out of the varieties you want. It happens.

Always sow seeds in a sterile, but good-quality starter mix, with mycorrhizea if you can find it; the cheap soil mixes tend to crust over as they dry, making it hard for seedlings to push through. I use plastic trays with clear plastic domes on top, opening them occasionally to make sure too much humidity doesn't build up. The Jiffy

Pots sold everywhere (they're flat until they puff up when you water them) have netting around them that doesn't disintegrate, so I don't use them. Since it's often cool in the house in February and March, I use heating pads on the lowest setting for bottom heat, which speeds germination considerably. If you can find one with a thermostat that turns on and off, that would be ideal, but most just turn off. Heat mats specifically for growing are also available. They're pricey but can be a good investment once you're serious about growing from seed.

Always water seedlings with warm water. As a preventative measure, or if your seedlings show signs of damping off (stems turn black, leaves droop, plant withers, or soil mix has a white fuzzy growth), spray with chamomile tea, which works well.

Tomatoes are much less fussy about transplanting than many other warm-season crops. Every time you pot up or plant out tomatoes, remove a lower branch or two and plant the stem deeply because roots will grow out from it. Some lay the plant out almost horizontally in the garden, burying the roots and half of the stem, but be careful; it's easy to break the plant doing this. Pinch off any lower branches that will be covered up. Add some mycorrhizea or kelp to the water and/or the planting hole, or spray with compost tea to give plants a boost.

Indeterminate types are tomatoes that sprawl all over the place and require a lot of room, while determinates grow more compactly. In any case, most tomatoes will need to be staked at some point and it's a lot easier to put a support structure in place while plants are small. Many tomato cages, especially the funnel-shaped ones that you stick in the ground, aren't strong enough or tall enough to support the weight of a mature tomato plant. T-posts or rebar with a doubled row of sturdy twine for the plant to grow in between is one method that allows you good access for picking the fruits—an important consideration. Make sure there will be enough space around the mature plant for you to get in there and pick!

Recommending tomato varieties is as subjective as recommending movies. Some do better than others in different years under different conditions. Here's a list of heirlooms favored by myself, gardener friends, or the Boulder Culinary Gardeners group: Black Krim, Jaune Flamme, Aunt Ruby's German Green, Green Zebra, Mortgage Lifter, Golden Egg, Taxi, Brandywine (red and yellow), Caspian Pink, Moskvich, Red Siberian, Black Prince, Sasha's Altai, and Silvery Fir Tree. The last five are good choices for the mountains, though above 7,000–7,500 feet tomatoes should be grown under cover at night.

Cherokee Purple does very well in Pueblo and the lower Arkansas Valley as well as farther north on the plains. Hybrids that many western gardeners like to grow include Celebrity, Fantastic, Early Girl, Better Boy, Sweet Baby Girl, Big Beef, and Sweet 100. Though not the best for eating fresh, Amish Paste and Oregon Spring are great for cooking and sauces. Likewise, Principe (Princess) Borghese, Juliet, San Marzano and the paste tomatoes are excellent for dried tomatoes.

OKRA

Okra is a warm-season vegetable that loves heat. It prefers the steamy climate of the southeastern United States (or India) but will grow here in our drier soil and air as long as it has lots of heat and good drainage. I love okra, especially in Asian dishes, but I've only grown it once and managed to harvest a grand total of three okra pods from very small plants. One night of temperatures dipping into the low 40s can stunt the plant's growth permanently, so maybe that's what happened.

Though I've seen a few okra plants at spring farmers' markets in the last couple of years, you'll probably have to start your own from seed. Soak the seeds overnight to soften them up for germinating. I've read that okra doesn't transplant well, so take extra care not to disturb the roots if you do. Gerald Miller, a great gardener from Pueblo who grows it successfully, says he starts it from seed in early May and plants it outside in the first week of June. Water teepees that warm the soil will give okra a good start and keep it warm at night. Plants should be about 15–18 inches apart and they will eventually get tall—4–5 feet or more if you're lucky.

Don't let weeds compete with okra plants, and mulch heavily once the soil warms up. Okra is in the hibiscus family and has a pretty yellow flower. Pick the pods when they're about 3 inches long. Once the plant starts producing, this will mean picking every couple of days. Like beans, it will slow or quit producing if you quit picking. Okra isn't a water hog and it's not a super-heavy feeder as long as the soil has been built well with organic matter and humus. This is a vegetable that will probably take some trial and error and may do better in some years than others.

My neighbor used to grow a lot of okra, and every bit of it was in demand every year.

By starting early using a traditional hotbed method he learned in France, his okra plants became very tall and productive by mid-July. A hotbed uses fresh manure (frowned upon by all cooperative extension experts because of potential pathogens, especially in feedlot manure). Chris got his from farmers he knows and animals that roam and eat grass in large pastures. He first created the hotbeds by piling up fresh manure and straw on the ground or in a bunker where it heats faster. He says the pile needs to heat up to 140 degrees or more, which can be checked with a soil thermometer. On top of the pile he created a framed-in planting bed 8–12 inches deep using good soil mixed with compost, and he covered it with old windows, just like a cold frame. He planted okra seed in a tray inside on top of the bed in mid-March, then transplanted it into the planting bed and covered the whole thing with plastic since the frame is leaky. The plants have no direct contact with the hot manure for at least four months, when their roots may extend down into it. He only removes the plastic cover later in the spring for ventilation when the plants are really getting too hot, even though temperatures outside are still cool. The hotbed method is still used for growing vegetables in Europe. It takes a lot of observation and monitoring, but the manure makes perfect compost for planting by the following year.

SUNFLOWERS

Grow your own sunflowers for seed (both for you and the birds), as windbreaks, and to support vining plants like pole beans. Commercial sunflowers are sprayed with some extremely poisonous pesticides. Furadan, or carbofuran, one of the most toxic pesticides available, was banned by the EPA in January 2010, though the manufacturer is suing to overturn the ban. It kills bees and birds that ingest a single grain, instantly. A Colorado sunflower grower was fined $30,000 in 2008 for deliberately applying it on the surface of his sunflower field instead of burying it, killing 2,200 migratory birds.

Grow tall sunflowers on the north side of the garden so they won't shade other plants, that is, unless you want to create shade. Plant in clumps 20 inches apart after the last frost, and cover the seeds with a loose netting to protect from birds. Thin each clump to the strongest plant.

Sunflowers need good drainage and do best with regular water, especially once flowers start to develop. The big ones that produce edible seed are very heavy feeders. Give them composted manure, slow-release fish fertilizer, and some liquid seaweed with trace minerals. Feed often but keep fertilizer off the stems so they don't rot. When heavy winds are predicted, withhold water so they're less likely to blow over. They don't usually need staking.

Climb a stepladder to cover the flower heads with a mesh bag or loose burlap bag to protect seed from birds after the petals fall off and the seeds start to swell. Harvest the flower head by cutting the stalk at the base. Remove seeds when they aren't soft or damp, and finish drying out of direct sunlight. You can rub the flower head across 1-inch wire mesh into a bucket to remove the seeds.

A great variety for seed is Sunzilla, a hybrid with a strong thick stalk that supports huge seed heads. Others are Mammoth Grey Stripe, Titan, and Kong.

Sweet corn

Corn has become the emblematic monoculture of the United States. Corn products are in much of our food, especially refined food products, as well as in lots of other things, from kitty litter to gasoline. The practice of doling out huge government subsidies to giant agribusiness companies to grow genetically modified field corn on millions of acres of land with systemic-pesticide-treated seed that harms pollinators, contaminates non-GMO corn, and requires vast quantities of water to grow in soil that has become lifeless in order to produce products like soft drinks that make us obese and unhealthy and litter for our pets to poop in seems absurd at best. If you like to eat corn, you had best find local, organically produced sweet corn or grow it yourself.

You'll need at least 75–100 sunny square feet and a raccoon-free or raccoon-proof plot. Fresh-picked corn, eaten before the sugars turn to starch, is a scrumptious treat.

But raccoons can seriously spoil the fun of homegrown sweet corn. Seriously. Lots of home gardeners, including myself, have thrown up their hands and quit after being beaten to the harvest by the little bandits too many times. After fifteen years I decided to try once more this summer. Tying into our existing hot wire around the pasture, I put up a three-strand hot wire tape fence around the planted corn at 6, 12, and 18 inches above the ground using plastic temporary fence posts that easily stick into the ground. That did the trick and no one got shocked—not even me!

If you grow grapes, which raccoons also love to plunder, and plant corn near the grapes, you can enclose both with the hot wire. You'll only need it for a few weeks as the corn and grapes ripen, then you can disconnect it until next year. It sounds like a much more difficult process than it actually is, though it is a project. Once you gather your materials, including a charger (solar chargers work very well), it will only take an hour or two to set it up. You can also put the hot wire on top of a taller wire fence, out of reach of people and pets, and disconnect it during the day. If you need help, your best bet is to find someone who has some experience with livestock. And if you're put off by the thought of electrocuting a raccoon, don't worry—you won't. Most animals detect the current and stay away, though a raccoon may loudly protest being denied access. Getting zapped is, well, shocking but not injurious, as I can personally attest.

Another method, gentler although less reliable, is to surround the corn patch with a thick band of winter squash as guard plants. They're prickly, which raccoons and skunks don't like, but it will also make it more difficult for you to get to your crop.

Corn is wind pollinated (though bees love to gather the pollen), so it's necessary to plant a stand that's dense enough for effective pollination to occur—at least two, three, or four rows, or several circles, as opposed to one long single row. If space constraints make that impossible and you still want to try, you can hand pollinate. This involves cutting off the tassels (the male flowers) at the top and shaking the pollen onto the silks below, which are female pollen tubes. Every single silk must receive some pollen in order to develop a fully-kerneled ear. An ear with gaps in the kernels has been poorly pollinated. The pollen is ready a few days after the silks emerge, when bees begin to visit (it's a brief window of a few days). Recent declines in bee populations mean that you may not be able to count on their appearance, though. Plant seeds every 4–6 inches and thin out the less-vigorous plants, leaving one about every 12 inches in rows about 30 inches apart, or every 18 inches on center. Too much crowding produces small ears. If climate or conditions are especially dry, thin plants to farther apart, which usually also increases the size of each ear. If side shoots develop, don't remove them. Given enough growing room, smaller ears sometimes form on the side shoots, a trait called tillering, which breeders usually try to eliminate. These side ears take an extra week or so to mature.

Seed will germinate in soil that's 60 degrees or warmer, usually in mid-May on the plains. The warmer the soil, the more quickly corn seeds will sprout, so it's worth waiting for soil to warm up. In the mountains, plant hardier short-season varieties in early June, or when the soil is warm enough. Flowering time is determined by day length. Northern varieties flower when days are long and nights are cool. Seedlings of most varieties are not frost tolerant, but a few (Extra Early Bantam, Fisher's Earliest, and Sugar Buns hybrid) will survive a light frost. Open-pollinated varieties tend to bounce back more quickly from frost damage than hybrids. A few are described as able to germinate in cooler soil.

Corn needs moderately rich, fertile soil with some aged manure and compost throughout the bed, not just in the planting holes, plus consistent water throughout

Traditional multicolored ornamental "Indian corn" is all starch and, while technically edible, tastes extremely bland.

the growing season. In our climate, corn is best planted in depressions to catch and hold water than in hills, where it runs off. Remove all weeds, and add some organic fertilizer in early July, when the plants have grown to at least 12 inches.

If earwigs become a problem (they're often present but don't harm the corn), you can apply a mixture of vegetable oil and a little soapy water to the tips of each ear a few days after the silks emerge. Bt is also effective.

Buy seed from a trusted company. All commercial corn used for livestock feed (field corn, not sweet corn) and some sweet corn seed is treated with pesticides that are systemic and harm bees. Plus, much sweet corn today is tainted through unavoidable crossing with commercial genetically modified corn. Some companies have signed the Safe Seeds Pledge, a commitment that they "do not knowingly buy or sell genetically engineered seeds or plants," and some test their corn seed for genetic contamination.

The terminology gets complicated, but normal or traditional American sweet corn varieties are classified as sugary (*su* on the seed packet). There are also sugary-enhanced (*se*, *su se*, or *se+* on the packet) or supersweets or extrasweets (*sh2* for "shrunken2"), which are two to three times sweeter, plus their sugar-to-starch conversion is slowed down so their sweetness holds longer. All these se and sh2 types are hybrids, except Candy Mountain (70 days), a very early nonhybrid supersweet variety recommended for the mountains or the plains, and a good one for saving your own seed.

Bodacious and Ambrosia (its bicolored version) are both se hybrids recommended by Larry Stebbins of Pikes Peak Urban Gardens.

Hybrid sweet corn varieties with bigger, fuller, more-uniform ears will always outperform OP types as far as the size of the ears and sweetness. Hybrid breeding focuses on taste, kernel size, the bicolor trait, and sugar-enhanced and supersweet characteristics. Some say nutrition is at odds with these since hybrid sweet corn produces more bulk with less nutrition than OP types. Small growers (like Alan Reed Bishop in Indiana and Joseph Lofthouse in Utah, as well as longtime researchers like James Brewbaker in Hawaii) are breeding OP multicolored, sugary-enhanced, pest-resistant, and drought-tolerant corn. Multicolored corn contains high levels of anthocyanins, amino acids thought to be important cancer fighters because they scavenge free radicals.

If you like sweet, juicy, traditional twentieth-century corn (who doesn't?) plant hybrids. But try planting a few OP types too. My recent crop was a beautiful multicolored OP variety called Painted Hills (different than the ornamental Painted Mountain) that were mostly tall and vigorous, with some smaller plants. It was very tasty but not supersweet, and, like many OP varieties, it didn't hold its tenderness very long on the stalk, though that may have been inept harvesting on my part. Picking corn at the right time (and planting in succession so

Painted Hills open-pollinated, multicolored, edible corn. Though not as supersweet as hybrids, it's very tasty *and* beautiful.

it doesn't ripen all at once) is crucial for best flavor. The husks had beautiful sunset tints, and each ear had a different distribution of colored kernels—light and dark blue, bright and pale yellow, and red. The ears were slimmer and some were shorter than the hybrid corn we're accustomed to, but I liked seeing all the variation.

Now I'm interested in trying some others: Spring Treat (71 days), an early yellow sugary-enhanced hybrid, and Blue Jade (70–80 days), a dwarf steel blue, tender sweet heirloom corn that produces 3–6 ears per plant and can be grown in containers.

Corn smut fungus turns normal kernels into large, gray-black distorted galls, harvested in Mexico while still immature as an earthy delicacy.

My Painted Hills developed some corn smut, probably a result of using a sprinkler and getting some of the lower ears wet. A friend who cooked some in an omelet said it tasted pretty good. He told me the gray-black fungus is considered a delicacy, known as "Mexican caviar." I tried it too, but was not convinced of its culinary worthiness.

Martian Jewels (80–90 days), a cross of several varieties, has a hardier, richer taste than most sweet corn, plus the cob is purple with white kernels. It's a Seeds of Change original, along with Rainbow Inca Corn.

Paying customers might not go for them yet, but home gardeners can afford to indulge

in experiments with older, more nutritious and vigorous varieties, and some of the newer crosses with them. After all, corn has been growing in the Americas for thousands of years. Hopi farmers planted theirs 8–12 inches deep, where moisture from winter and spring storms remained in the sandy soil. The seedlings quickly elongated, pushing through a foot of sandy soil, and survived just fine until the summer rains materialized. Thanks to its quick adaptations and mutations, corn has become the most widely planted crop in US agriculture and, ironically, the most uniform monoculture in existence.

EASY-TO-GROW HERB COMPANIONS

Easily grown annual herbs are a great addition to the vegetable garden, and many attract beneficial insects. **Cilantro** is an easy-to-grow cool-season green that self-sows freely. **Dill** attracts lots of beneficial insects. **Basil** is a great warm-season companion plant for tomatoes, said to improve their flavor, while

Dill weed attracts lots of beneficial insects. It's a host plant for the black swallowtail butterfly larva (caterpillar).

A bed of Holy basil or Tulsi tea (*Ocimum tenuiflorum*) between rows of sweet basil (*Ocimum basilicum*).

Both German and Roman chamomile are helpful in some way to nearly every plant in the garden.

vegetables. It attracts loads of bees and other pollinators, adds trace minerals to the soil, and freely self-sows. **German chamomile** is an annual said to improve the flavor of many crops, especially cabbage and onions, plus it accumulates minerals, which are then returned to the soil. **Roman chamomile** is a tougher perennial that will grow in poorer soils. Both are considered helpful to almost every plant in the garden.

Parsley is a vitamin-rich perennial.

And there are many other perennial herbs. **Sorrel** grows wild in the mountains. The garden variety is a power-packed, nutritious, somewhat bitter green that makes excellent soup. It's a vigorous grower so I removed it from the garden bed and gave it its own separate spot. **Parsley** is a vitamin-rich, health-giving perennial that doesn't like to be moved and gets along well in the asparagus bed. **Mints** and, to a lesser degree, **oregano** are aggressive growers so should be contained in some way or grown in an area separated from the vegetable beds. A mulch

the tomatoes can in turn provide welcome afternoon shade. Italian mountain basil (from Seeds Trust) is delicious and can absolutely take the cold nights in the mountains. **Borage** is a great companion plant for most

What to Grow 179

of mint clippings is said to help beets grow. **Bronze fennel** and **tarragon** are two other tasty perennial herbs that are less aggressive. **Comfrey** is a deep-rooted aggressive grower that can be easily propagated by dividing the root; just slice some off with a shovel and plant. It has several garden uses, including a great compost and fertilizing plant that adds nutrients to garden soil. It's also invaluable as a healing herb for injuries with inflammation and swelling, wounds, and burns. Contain it

Mints are invasive growers beloved by bees. Grow in containers or in their own spot away from the vegetable garden.

so it doesn't spread, unless you want to grow a lot of it. Finally, the West is sage country and, though from the Mediterranean originally, **culinary sage** does very well in western gardens with little care, especially with a little afternoon shade.

PERENNIAL VEGETABLES
Asparagus, rhubarb, Jerusalem artichokes, and horseradish are the most familiar perennial garden plants. But there is a movement afoot to grow more perennial grains and vegetables for food so that land doesn't have to be plowed up every year and fertilized for annual crops. Wes Jackson at the Land Institute in Kansas has been spearheading the research on grains for a number of years. For gardeners, Eric Toensmeier has written a guide to more than a hundred perennial vegetables that produce for at least three years and aren't just novelty plants.

I've grown **asparagus** both from roots (crowns) and seeds, which only take one additional year. Since a healthy asparagus bed will be productive for twenty to thirty years, it's worth building healthy soil, finding the best sunny location where the plants won't be disturbed by digging or growing other crops, and planting fresh healthy roots or seeds of productive varieties.

Asparagus likes fertile soil but doesn't need a lot of nitrogen. It also needs frequent deep watering until it's established, which takes about three years. Good drainage is very important too, so the roots won't rot. Create beds where corn or asparagus hasn't grown previously. Wherever a cover crop has been grown and turned under would be ideal.

Because asparagus is both a deep-rooted perennial and a heavy feeder, it greatly benefits from double-digging, if you're able and willing, and from forking in some extra nutrients like composted manure, coffee grounds, kelp, bone meal, blood meal, or alfalfa meal, or a combination of some of these. Locating the bed where you've sheet mulched for a year or two is another good approach, or you can plant asparagus in raised beds filled with planting soil to a depth of at least 12 inches with some extra organic amendments and nutrients. In short, invest some time and energy into creating the best possible bioactive bed and you will reap the benefits of delicious, productive asparagus for many years to come.

The main reason asparagus beds degenerate over time is because they get too crowded. Either they were planted too closely to begin with or the female plants drop their ripe red berries, which are seed-balls, into the bed every fall where they sprout and quickly start competing with the mature plants. To prevent this (or unless you *want* to propagate asparagus from seed), dig up and remove the entire crown and roots of the female plants—the ones with berries—before the berries turn bright red and drop. Do this continually until you have a bed that's all male plants, about 24 inches apart. The males live longer and produce earlier than the female plants, their spears are bigger, and the plants are more productive because they don't expend energy making seeds. Always remove grass and weeds from the bed every year while they're still small. If your asparagus bed has become overgrown and unproductive, rejuvenate it by carefully digging up and separating crowded plants. Use the extras to start another or give them to friends.

There are several hybrid varieties of asparagus now available that have just male plants, which saves you the trouble of culling the females: Jersey Supreme, Jersey Prince, Jersey Giant, Jersey King, and Jersey Knight, all developed by Rutgers University researchers (in New Jersey). They are billed as doubling or tripling the yield of the standard OP variety, Mary Washington. However, as a heads-up, Steve Solomon

mentioned in *Gardening When It Counts* that growers of all male asparagus varieties have reported some disease problems.

Through selective breeding, at least two other OP varieties have been developed: Mary Washington Improved (80–90 days, very hardy and productive, better yields and tighter tops, but less disease resistant than the original), and UC-72 (110–120 days, 70 percent male plants, heavy yields, a little larger than Mary Washington). There are also a few types of purple asparagus, which is sweeter: Purple Passion and Sweet Purple are heirlooms with both male and female plants, and there is at least one hybrid available.

I've planted seed right in the well-amended, weed-free, permanent bed, as well as crowns. It's often recommended to seed a nursery bed and then transplant after a year, but I don't see the point. I also don't plant in the bottom of a trench and gradually fill in the soil each year as I've read. Too much trouble, though it might be a perfectly good method. If you're growing a variety with all or predominantly male plants, the seed (if you can get seed) will be more expensive, and you won't be removing any female plants so you might want to plant them farther apart at the outset instead of thinning so many. Eventually, the mature plants should be spaced about 24–30 inches apart. If you have or can create a situation where weeds won't encroach and be a constant problem, you can also just plant asparagus here and there around the garden or in an orchard.

Rhubarb. Unless you're a big fan of rhubarb and have a lot of room, one plant should be plenty for most home gardens. When I read in gardening books about how to space rhubarb plants in rows, I wonder what they must be thinking. It's a giant in the vegetable garden and a heavy feeder. Rhubarb needs well-drained soil with an extra amount of organic matter—more than most other vegetables—and a sunny spot where it won't be in the way. It does better when the planting area has been amended well before digging the hole.

During cooler conditions in the spring and fall, it thrives; when it's hot, growth slows. Sometimes an impressive seed stalk forms, but you should cut this off.

Plant crown divisions in early spring and dig a big hole, ideally 3 feet wide and at least 2 feet deep, so the large, mature root system will have plenty of room. You can divide a mature plant by slicing off a chunk of the root and making sure each division has at least one eye (bud).

Water rhubarb consistently, even when it's dormant, so the roots won't dry out, but check the soil to make sure it isn't wet. Side dress with compost in summer and fall, and apply mulch.

Don't harvest at all during the first year. Harvest stalks that are at least an inch thick in the second and third years and go easy. By the fourth year, you can harvest all you want, but don't take more than half of the stalks at one time. Always discard the leaves, which contain toxic amounts of oxalic acid and are poisonous.

A friend who lives near 9,160 feet has the biggest, most amazing and prolific rhubarb patch I've ever seen. He throws all his wood ashes on it. Maybe his mountain soil is acidic because despite all the potassium and calcium they contain, highly alkaline wood ashes concentrate salts and are considered

a gardening no-no on the plains, where the soil is alkaline to begin with. But his plant sure loves those ashes!

Jerusalem artichoke, or **sunchoke,** is a tall plant in the sunflower family, native to North America and grown for its tasty vitamin- and mineral-rich tubers, much like a

Jerusalem artichoke, or sunchoke, is an easy-to-grow North American native perennial grown for its tubers.

potato except they contain inulin (not insulin) instead of starch. They are good raw, thinly sliced in stir-fry or salads, roasted or baked like potatoes, plus they make a killer dip.

The plant actually prefers medium-heavy soils, so it's an easy one to grow without much fuss if it has sun. They spread rapidly so give them their own spot, separated from other garden plants. When the leaves die back after the first frost, dig up and harvest the tubers as needed. As your patch multiplies, dig them up and give them away to gardener friends. Plant tubers 3 inches deep

Horseradish is an extremely vigorous, mineral-rich root that also makes an effective pesticide.

Heirloom Moon and Stars watermelon was considered extinct until 1980. It grows huge with long, hot growing seasons, but mine still tasted great.

and 2–3 feet apart in early spring (or as soon as you get them from a friend). Unlike potatoes, they don't keep well out of the ground, so either keep them moist or leave them in the ground.

Horseradish does very well in most climates—almost too well. It's vigorous to the point of invasive. Plant in a location where it will be naturally contained by something impenetrable, like concrete, or grow it in a big container and keep a lookout for signs of spreading from the bottom. It's a valuable nutritious and medicinal plant, used for thousands of years because it contains minerals—potassium, calcium, magnesium, and phosphorus—and antibacterial oils. Once dug for harvesting, the root should be used immediately since it doesn't keep. Early leaves are good in spring salads, and roots should be harvested after growth stops in the fall. It makes an effective pesticide for voracious blister beetles and Colorado potato beetles.

FRUITS

There are many fruits that a home gardener in the West can grow. Growing tree fruits and shrubs like cherries, apples, peaches, plums, mulberries, grapes, currants, and so forth provides enough material for an entire book. But here are a few fruits that many home gardeners love to grow with or near the vegetable garden and so are worth including.

Melons and watermelons. Melons need very warm soil to germinate, with best results from 75–95 degrees. They will sprout in cooler soil down to 60 degrees, but it takes longer. Rocky Ford, Colorado, at an elevation of 4,871 feet, is famous for its cantaloupes grown from greenhouse-sown transplants, mostly using drip irrigation and black plastic mulch to keep the soil warm and the weeds down. (More accurately they are muskmelons, a name marketers apparently dislike; cantaloupes are smooth skinned or have a few ridges and very light netting.)

An item under the heading "Cantaloupe Eccentricities" in the April 29, 1908 *Market Growers Journal* speaks to the special qualities that our western climate imparts to irrigated melon crops:

> It seems next to useless for the eastern grower to attempt to seriously compete with the westerner. Eastern cantaloupes are frequently well flavored, but they seldom, if ever, possess the inviting spice of the western product of perpetual sunshine coupled with irrigation.

Depending on the variety, most muskmelons need two to three months of warm temperatures (80 degree or higher during the day and above 60 degrees at night) to produce the sugars that create great-tasting melons. Jacquie Monroe of Monroe Organic Farms, known for its delectable melons, says muskmelons like our cooler nights and dry climate. They don't grow true cantaloupes at their farm anymore because the flavor was never as good as muskmelons; however, they do grow delicious honeydew melons. Though my experience is admittedly limited to a few varieties and a few years, I've grown Oka muskmelon (83 days, a sweet, delicious heirloom) and Moon and Stars watermelon (I only got one melon, but love that pattern on the rind) from transplants sown inside

in late April. My best-ever watermelons were round Winter Queens, the size of basketballs, from a plant purchased at a sale. They're known for being good keepers; we ate the last one on Thanksgiving and except for chilling just before eating, it wasn't ever refrigerated. As with winter squash, there are many, many different kinds to try.

Tractor tires warm up the soil for melons, which need a warm start.

Here are a few that gardener friends with amended clay soil have grown and recommend: Tigger (a small Asian melon that's crisp like an apple, but not especially flavorful); Collective Farm Woman (Ukranian heirloom with pale yellow flesh); Jenny Lind (76 days, heirloom, sweet green flesh); Rocky Ford Green Flesh (85 days, heirloom); Hannah's Choice (hybrid muskmelon from Cornell's breeding program); and Goddess (68 days) and Earlichamp (75 days), two hybrids with good disease resistance. Athena is a honeydew with light green flesh. Orange Dew, with orange flesh, is offered by Golden Harvest Organics Seed Company.

At lower altitudes on the plains, try both direct seeding and transplants, without disturbing the roots. Melons like humus-rich soil and nitrogen, so if you haven't already well amended your soil with composted manure, mix some (or a little bone meal and blood meal) into the planting hole. You can also plant where nitrogen-fixing beans have grown previously. If you have sandy loam soil and plenty of sun, you will no doubt have great success growing melons. They are susceptible to powdery mildew and wilts, so plant disease-resistant varieties and if you're not using drip, don't let the leaves get wet when you water.

Row cover will speed up growth in the beginning of the season and during cold snaps, but for melons, support the cover so it doesn't touch the plants, and remove it as soon as buds start to develop so pollinators can reach the flowers. It's best to wait for a warm spell before seeding and setting out plants since a cold beginning can stunt the plants permanently. As the melons ripen you can put bricks, flat stones, or flakes of hay under them.

Burrell Seeds, in Rocky Ford, has been in business for 110 years. Though it was sold to new owners recently, they still specialize in melon seed, both heirlooms and hybrids, and give the following growing advice:

Melons growing on top of water-filled barrels in Barbara Miller's greenhouse.

If planted in hills the rows should be 5–6 feet apart. Plant 10–12 seeds per hill 2 inches deep and thin to one or two plants when they have 5–6 leaves. Keep free from weeds and cultivate (hoe) around the plants often, 8–10 times or more. (Hoe shallowly close to the plants, more deeply farther out.) If under (furrowed/flood) irrigation, cantaloupes should be watered about every two weeks. Continue watering throughout the season but as the melons become softball-sized or larger stop watering them to avoid fruit rot.

Melons are a difficult crop in the mountains unless you've got a greenhouse, but Seeds Trust's catalog, which states that they've searched the world for the fastest-maturing melons, offers Sugar Baby Watermelon (73 days, drought resistant) and Minnesota Midget cantaloupe (75 days) for higher altitudes. Foliar feeding will speed ripening. A light spray of compost tea or a fish/seaweed product that has time to dry before late afternoon won't harm the leaves.

Who doesn't notice a huge difference between supermarket **strawberries** and home garden grown? Strawberries are one of the most pesticide-intensive commercial crops, and even the organic ones don't come anywhere close to the melt-in-your-mouth flavor of your own fresh picked. This makes sense when you consider how tough they have to be to hold up through picking, packing, transport from California, unpacking, and display.

Monroe Organic Farms consistently has delicious fresh strawberries for sale at the farmers' market in the spring and the fall.

They're not cheap, nor should they be for that quality and taste. Their secret? It's the soil—old river-bottom sandy loam on the northeastern plains. They amend it every year, adding manure and compost, replacing and building up nutrients, and feeding the microbial soil life, instead of just taking whatever they can get.

But even without sandy loam, you too can grow strawberries at home that are more delicious and tender than any you'll ever find at stores. And though some experienced mountain gardeners have told me that, except for the tiny alpine strawberries, they are unable to grow "soft fruits" including strawberries at high elevations, Penn Parmenter disagrees—vehemently. She has seen some amazing, prolific, and even naturalized strawberry patches in gardens at 8,000–9,000 feet in the Wet Mountains with delicious, sweet berries as big as any in the stores. So don't underestimate the gifts of the mountains. Not all soil is sparse and rocky; there are rich pockets of glacial and river bottom soils. The sunlight is extremely intense. The season may be short, but conditions in some microclimates at very high altitudes support rapid growth of some of the most nutritious, high-quality food anywhere.

Not including the alpines, there are three strawberry growing types: June bearing, everbearing, and day neutral. Despite the name, most June bearers actually ripen heavily in July in most of Colorado. They are often said to be the most flavorful type, and though they produce for a shorter time than everbearers, their overall yield is larger, unless a late spring frost hits the flowers, in which case there won't be many to harvest. If you want a big crop all at once, this is the type to plant. Varieties recommended by CSU Extension include Honeoye, Kent, Guardian, Jewel, Redchief, Delite, Mesabi, AC Wendy, Cabot, and Bloomiden.

Profumata di Tortona and Capron Musk are a couple of June bearing musk strawberries from Italy. Native to Europe and genetically different from both alpines and other garden strawberries, they are said to be profoundly delicious and aromatic, with hints of raspberry and pineapple. "Said to be," because I don't personally know anyone who grows them. The plants are bigger than other strawberries—about 18 inches high—and they require a little more water and nutrients. The fruit is more rounded. In the first two years, musk strawberries don't produce much but then they bear heavily, though briefly, in June (probably into July in the semiarid West). Because they aren't self-pollinating, both varieties must be grown together; a ratio of five Profumata to one Capron is recommended. These are gourmet berries and more expensive than other strawberry plants.

Everbearing types are the hardiest in our region. They produce reliably the first year in June and again in the fall, with a few in between. Fort Laramie, Ogallala, and Ozark Beauty (probably the most popular), all everbearers, are the ones sold most often in garden centers.

Day-neutral types flower and fruit more consistently over the entire growing season than everbearers. Tristar, Tribute, and Fern are three recommended by CSU. Mara des Bois strawberries were introduced by a French nursery in 1991. Favored by chefs and sought after by gardeners who have tasted it, this strawberry has caused several of my gardening friends to ruthlessly rip out all their other varieties, which they say pale in comparison. Mara des Bois has a medium-sized fruit with a sweet aromatic flavor and is too tender for shipping, so it will never be available commercially. And there are others; I'm trying one called Sparkle this year.

Strawberries need sun; eight hours is usually recommended, though some shade, especially in the afternoon, benefits them in my plains garden. They like a moderately rich, loose soil with good tilth that drains well. It's usually said that strawberries need plenty of water, but if you use a drip system and give them small amounts consistently so they never dry out, they'll grow beautifully. Year-round mulching is very beneficial, especially with the addition of fall leaves. I shred leaves in the fall so they'll break down more quickly and put them under thick straw or hay mulch along with some compost. Keep on top of the weeds; mulch helps a lot. Lettuce and spinach are good garden companions for strawberries. Every few years (three to four) you will probably need to rejuvenate strawberry plants by moving them to another bed, transplanting the runners and newer plants. One gardener friend moves some Mara des Bois inside in pots in late fall and manages to pick some winter berries since it's a day-neutral type.

The biggest challenge to growing strawberries in my garden, and I know this is even more true for mountain folk, is defending the crop from birds, or at least working out some kind of sharing arrangement. A chicken-wire enclosure is the most secure solution.

Like strawberries, **raspberries** are perennials, and there are two different growing types. The crown and roots of raspberries

Raspberries like lots of organic matter, good drainage, and consistent water. Many can still produce with some shade.

come back every year, but the canes that grow aboveground typically live for just two years and are biennials. In what used to be the standard varieties, known as summer-bearing raspberries, the canes don't flower and produce fruit until July of their second year. These second year fruiting canes are known as floricanes.

Wild raspberries, on the other hand, often flower and produce inferior, seedy berries during their first year on first-season canes, called primocanes. Breeders used this trait to develop fall-bearing or primo-cane-bearing raspberries (also known as

everbearing) that flower and develop viable fruit the first year on the top portions of the canes. Today, most of the raspberries grown in Colorado are primocane-bearing variet-ies. In general, this type grows better along the Front Range, while both types grow well on the Western Slope.

What makes the fall-bearing types simple to grow is that you can just cut off or mow down the old canes every winter, because new fruiting buds will develop on new canes the following spring. Don't compost the spent canes—dispose of them, because they can contain pests or disease.

But if you grow some of both types, summer-bearing varieties that are hardy here and fall-bearing varieties, you can extend the raspberry season from July until fall freeze.

Joel Reich from the Boulder County Extension office says that by pruning off just the top fruiting portions of the fall-bearing canes in late fall, you will also get some fruit in July from the lower canes of the fall-bearers, while the new primocanes are still developing. But the earlier, secondary crop may be at the expense of the fall crop

Summer-bearing varieties recommended by CSU Extension for the Colorado Front Range include Nova and Boyne. On the Western Slope, add Killarney, Latham, Newburgh, and Titan to those two. The following fall-bearers do well throughout the state, at elevations up to 8,500 feet: Autumn Britten, Anne (yellow-fruited), Polana, Jaclyn, Joan-J (nearly thornless), Himbo-Top, Redwing, August Red, Heritage, Fall Red, Fall Gold (yellow-fruited), and September. Always buy disease-free varieties.

Black and purple raspberries are considered less hardy, but my four-year-old Jewel Black (hardy to zone 4) is doing fine so far and fruiting well. A friend has a very old and huge thornless blackberry that's sweet (many are not) and climbs all over a trellis. He has no idea what variety it is, and though I and others have tried several times to propagate cuttings, we have yet to succeed. Triple Crown is one of the best blackberries for western climates.

Raspberries like lots of organic matter in the soil and good drainage. I'm fortunate to live near an organic dairy, so I buy some of their composted cow manure (which they test for salts) for my garden and my raspberries, and I use straw or hay for mulch. Raspberries like consistent water; especially when it's hot, don't skimp! But hold off on watering after a frost so they can harden off. Along with all your trees, especially fruit trees, give them a good soak in late November and maybe once a month after that to help them through our typically dry winters.

Raspberries can take some shade, though it may depend on the variety. Mine get about six hours of sun, and are in filtered shade after that. A friend in Denver grows some on the north side of the house and gets a decent crop of berries. Some grow better with trellising support (put it in place before they grow large) as well as periodic thinning to stay productive and allow you to reach the fruit. Amazingly, birds don't like raspberries, but, as I discovered, horses will devour the plants. The dried leaves make an excellent vitamin- and mineral-rich tea.

Chapter 12
Saving Seeds

The tradition of saving our own garden seeds almost disappeared in the latter part of the twentieth century, but gardeners today are starting to recognize its importance and take up the practice.

Humans have been savings seeds for thousands of years. Just a century ago, our food came from roughly 1,500 plants, plus thousands of different cultivated varieties. People saved their own seeds because there was no other choice, and they selected the best plants from the varieties they liked because they tasted good, yielded early, kept their kids healthy, resisted pests, thrived with less water, tolerated early frosts, or any number of other reasons.

The United States is a country of immigrants. Many brought seeds with them from their homelands and passed these heirlooms on through the generations. Pots of planted vegetables even filled the fire escapes of city tenements.

But the tradition and art of seed saving almost disappeared in the latter half of the twentieth century. As more people moved to urban areas and suburbs, home food gardening became less popular than lawn care. People were buying their food in supermarkets, with produce trucked or flown in. Fast food and junk food replaced vegetables in our national diet. The continuing disappearance of small family-owned farms overshadowed a back-to-the-land movement in the early 1970s. Today, just four plants—wheat, rice, corn, and soybeans—provide more than 75 percent of the calories humans consume, and that diverse pool of 1,500 food plants has shrunk to about 30.

As more-profitable hybrids came to dominate the seed industry, many of the smaller seed companies that had carried collections of unique home garden, open-pollinated vegetable varieties went belly-up. Big seed companies swallowed up little ones.

In 1975, Seed Savers Exchange was founded in an effort to locate and preserve heirloom seeds. Today, some thirty-five years later, a renaissance in food gardening is under way, based largely on a desire for more sustainable healthy living, but also on survivalist fears of possible future food shortages. Whatever the reason, seed saving is finally beginning to catch on again.

Saving seeds is both simple and complex. The act of harvesting and saving seeds is simple. And the reproductive systems and genetics of some plants make it easy to know for sure that the seeds you collect will produce the plants you want. But wherever diversity exists, there is complexity in plant sexual reproduction and more possibility for genetic variation. It isn't always straightforward.

The seeds worth saving come from open-pollinated varieties, not hybrids. Seed from hybrid varieties does not produce plants that come true and have the same traits and characteristics as the parent plant, and in most cases hybrid offspring will be plants that disappoint.

Vegetables like lettuce and tomatoes are annuals that produce seed in their first year. Carrots and beets are biennials that flower and produce seed in their second year. Some plants have both male and female flowers on the same plant, while others have just female or just male flowers. Some are "perfect flowers," meaning they have both male stamens that produce pollen and a female pistil that receives pollen. Some plants are self-pollinating, while others won't accept their own pollen. Insects (mostly honeybees) pollinate most flowers, but the wind manages it for all the grasses, including corn.

Because different varieties of some species will cross readily with each other, it's necessary to isolate them in some way, either by physical distance, or by planting them to mature and flower at different times. For example, all of the brassicas (broccoli, cabbage, Brussels sprouts, kale, and so forth) will cross with one another. Squash types and varieties within the same species will cross; acorn will cross with delicata, but not with hubbard or butternut.

Physically separating plants any significant distance is very difficult in a small garden and where neighbors' gardens are next to each other in adjoining lots.

The list below includes the easiest, most straightforward vegetables for seed saving, which is a good place to start. (For more advanced and detailed seed-saving techniques, see *Seed to Seed* by Suzanne Ashworth and *Basic Seed Saving* by Bill McDorman.)

Once harvested and cleaned (if necessary), seeds should be kept in a cool, dark, and, most important of all, dry place for storing. Put seeds in plastic bags and put the bags in airtight glass jars. Old vitamin bottles with silica packets work well too. Label them right away so you don't forget what you have collected.

Easiest Vegetables for Seed Saving
(Ideal separations listed are for commercial growing. Viability numbers assume proper storage.)

Beans (*Phaseolus vulgaris,* or common bean). Flowers of common green beans are perfect and self-pollinating, and cross-pollination by insects is rare. Ideal separation: 150 feet. Home garden reality: Don't grow two different varieties side by side, and never grow two different white-seeded varieties next to each other because you won't be able to tell if crossing has occurred.

Allow pods to dry brown and harvest

about 6 weeks after the eating stage. If a freeze is expected before pods are ready (and row cover or other protection won't suffice), pull up the whole plant by the roots and hang it upside down in a warm, dry place until pods are brown. Break pods by hand or flail (crush) larger amounts.

Viability: 4 years

Lettuce (*Latuca sativa*). Perfect, self-pollinating flowers form in small heads of 10–25 flowers. All open on the same day for a short time, usually in the morning, and form one seed each. Ideal separation: 20–24 feet. Home garden reality: 12–20 feet for different varieties.

Seeds ripen at different times over a period of 12–24 days after flowering. Harvest when half the head has gone to seed. Shake seeds into a paper bag, or cut off the top of the plant and let it dry upside down in a paper bag. Screen if necessary to remove the chaff (dry plant debris).

Viability: 3 years

Peas (*Pisum sativum,* garden and edible pod pea). Perfect, self-pollinating flowers; cross-pollination by insects is rare, but possible. Ideal separation: 50 feet, or grow another crop that flowers at the same time in between different varieties. Home garden reality: Pea varieties rarely cross-pollinate.

Allow pods to dry brown, four weeks after eating stage. If a freeze is expected and row cover won't suffice, pull up the whole plant by the roots and hang it upside down in a warm, dry place until pods are brown. Open pods by hand or flail (crush) larger amounts.

Viability: 50 percent germination for 3 years

Peppers (*Capsicum annuum*). Perfect, mostly self-pollinating flowers, but honeybees and solitary bees also pollinate them. Studies show up to 80 percent crossing. Ideal separation: 400 feet. Home garden reality: 50 feet with a tall flowering crop in between.

Harvest fully ripe peppers for eating and save the seed. Most peppers start out green and change color (turning yellow, orange, red, purple, or black) when fully ripe. If a freeze is expected and row cover won't suffice, pull up the whole plant by the roots and hang it upside down in a warm, dry place. Cut off the bottom of the fruit and reach in to harvest the seeds in the center.

Viability: 50 percent germination for 3 years

Tomatoes (*Lycopersicon esculentum*). Perfect, self-pollinating flowers. Most modern varieties have short (retracted) styles so cross-pollination is very rare; in heirlooms and older varieties with longer styles it is more common, so greater separation is needed. Use a magnifying glass to examine the flowers. Don't save seed from varieties with double flowers since they're more prone to insect pollination. Ideal separation: 10 feet for short-style varieties, 100 feet for long-style varieties. Home garden reality: Extent of crossing is controversial and opinions differ. Some growers don't see crossing even when tomatoes are grown next to each other.

Allow tomatoes to fully ripen before harvesting for seed. If that isn't possible, pick the unripe green fruit and let it slowly ripen in a cool dry place. Let it change color before harvesting seed. Cut the tomato into halves across the middle (equator) and squeeze out the jellylike substance with the seeds into a small glass or jar with a little water. Loosely cover and put in a warm place for about three days, stirring once a day.

A layer of fungus will appear on top— this is a good thing. After three days, fill the container with warm water and allow contents to settle. Carefully pour out the water, tomato pulp, and floating immature seeds. Repeat until water is almost clear. Pour clean, viable seeds at the bottom of the jar into a strainer to drain. Dump seeds out onto a paper towel to dry thoroughly for a day or two, break up the clumps, and store.

Viability: 4–10 years, depending on variety

Other easy vegetables, flowers, and herbs for seed saving are chives, mizuna, arugula, orach, marigolds, cosmos, dill, nasturtium, gaillardia, bachelor buttons, zinnia, basil, penstemon, rose mallow, and calendula. When you harvest your own seeds and plant them out the next year, you help plants adapt to local conditions over time. Bill McDorman, owner of Seeds Trust

high-altitude-seed company, who traveled to Siberia to collect vegetable seed, tells the story of a gardener there who had been given watermelon seeds from a well-meaning American. Since watermelons grow best in long, hot seasons, Siberia is not the climate of choice for growing them. But Sasha tried anyway, reaping golf ball–sized melons the first year. He planted those seeds and grew tennis ball–sized melons the next year. He did this for several years until he was finally able to grow full-sized watermelons.

By buying seeds each year that are grown in other climates and locations, we actually deprive plants of their genetic adaptability. Seed libraries are a good way to keep local plants' genetics in our communities at the grassroots level. I know of several that have been started by home gardeners recently in different parts of Colorado. Gardeners check out seed for free, grow out a few of the plants for seed, and return twice as much as they originally took from the library. It's another demonstration of the abundance of nature. Now if we could just get over that twisted need for domination.

Appendix
Best Plants for Pollinators

Grow some easy, climate-appropriate flowers and western natives for native pollinators along with your vegetables. Annual bachelor's button or cornflower (*Centaurea cyanus*) is easy from seed and now endangered in its native habitat in England. Bees love it.

POLLINATOR CONSERVATION POINTERS

- Plant a lot of flowers. Some newer, fancy hybrids, especially those with double flowers, have lost their effectiveness as hosts for pollinators, so stick close to the original species.
- Plant several of one species of flower for pollinator efficiency. Access to pollen and nectar is different for each species and pollinators have to learn how for each one.
- While honeybees are generalists that visit many different types of flowers, native pollinators (bumblebees, solitary bees, and so forth) visit specific, host plants—mostly natives. Plant as many native species as possible to support them.
- Don't use pesticides.
- Don't treat trees with trunk injections of systemic neonicotinoid pesticides like imidacloprid, which has been linked to colony collapse disorder and has been banned in several European countries.

BEST PLANTS FOR POLLINATORS

All plant species listed are visited by honeybees, which are generalists for nectar or pollen. Additionally, those species that support and are pollinated by (sometimes more effectively) bumblebees or hummingbirds are indicated by **B** and **H**, respectively. Native plants, indicated by **N**, are visited by all bees (honeybees, bumblebees, and native bees).

TREES

Ash (*Fraxinus* spp) good pollen, some nectar, much propolis

Aspen (*Populus tremuloides*) pollen, much propolis **N**

Black locust (*Robinia pseudoacacia*)

Buckeye/horse chestnut (*Aesculus glabra/ hippocastanum*)

Buffaloberry (*Shepherdia argentea*) early **N**

Catalpa abundant nectar including from nectaries on underside of leaves a week before flowers bloom, thru the bloom period and about ten days afterward

Chokecherry (*Prunus virginiana*) **N**

Crab apple

European spindle tree (*Euonymus europeus*)

Golden raintree (*Koelreuteria paniculata*)

Hackberry (*Celtis occidentalis*)

Hawthorn (*Crataegus*) generally good nectar quality, like tree fruits where sufficiently planted

Honey locust (*Gleditsia triacanthos*) not as good as black locust

Japanese pagoda tree (*Sophora japonica*) bees love it, good for nectar but depends on soil and other conditions

Beautiful western native shrub *Purshia mexicana*, or cliffrose, was first collected in Montana on the Lewis and Clark expedition in 1806.

Linden/basswood (*Tilia americana*)

Mayday tree (*Prunus padus commutata*)

Oak (*Quercus*) good for pollen

Pussywillow (smaller *Salix*)

Russian Olive (*Elaeagnus angustifolia*) one of best spring honey plants

Willow (*Salix*) much early nectar and pollen **N**

SHRUBS

Abelia **B**

Antelope brush (*Purshia tridentate*) **N**

Apache plume (*Fallugia paradoxa*) **N**

Blue mist spirea (*Caryopteris*) **B**

Boulder raspberry (*Rubrus deliciousus*) **N**

Brooms (*Cytisus*)

Buddleia butterfly bush **H**

Cliffrose (*Cowania mexicana*) **N**

Cotoneaster

Desert false indigo (*Amorpha fruticosa*) **N**

Lilac **B**

Mahonia (*Mahonia repens*, *M. fremontii*) **N**

Manzanita or bearberry (*Arctostaphylos*)

Mountain lilac (*Ceanothus*) closely related to buckthorns, honey and pollen, rarely surplus

Mountain mahogany (*Cercocarpus*) **N**

Redbud (*Cercis canadensis* or *occidentalis*) early spring brood rearing

Rose (wild and cultivated) much pollen **N**

Saint-John's-wort (*Hypericum kouytcherise*) **B**

Sand cherry (*Prunus pumila*) early nectar and pollen **N**

Serviceberry/Juneberry (*Amelanchier*) pollen and nectar **N**

Siberian peashrub (*Caragana*)

Snakeweed

Snowberry (*Symphoricarpos albus*)

Spirea

Sumac (*Rhus glabra*, *R. trilobata*) **N**

Viburnam (North American varieties *dentatum*, *lentago*, *trilobum* or *Viburnum opulus* var. *americanum*)

Wolfberry (*Symphoricarpos occidentalis*)

FRUITING TREES, SHRUBS, PLANTS

Apple

Apricot (especially Asian) **B**

Blackberry

Cherry (wild and cultivated) **N**

Currant (*Ribes*) pollen and brood rearing **B**
Elderberry (*Sambucus canadensis*) pollen
Grape (*Vitis*) pollen, some honeydew from leaves
Gooseberry (*Ribes hirtellum*)
Nanking Cherry (*Prunus tomentosa*)

Wolfberry (*Lycium pallidum*), native to semidesert western
US shrublands is beloved by many different pollinators,
especially butterflies. (Not to be confused with
Symphoricarpos occidentalis, also called wolfberry.)

Plum (wild and cultivated) early **N**
Peach often too early for bees
Pear much nectar
Raspberry
Strawberry
Wolfberry/goji berry (*Lycium barbarum* or *L. chinense*)

COVER CROPS
Alfalfa
Buckwheat
Clover **B**
Cowpea (*Vigna sinensis*)

HERBS
Anise hyssop
Basil
Bee balm/bergamot
Borage
Catnip
Chives
Comfrey
Coriander
Dill
Fennel
Lavender **B**
Marjoram
Mint (all)
Motherwort
Oregano
Rue
Sage
Santolina
Sorrel (*Rumex acetosella*)
Thyme
Wormwood (*Artemisia ludoviciana*)

VINES
Virgin's bower (*Clematis virginiana*) **N**
Honeysuckle **B**
Hops
Hyacinth bean **H**
Silver lace vine (*Polygonum aubertii*)
Trumpet vine (*Campis radicans*) **H**
Virginia creeper (*Parthenocissus quinquefolia*)
Wild grape (*Vitus*) **N**

VEGETABLES (WHILE IN FLOWER)
(All plants in this section also attract native bees.)
Beans
Broccoli
Corn good pollen source (if not toxic)
Cucumber
Kale (overwintered) **B**

Melon

Mustard (*Brassica campestris*) pollen and nectar

Onion (flowers) pollen and honey

Parsnip where grown for seed

Squash

Turnip where grown for seed

WILDFLOWERS AND NATURALIZED WEEDS

(All plants in this section also attract native bees.)

Broomweed

Chickweed

Chicory

Cleomella (*Cleomella angustifolia*)

Dandelion

Figwort (*Scrophularia marilandica* Simpson honey plant)

Fireweed or willow herb (*Epilobium angustifolium*)

Gumweed

Heartease (*Polygonum*)

Locoweed (*Astralagus* spp.)

Milkweed

Mustard

Phacelia

Rocky Mountain bee plant (*Cleome serrulata*)

Showy rosinweed (*Silphium speciosum*)

Teasel

Thistle **N**

Vervain

Viper's bugloss (*Echium vulgare*) **B**

Wild cucumber/manroot

Wallflower

PERENNIALS AND GARDEN FLOWERS

Agastache hyssop **B, H**

Agave **H**

Ajuga bugleweed

Aster **B**

Bee balm (*Monarda fistulosa*) **N**

Butterfly weed (*Asclepias tuberosa*)

Campanula

Catmint (*Nepeta*) **B**

Centaurea montana

Cerinthe

Columbine **B, H**

Coreopsis **B**

Common native blanketflower (*Gaillardia aristata*)

Crown vetch (*Coronilla varia*)

Cyclamen **B**

Datura **B**

Delphinium **B**

Eriogonum

Foxglove (*Digitalis*) **B**

Echinacea

Goldenrod (*Solidago*) **B**

Globe thistle (*Echinops sphaerocephalus* Chapman honey plant)

Sea holly (*Eryngium maritimum*)

Euphorbia

Gaillardia

Gaura **B**

Hellebores **B**

Geranium (wild) **N**

Germander (*Teucrium canadense* or *lacinatum*)

Hollyhock (*Alcea rosea*)

Indigo weed (*Baptisia tinctoria*)

Joe-pye weed **B**

Lamb's ears (*Stachys lanata*)

Lamium/nettle

Larkspur

Liatris gayfeather **N**

Lupines

Malva mallow

Monkshood **N, B**

Mullein (*Verbascum*) **N**

Penstemon **N, B, H,**

Peony (single flowered only)

Phlox **B**

Polygonum

Poppies (especially California poppies)

Prairie coneflowers (*Ratibida angustifolia, pinnata,* or *columnifera*) **N**

Prickly pear cactus (*Opuntia*)

Prunella selfheal

Purple prairie clover (*Dalea purpurea*) **N**

Rocky Mountain bee plant (*Cleome serrulata*) **N**

Russian sage **H**

Sage **H**

Salvia **N, B, H**

Sea lavender (*Limonium latifolium*)

Stonecrop (*Sedum*)

Sempervivum (hens and chicks)

Spiderwort **B**

Veronica **B**

Yucca **N, H**

Bulbs and Roots

Crocus

Daffodil **B**

Tulip **B**

Dahlia

Gladiolus

Annuals

Bachelor's button/cornflower (*Centaurea cyanus*)

Cleome

Cosmos (single flowered only)

Lavatera rose mallow

Marigold

Morning glory

Portulaca rock rose

Snapdragon

Sunflower

Tithonia

Zinnia

Sources

Ashworth, Suzanne. *Seed to Seed: Seed Saving and Growing Techniques for Vegetable Gardeners.* 2nd ed. White River Junction, VT: Chelsea Green, 2002.

Bradley, Fern Marshall. *Rodale's Ultimate Encyclopedia of Organic Gardening.* Emmaus, PA: Rodale Press, 2009.

Braun, Elizabeth. "Reactive Nitrogen in the Environment: Too Much or Too Little of a Good Thing." *United Nations Environment Programme,* 2007.

Coleman, Eliot, and Barbara Damrosch. *Four Season Harvest: Organic Vegetables from Your Home Garden All Year Long.* White River Junction, VT: Chelsea Green, 1999.

Darwin, Charles. *The Formation of Vegetable Mould, Through the Action of Worms, With Observations on Their Habits.* London: John Murray, 1881.

Davis, Jeanine, Sue Ellen Johnson, and Katie Jennings. "Herbicide Carryover in Hay, Manure, Compost and Grass Clippings: Caution to Hay Producers, Livestock Owners, Farmers, and Home Gardeners." North Carolina Cooperative Extension, 2010, www.ces.ncsu.edu/fletcher/programs/ncorganic/special-pubs/herbicide_carryover.pdf.

Flowerdew, Bob. *The No-Work Garden.* London: Kyle Cathie, 2004.

Gammon, Crystal, and Environmental Health News. "Weed-Whacking Herbicide Proves Deadly to Human Cells." *Scientific American Magazine,* June 23, 2009, www.scientificamerican.com/article.cfm?id=weed-whacking-herbicide-p.

Hooper, Ted, and Mike Taylor. *The Beekeeper's Garden.* London: A & C Black, 1988.

Jeavons, John. *How to Grow More Vegetables (and fruits, nuts, berries, grains, and other crops) Than You Ever Thought Possible on Less Land Than You Can Imagine.* Berkeley, CA: Ten Speed Press, 2002.

Lanza, Patricia. *Lasagna Gardening: A New Layering System for Bountiful Gardens: No Digging, No Tilling, No Weeding, No Kidding!* Emmaus, PA: Rodale Press, 1998.

Logan, William Bryant. *Dirt: The Ecstatic Skin of the Earth.* New York: Riverhead Books, 1995.

Lovell, Harvey B., and Lawrence R. Goltz. *Honey Plants.* Rev. ed. Medina, OH: A. I. Root, 1977.

Lowenfels, Jeff, and Wayne Lewis. *Teaming with Microbes: A Gardener's Guide to the Soil Food Web.* Portland: Timber Press, 2010.

McDorman, Bill. *Basic Seed Saving.* Sedona, AZ: Seeds Trust, 1994.

National Science Foundation. "Too much of a good thing: Human activities overload ecosystems with nitrogen." PhysOrg.com, October 7, 2010, www.physorg.com/news205680251.html.

Pearce, Fred. "The Nitrogen Fix: Breaking a Costly Addiction." *Yale Environment 360,* November 5, 2009, http://e360.yale.edu/content/feature.msp?id=2207.

Pellet, Frank. *American Honey Plants.* Hamilton, IL: Dadant & Sons, 1976.

Solomon, Steve. *Gardening When It Counts: Growing Food in Hard Times.* Gabriola Island, BC: New Society, 2006.

Stewart, Amy. *The Earth Moved: On the Remarkable Achievements of Earthworms.* New York: Algonquin Books of Chapel Hill, 2003.

Stout, Ruth, and Richard Clemence. *The Ruth Stout No-Work Garden Book: Secrets of the Famous Year-Round Mulch Method.* Emmaus, PA: Rodale Press, 1971.

Townsend, Alan R., and Robert W. Howarth. "Fixing the Global Nitrogen Problem." *Scientific American Magazine* 302.2 (2010): 64–71.

Townsend, A. R., R. W. Howarth, M. S. Booth, C. C. Cleveland, S. K. Collinge, A. P. Dobson, P. R. Epstein, E. A. Holland, D. R. Keeny, and M. A. Malin. "Human Health Effects of a Changing Global Nitrogen Cycle." *Frontiers in Ecology and the Environment* 1 (2003): 240–246.

Wargo, John, Nancy Alderman, and Linda Wargo. "Risks from Lawn-Care Pesticides Including Inadequate Packaging and Labeling," 2003, www.ehhi.org/reports/lcpesticides/lawnpest_full.pdf.

Weinberg, Julie Behrend. *Growing Food in the High Desert Country.* Santa Fe: Sunstone Press, 1985.

Wolfe, David. *Tales from the Underground: A Natural History of Subterranean Life.* Cambridge, MA: Da Capo Press, 2002.

Wright, Kenneth. *Water Rights in the 50 States and Territories.* Denver: American Water Works Association, 1990.

Resources

Books and Publications

Deppe, Carol. *Breed Your Own Backyard Garden Vegetables*. New York: Little Brown & Co., 1993.

Gladstar, Rosemary, and Tammi Hartung. *Homegrown Herbs: A Complete Guide to Growing, Using, and Enjoying More than 100 Herbs*. North Adams, MA: Storey, 2011.

Hemenway, Toby. *Gaia's Garden: A Guide to Home-Scale Permaculture*. 2nd ed. White River Junction, VT: Chelsea Green, 2009.

Hooper, Ted, and Mike Taylor. *The Bee Friendly Garden: Bring Bees to Your Flowers, Orchard, and Vegetable Patch*. Somerset, UK: Alphabet and Image, 2006.

Hooper, Ted, and Mike Taylor. *The Beekeepers Garden*. New York: Alphabooks, 1988.

Lancaster, Brad. *Rainwater Harvesting for Drylands and Beyond*. Vol. 1, *Guiding Principles to Welcome Rain into Your Life and Landscape*. Tucson: Rainsource Press, 2006.

Lancaster, Brad. *Rainwater Harvesting for Drylands and Beyond*. Vol. 2, *Water-Harvesting Earthworks*. Tucson: Rainsource Press, 2007.

Magdoff, Fred, and Harold van Es. *Building Soils for Better Crops*. 2nd ed. Washington, DC: Sustainable Agriculture Network, 2002, www.soilandhealth.org/03sov/0302hsted/030218bettersoils.pdf.

Marr, Charles W., Rhonda Janke, and Paul Conway. "Cover Crops for Vegetable Growers." Manhattan, KS: Kansas State University Cooperative Agricultural Extension Service, 1998, www.ksre.ksu.edu/library/hort2/MF2343.pdf.

Mollison, Bill, with Reny Mia Slay. *Introduction to Permaculture*. Sisters Creek, Tasmania: Tagari Publications, 1994.

Rodale, Mari. *Organic Manifesto: How Organic Farming Can Heal Our Planet, Feed the World, and Keep Us Safe*. New York: Rodale, 2011.

Sammataro, Diana, and Alphonse Avitabile. *The Beekeepers Handbook*. 3rd ed. Ithaca, NY: Comstock Publishing Associates, 1998.

Stout, Ruth. *Gardening without Work: For the Aging, the Busy, and the Indolent*. New York: Devin-Adair, 1963.

Stout, Ruth. *How to Have a Green Thumb without an Aching Back: A New Method of Mulch Gardening*. New York: Exposition Press, 1955.

Thun, Maria. *The Biodynamic Year: Increasing Yield, Quality and Flavor (100 Helpful Tips for the Gardener or Smallholder)*. Sussex, UK: Temple Lodge Publishing, 2008.

Xerces Society. *Attracting Native Pollinators: The Xerces Society Guide to Conserving North American Bees and Butterflies and Their Habitat*. North Adams, MA: Storey Publshing, 2011.

Websites

ATTRA's National Sustainable Agriculture Information Service and Resource Guide to Organic & Sustainable Vegetable Production—https://attra.ncat.org/attra-pub/vegetable-guide.html

Beyond Pesticides—www.beyondpesticides.org

Gary Nabhan—http://garynabhan.com

Institute of Science in Society—www.i-sis.org.uk

The Land Institute, Salina, Kansas—www.landinstitute.org

National Climatic Data Center, US Department of Commerce—www.ncdc.noaa.gov/oa/climate/regionalclimatecenters.html

Nitrogen News, a resource for journalists and bloggers covering nitrogen science and management policy—www.nitrogennews.com

Organic Materials Review Institute—www.omri.org

Organic Seed Alliance—www.seedalliance.org

Permaculture Institute—www.permaculture.org

Rainwater Harvesting for Drylands and Beyond—www.harvestingrainwater.com

Spikenard Farm and Honeybee Sanctuary—http://spikenardfarm.org

Western Regional Climate Center—www.wrcc.dri.edu

Western State University Extension Gardening Resource Websites

Colorado State University Extension (Fact Sheets and more)—www.ext.colostate.edu

Montana State University—http://gardenguide.montana.edu

New Mexico State University Extension— http://extension.nmsu.edu/yard_garden.html

University of Arizona—http://extension.arizona

.edu/topics/agriculture-and-natural-resources/
home-garden-landscape

University of Idaho—www.extension.uidaho.edu/
homegard.asp

University of Wyoming—www.uwyo.edu/barn-
backyard/info.asp?p=10459

Utah State University—http://extension.usu.edu/
yardandgarden

Regional and Heirloom Seed Catalogs
Look for companies that honor The Safe
Seed Pledge:

"Agriculture and seeds provide the basis
upon which our lives depend. We must
protect this foundation as a safe and genetically stable source for future generations.
For the benefit of all farmers, gardeners
and consumers who want an alternative:

We pledge that we do not knowingly
buy or sell genetically engineered seeds or
plants. The mechanical transfer of genetic
material outside of natural reproductive
methods and between genera, families
or kingdoms, poses great biological risks
as well as economic, political, and cultural threats. We feel that genetically

engineered varieties have been insuf-
ficiently tested prior to public release.
More research and testing is necessary to
further assess the potential risks of genetically engineered seeds. Further, we wish
to support agricultural progress that leads
to healthier soils, genetically diverse agricultural ecosystems and ultimately healthy
people and communities."

AlPlains (Western natives)
Baker Creek Heirloom Seeds
BBB Seed
Botanical Interests
Burrell's Better Seeds
Fedco
Golden Harvest Organics
Johnny's Garden Seeds
Native Seeds Search
Nichols Garden Nursery
Pinetree Garden Seed
Plants of the Southwest
Renee's Garden Seeds
Seed Savers Exchange
Seeds Trust
Western Native Seed
Westwind Seeds

Index

for, 8–9, 82, 119–122; as protein source for higher animals,
49–50; in sheet-mulched gardens, 65; toads as predators of,
118; wasps, 8, 119, 120, 149.
See also honeybees
in-stream flows (water law), 126
insulation for garden structures,
87, 96
interdependency, 49
interplanting, 119
invertebrates, microscopic, 30
irrigation, 35, 106, 107, 126–
127, 130–132
irrigation projects, 22–23

J
Jackson, Wes, 180
Japanese mustard spinach (kom-
atsuna), 142
Jay Hill Farm, 169
Jerusalem artichoke (sunchoke),
182–183
Johnson, Don, 65
Jones, Curtis, 71
June bearing strawberries,
186–187
Jutras, Joe, 167

K
kale, 149, 153
kelp spray, 119, 122
kitchen scraps, 63–64, 66, 67
kohlrabi, 153–154
Kölreuter, Joseph Gottlieb, 51
komatsuna (Japanese mustard
spinach), 142
Köppen, Wladimir, 13
Krischik, Vera, 54

L
labeling requirements, 9, 105
lacewings, 95
lady beetles, 93, 94
Lancaster, Brad, 128
Land Institute, 180
landscape design for water conservation, 128–129
Langstroth hives, 50–51, 59
Lanza, Patricia, 64
Lasagna Gardening (Lanza), 64
lawns: converting to gardens,
63–70; and loss of biological
diversity, 103; and nitrogen

pollution, 46; pesticide use on,
54, 104; and water use, 127
L-dopa, 155
lead testing kits, 73
leaf celery, 154
leaf vacs, 62
leaf-cutter bees, 55, 57
learning, 2, 9
leaves, 36–37, 38, 62–63, 66
leeks, 86, 145–146
legumes, 32, 38, 39, 41, 43
lettuce, 59, 82–83, 137, 141–
142, 193
lima beans, 161
llama manure, 37
loam, 28, 29, 135–136
loose-leaf lettuce, 141–142
Lycopersicon esculentum (tomatoes).
See tomatoes *(Lycopersicon
esculentum)*

M
mâche (corn salad), 137–139
mantids, 96, 121
manure tea, 37
manures, 37–39, 62, 66,
105–106
Martinez, Florentino, 34
mason bees, 56–57
McDorman, Bill, 141, 192, 194
MCPP, 104
medicinal uses of garden plants:
brassicas, 149; cabbages, 151;
chicories, 144; comfrey, 180;
cucumbers, 165; fava beans,
155; greens, 139; potatoes,
158
melons, 58, 72, 137, 183–186
mentoring of future gardeners,
2, 9
Mexican bean beetles, 93, 121
Mexico Agricultural Program, 44
microbes in soils, 29–33, 61, 62,
73, 108
microclimates, 78–79
microcreatures (microherd),
29–30
milk spray, 121
Miller, Barbara, 7, 160, 163
Miller, Gerald, 173
miller moths, 120
mineral nutrients: availability to
plants, 62; calcium, 62; nitrogen, 31, 62–63; phosphorus,

32, 39, 62, 160, 170; potassium, 46, 62; in wood ashes,
38, 182
miner's lettuce (claytonia), 141
minitunnels, plastic, 81, 83
mint, 74, 179–180
mint sprays, 121
mizuna, 142–143
Mohr, Pete, 167
moisture, winter, 65, 66, 67
monochoid nematodes (round-
worms), 29
monoculture crops: and conventional agriculture, 50, 53,
108, 175; effect on biological
diversity, 108; large-scale pollination of, 53
Monroe, Jacquie, 184
Monroe Organic Farms, 184,
186
Monsanto, 6
mountain gardens: choos-
ing plant varieties for, 78,
136–137; conditions in, 14,
16–17, 18
mountain peat, 29
mountain spinach (orach), 143
mulches: biodegradable, 83, 84;
carbon-rich, 31; for container
gardens, 74; for moisture
retention, 108; no-till sheet
method, 7, 63–68; plastic
sheeting, 83–84; and sustainable agriculture, 6; and water
conservation, 129–130, 132;
for weed prevention, 107; for
winter soil protection, 17
municipalities: composting programs in, 36–37; hazardous
household waste dropoff programs, 9; providing water for,
126–127; snowmelt as water
source, 15, 16
muskmelons, 184
mustard, 41
mustard, Chinese, 119, 121
mustard greens, 137, 142–143,
149
Mycobacterium vaccae, 30–31
mycorrhizal fungi, 31–32, 133

N
Nabhan, Gary, 129
Nantes-type carrots, 156

Napa cabbage, 152
National Resources Defense Council (NRDC), 53
National Sustainable Agriculture Information Service and Resource Guide to Organic & Sustainable Vegetable Production (ATTRA), 122
native bees, 56–57, 63
native peoples, strategies for low-water gardening, 15, 129
native plants: attracting native bees with, 57; attracting pollinators with, 51, 58; loss of, 54; planting for biodiversity, 108; soils for, 25
native prairie grasses, 14, 21–22
Native Seeds/SEARCH, 129
native soils, 13, 17, 21–22, 27
Navajo people, strategies for low-water gardening, 129
nectar, 55, 119
neem oil, 119
neighbors, consideration for, 68
nematodes, 29, 32, 121
neonicotinoid pesticides, 52–54
netting, bird, 117
nettle spray, 119, 120
neurotoxins in pesticides, 104
New, Paul, 158
newspaper, 66, 71
nightshades, 121, 137, 169–173
Niles, Meredith, 23
niter (potassium nitrate), 46
nitrates, 34, 35–36, 43–44, 45, 46
nitrification, 44
nitrogen, 31, 62–63
nitrogen, synthetic, 44–46
nitrogen cycle, 43–44
nitrogen pollution, 44–46
nitrogen-fixing plants, 32, 41, 160
NOLO bait, 121
nonselective herbicides, 104
Nosema locustae, 121
no-till sheet mulch method, 63, 66–67
NPK (nitrogen, phosphorus, potassium), 43
NRDC (National Resources Defense Council), 53
nutrient concentrations of organic materials, 38

nutrients, soil: availability to plants, 108; and beneficial microbes, 29–33; and cation exchanges, 34–35; role of nitrogen in, 43–44; and soil amendments, 25–26, 28–29, 36–41; and soil chemistry, 34–36; and soil structure, 28. See also soil food web
nutrition, and organic gardening, 5

O
oats, 41
okra, 173–174
ollas, 74
onion sprays, 121
onions, 58–59, 82–83, 136, 146–148
open-pollinated (OP) plant varieties, 138, 177, 192
orach (Atriplex hortensis), 143
oregano, 179
organic, use of term, 6
organic gardening: author's experience with, 1–3, 40; interpretations of sustainability, 5–6; motivation for, 3; permaculture approach to, 6–9; popularity of, 5; and small-scale food gardening, 1, 9–10, 61–63; and understanding of ecological principles, 27
Organic Gardening Magazine, 6
organic herbicides, 106, 107
Organic Materials Review Institute, 122
organic matter: and microbes, 33; in native soils, 13, 25, 27; raw materials for, 38, 61–63, 105–106; role in soil building, 25, 36; and soil pH, 35; and soil structure, 28. See also amendments
overhead watering, 131
overwintering, 83
owls, 110
oxygen, 25, 28, 49, 129

P
paper wasps, 8, 149
parasitic mites, 53
parasitic wasps, 8, 119, 120, 149
Parmenter, Cord, 112

Parmenter, Penn, 85, 88–89, 112, 143, 147, 152, 154, 163, 186
parsley, 58–59
peas, field, 41
peas, garden (Pisum sativum), 155, 193
peat, mountain, 29
peat, sphagnum, 73
Penncap-M, 52
pepper sprays, 111, 116
peppergrass (cress), 141
peppers (Capsicum annuum): growing requirements, 137, 169–171; insect pollination of, 58; saving seeds, 193; soil warming techniques, 84; varieties for containers, 74
perennial herbs, 179–180
perennial vegetables, 180–183
perennial weeds, 107
permaculture approach to organic gardening, 5, 6–9
permaculture remediation programs, 108
pesticide contamination, 52–54
pesticides: availability of banned products, 106; avoiding in food gardens, 36; and depletion of topsoil, 27; effect on beneficial insects, 93; insecticides, 52, 54, 104–105; overuse on lawns, 59, 104; persistence of, 105; role in bee deaths, 5, 51–54, 174; and small-scale food gardening, 6–10, 50. See also herbicides, chemical
pests: attitudes toward, 6, 103; control in balanced soils, 108; insects, 118–122; weeds, 104–109. See also wildlife
pH, soil, 35, 62
phosphates, 34, 35, 38, 170
phosphorus, 32, 39, 62, 160
photosynthesis, 49
Physalis sp. (tomatillo), 171
physiological effects of soil microbes, 30–31
phytochemicals, 138, 151
Pikes Peak Urban Gardens, 155
Pimentel, David, 27
pine needles, 62, 66
Pisum sativum (garden peas), 155, 193

urea-based fertilizers, 43, 45. *See also* synthetic fertilizers

US Department of Agriculture (USDA): Cheyenne Horticulture Station, 125; Economic Research Service, 9; herbicide statistics from, 104

US Fish and Wildlife Service on domestic pesticide use, 104

US Geological Survey (USGS): on groundwater contamination, 105; and western exploration, 19

UV (ultraviolet) light, 18

V

vegetables: choosing varieties and cultivars, 138–139; cool season, 135, 136–137; heirloom, 5, 58, 138, 166; perennial, 180–183; warm-season, 135, 137–139. *See also* plant varieties; *specific vegetables*

ventilation for garden structures, 83, 85–86, 87

vermicompost (worm castings), 32, 33

verticillium fungi, 122

vetch, 41

Vicia faba (fava beans), 137, 154–155

vinegar spray, 122

virus protective spray, 122

viruses, plant, 122

W

Wall o' Waters, 68, 84

warm-season vegetables: cucurbits, 137, 162–165; eggplant, 169; globe artichokes, 167–168; growing requirements, 135, 137–139; insect pollination of, 58; okra, 173–174; peppers, 58, 74, 84, 137, 169–171, 193; and soil warming, 68, 84; sunflowers, 174; sweet corn, 58, 109, 111, 137, 175–178; tomatillos, 171. *See also* beans, garden; tomatoes *(Lycopersicon esculentum)*

Warren, Susan, 167

wasps, predatory, 8, 119, 120, 149

water bears (tardigrades), 30

water conservation: collecting and harvesting, 127–128; designing landscapes for, 128–129; lessons from native peoples, 129; strategies for, 15, 28–29, 129–133

water diversion projects, 126

water issues, 125–127

water quality, 127–128

water rights, 20

water shortages, 23, 125

water teepees, 68, 84, 172

watering: for containers, 73–74; by hand, 132; irrigation methods, 35, 106, 107, 126–127, 130–132; overhead, 131; and plant diseases, 130–131; and slug control, 122; and winter moisture, 65, 66, 67

watermelons, 183–186

water-retaining crystals, 73

watersheds, 19–20

weather cycles, 14, 77, 125

weather extremes, 15–17, 88–90

weed barrier cloth, 70

weeds: in balanced soils, 108; benefits of, 9; controls for, 39, 41, 65–66, 104–109

western climates: availability of water in, 14–15; classifications of, 13–14; described, 77; and global climate change, 23; historical effects of settlement, 19–23; seasons, 17–19; sunshine as asset in, 14–15; weather extremes, 15–17

western slopes of mountain ranges, 16, 17

western United States, 19–23

western water law systems, 125–126

White, Bessie, 129

White Mountain Farm, 158

Wilber, Charles Dana, 21

wildfire, 17

wildlife: bears, 113–114; and biological diversity, 109; birds, 2, 8, 109, 110, 116–118; deer and elk, 112; foxes, 109, 110, 111–112; rabbits, 82, 116, 163; raccoons, 84, 109–111, 175; skunks, 109, 110, 114–116; snakes, 118; squirrels, 111; toads, 118

Wilson, E. O., 30

wilt diseases, 122, 170, 171, 185

wilting, 18, 74, 78, 131, 170

wind: chinook, 17, 79; drying effects of, 17, 18; protection from, 78, 88–89; in western climates, 13

windbreaks and windscreens, 78, 89

winter, 17

winter purslane (claytonia), 141

winter squash, 162–163, 166–167, 175

wood ashes, 38, 182

wood chips, 62–63

worker bees, 55–56

worm castings (vermicompost), 32, 33

worms, 33–34, 62

X

Xerces Society, 9

Y

yard waste, 66

yellow jackets, 8

Z

Zeleus sp. (assassin bugs), 97

zucchini, 165–166

About the Author

Jane Shellenberger is an eclectic gardener. She is publisher and editor of the regional gardening magazine *Colorado Gardener*, a thinking-gardener's companion, which she founded in 1997. She is also a member of the Garden Writers Association. Shellenberger lives on a five-acre farmette on the plains between Boulder and Longmont, Colorado.